D0203499

LETHAL POLITICS

LETHAL POLITICS

Soviet Genocide and Mass Murder
since 1917

R. J. Rummel

Transaction Publishers
New Brunswick (U.S.A.) and London (U.K.)

947.084
R932

Copyright © 1990 by Transaction Publishers,
New Brunswick, New Jersey 08903

All rights reserved under International and Pan-American Copyright
Conventions. No part of this book may be reproduced or transmitted in
any form or by any means, electronic or mechanical, including pho-
tocopy, recording, or any information storage and retrieval system,
without prior permission in writing from the publisher. All inquiries
should be addressed to Transaction Publishers, Rutgers–The State University, New Brunswick, New Jersey 08903.

Library of Congress Catalog Number: 89-28836
ISBN: 0–88738–333–5
Printed in the United States of America

Library of Congress Cataloging-in-Publication Data

Rummel, R. J. (Rudolph J.), 1932–
    Lethal Politics: Soviet Genocide and Mass Murder
      Since 1917 / R.J. Rummel.
      p. cm.
    Includes bibliographical references.
    ISBN: 0–88738–333–5
    1. Soviet Union—Politics and government—1917–   2. Genocide—
Soviet Union—History—20th century. 3. Political persecution—
Soviet Union—History—20th century. 4. Soviet Union—Population—
History—20th century. I. Title.
DK266.3.R86   1990   89-28836
947.084—dc20   CIP

Contents

UNIVERSITY LIBRARIES
CARNEGIE MELLON UNIVERSITY
PITTSBURGH, PA 15213-3890

Tables and Figures

Preface

This book is part of a project on government genocide and mass killing in this century. The aim is to test the hypothesis that the citizens of democracies are the least likely to be murdered by their own governments; the citizens of totalitarian, especially Marxist systems, the most likely. The theory is that democratic systems provide a path to peace, and universalizing them would eliminate war and minimize global political violence. This was the conclusion of my *Understanding Conflict and War*,[1] and has been further confirmed by systematic, empirical tests since.[2]

In the process of that research, I discovered that governments have murdered tens of millions of their own citizens, and that in some cases, the death toll may have actually exceeded that of World War II. To get some idea of the numbers involved, I surveyed the extent of genocide and mass killing by governments since 1900. The results were shocking: according to these first figures—independent of war and other kinds of conflict—governments probably have murdered 119,400,000 people—Marxist governments about 95,200,000 of them. By comparison, the battle-killed in all foreign and domestic wars in this century total 35,700,000.[3]

These monstrous statistics sharply reoriented my research. For more than thirty years as a political scientist and peace researcher, I had focused my research on the causes and conditions of war, conflict, and peace. I had believed that war was the greatest killer and that nuclear war would be a global holocaust. Now I have found that the total killed by government in cold blood was almost four times that of war. *It was as though a nuclear war had already occurred.*

Surprisingly few had recognized this. While much had been published on individual genocides, such as those of the Jews or Armenians, and some general analyses had been done, as by Kuper,[4] up through 1987 virtually no research had been published on the total amount of genocide and mass murder among nations.[5] The one exception was Elliot's *Twentieth Century Book of the Dead*, which arrives at a figure of about 100,000,000 killed in this century, including war. The work, however, omitted many small genocides and was limited in its treatment of killing by Marxist governments.

For these reasons, with a grant from the United States Peace Institute, I undertook in 1988 a project to refine and elaborate my findings, to determine empirically the conditions and causes of government genocide and mass killing, and to assess the role of democratic versus autocratic institutions. The aim was to provide a comprehensive overview of such governmental murder; to test further whether the more democratic a nation, the more secure its citizens from such killing; and to publish the results in a major monograph.

Among the first studies undertaken was that of Soviet genocide and mass murder. This was a very difficult task, for while widely different estimates were available on such Soviet institutions as the labor camp, such polices as collectivization or the Red Terror, or such events as the deportation of Poles in 1939 through 1941, few experts had tried to systematically accumulate and total them over Soviet history. To my knowledge, there are only two major works in English attempting to tally the toll in some systematic manner.[6] Robert Conquest gives a carefully accumulated total for the Stalin years (at least 20,000,000 killed);[7] and in his samizdat, translated into English, Soviet geophysicist Josif Dyadkin did a demographic analysis of excess Soviet deaths from 1926 to 1954 and concluded that Soviet repression killed 23,100,000 to 32,000,000 Soviet citizens over this 29-year period.[8]

Scattered here and there in one book or another are estimates of the number murdered. For example, Dimitri Panin claims that 57,000,000 to 69,500,000 people were killed and says that estimates of authors in the West vary from 45,000,000 to 80,000,000.[9] Aleksandr Solzhenitsyn mentions a figure of 66,000,000 calculated by an émigré professor of statistics.[10] And D.G. Stewart-Smith gives an estimate of 31,000,000 killed in repression.[11] Like Dyadkin's, some estimates have been based on demographic analyses, as Medvedev's 22,000,000 to 23,000,000 total (1918–53).[12]

For lack of a thorough statistical accumulation and analysis of Soviet genocides and mass murders from 1917 to recent years, I had to undertake at least an initial effort in this direction. At first, the result was to be a chapter in a monograph on twentieth-century genocides and mass killing. But it soon became clear that the Soviets themselves are responsible for so many genocides and that so many different kinds of mass killings had occurred that to unravel and present the detailed events, institutions, and related statistics involved would require a monograph itself. Thus I wrote this book.

In order to best present the historical details, statistical analyses, and various figures and sources—and yet make the book readable and useful to various publics—I have divided this volume in the following way. First, the statistical data, sources, and analyses have been separated from the historical "when, what, and why" of the estimates. This provides an explanation and understanding of the deaths being reported and historical narrative for those uninterested in the statistical details while also making available the statistical material for specialists. Second, rather than putting all the statistics in one long appendix at the end of the book, I have prepared a separate appendix for each historical period, thus keeping the historical narrative and related statistical material together. Third, each historical period has been treated as a chapter, with the associated statistical appendix at the end. Finally, a historical overview and analysis and presentation of the final results have been incorporated into the first chapter, which constitutes an executive summary. Its appendixes summarize the statistical data, compare these to estimates in the literature, and simulate the result of altering some important assumptions.

I should note that there is a clear division in style between the appendixes and the historical narrative. In the appendixes, I have tried to be objective, neutral, and prudent, recognizing that we all have biases that work against our best intentions in surprising ways. The methodological appendix spells out the principles and procedures guiding the preparation of the estimates and totals in the other appendixes. In the narrative I have been less dry and disinterested, however, than some specialists and historians might desire. If this be so, then I can only say that it is to others I must leave writing with dispassion about the murder of tens of millions of human beings.

Throughout the narrative, I have tried to keep a clear distinction between government (or party) and the people. It is a government elite that is directly responsible for the genocides and mass murders recorded here, not the Russian or Ukrainian or German people. In the case of the Soviet Union this distinction is maintained by the use of "Soviets," as in the "Soviets shot. . . ," or "killed 50,000. . . ," or "invaded. . . ." While this may seem hardly controversial for the Soviet Union, it may be in the use of "Nazis," instead of "Germans," in describing mass killing during World War II. Thus, the "Nazis massacred 25,000 inhabitants . . . ," rather than the "Germans. . . ." While some may feel that this ignores the responsibility the German people allegedly share for Nazi aggression and murders, this is not an issue that I can treat seriously here. In any case, the Nazi and Soviet regimes bore first responsibility for their killing, and the narrative recognizes this.

One final comment on the term *murder*. If anything may appear to display an anti-Soviet, less-than-professional bias, it may be the consistent accusation that the Soviets have murdered all these millions and the use of the term in the title of this book. I am doing this, however, because I believe the technical meaning of murder fits what the Soviets did. To murder someone means to unlawfully and purposely kill him, or to be responsible for his death through reckless and depraved indifference to his life (as in Soviet deportations or the labor camps). As established by the Nuremberg War Crimes Tribunal after World War II, "crimes against humanity" consist of

> murder, extermination, enslavement, deportation and other inhuman acts done against any civilian population, or persecutions on political, racial or religious grounds, when such acts are done or such persecutions are carried on in execution of or in connexion with any crime against peace or any war crime.[13]

When the Nazis invaded Poland and began World War II, their massacre of Jews and others, deportation of civilians, atrocities in occupied territory, execution of opponents at home, and so on were thus crimes against humanity. Similar acts by Soviet authorities during their own civil and international wars were also such crimes.

As for Soviet genocides, massacres of civilians, deportations, and the like, the Genocide Convention, passed by the General Assembly of the United Nations in 1948, covers much of that in peacetime. By Article I:

> The Contracting Parties confirm that genocide, whether committed in time of peace or in time of war, is a crime under international law which they undertake to prevent and to punish.[14]

The Soviet representative, among others, successfully fought to limit the interpretation of genocide to national, religious, ethnic, and language groups.[15] The massacre of political groups and opponents are purposely excluded. But a prior resolution of the General Assembly passed in late 1946 explicitly covers them. According to this resolution,

> genocide is a denial of the right of existence of entire human groups, as homicide is the denial of the right to live of individual human beings. . . . Many instances of such crimes of genocide have occurred, when racial, religious, political and other groups have been destroyed, entirely or in part. . . .
>
> The General Assembly Therefore, Affirms that genocide is a crime under international law which the civilized world condemns, and for the commission of which principals and accomplices—whether private individuals, public officials or statesmen, and whether the crime is committed on religious, racial, political or any other grounds—are punishable.[16]

All this covers what the Soviets did in killing their own or subject people. According to the international community, these were crimes against humanity. They were illegal. If ever the responsible actual or former Soviet officials were tried before an international tribunal for these crimes, they could be punished as murderers.

While trying to be as historically objective as possible, we also should not fear calling a murderer a *murderer*—and murder *murder*.

Notes

1. Rummel (1975–1981).
2. See Rummel (1983, 1984, 1985).
3. Rummel (1986, 1987, 1988).
4. Kuper (1981).
5. Some have begun to recognize and try to fill this research hole. For example, Barbara Harff and Ted Robert Gurr (1988, p. 359) pointed out that "there has been no comprehensive and systematic survey of such events," and then presented a comprehensive collection of those genocides and politicides occurring since 1945. They conclude that between 7 and 16 million people have been so killed. As will be shown here, this is most likely an underestimate, since in the Soviet Union alone probably over 22 million were killed in genocides and mass murders during this period.
6. Melgounov (1925) and Maximoff (1940).
7. Conquest (1968, appendix A). In a report written for the United States

Senate Committee on the Judiciary (1970), Conquest attempts to estimate the number killed since 1917, which he concludes would have to be more than 22,000,000 citizens (p. 25). This effort is much less systematic than in the work cited.

8. Dyadkin (1983, p. 60). An assumed 20 million war dead for World War II and 40 thousand for the Soviet-Finnish War are subtracted from Dyadkin's figures.
9. Panin (1976, p. 93n).
10. Solzhenitsyn (1975a, p. 10).
11. Stewart-Smith (1964, p. 222). Includes the "1933–35" famine.
12. Medvedev (1979, pp. 140–41); from Soviet demographer M. Maksudov.
13. Falk, et al. (1971, p. 108).
14. Kuper (1981, p. 210).
15. Ibid., Chapter 2.
16. Quoted in ibid., p. 23.

Acknowledgments

I am indebted to the United States Institute of Peace for a grant to my project on comparative genocide, of which this book is a part. The views expressed here are those of the author and do not necessarily reflect those of the Institute or its officers.

I also wish to thank George Kent for his helpful comments on the draft of chapter 1; Ernest Lefever and Manfred Henningsen for causing me to reconsider and revise the narrative style; and Helen Fein, Barbara Harff, and Ted Robert Gurr for helpful comments on the whole draft. As in all my work, I owe many thanks to my wife, Grace, for her comfort, honesty, and thorough editing. I hasten to add, that I alone am responsible for what follows.

1

61,911,000 Victims: Utopianism Empowered, 1917–1987

When we are reproached with cruelty, we wonder how people can forget the most elementary Marxism.

—Lenin

"How long will you keep killing people?" asked Lady Astor of Stalin in 1931.
Replied Stalin, "the process would continue as long as was necessary" to establish a communist society.

Probably 61,911,000 people, 54,769,000 of them citizens, have been murdered by the Communist party—the government—of the Soviet Union. This is about 178 people for each letter, comma, period, digit, and other character in this book.

Old and young, healthy and sick, men and women, and even infants and the infirm, were killed in cold blood. They were not combatants in civil war or rebellions and they were not criminals. Indeed, nearly all were guilty of . . . nothing.

Some were from the wrong class: bourgeoisie, land owners, aristocrats, kulaks. Some were from the wrong nation or race: Ukrainians, Black Sea Greeks, Kalmyks, Volga Germans. Some were from the wrong political faction: Trotskyites, Mensheviks, Social Revolutionaries. Or some were just their sons and daughters, wives and husbands, or mothers and fathers. Some were those occupied by the Red Army: Balts, Germans, Poles, Hungarians, Rumanians. Then some were simply in the way of social progress, like the mass of peasants or religious believers. Or some were eliminated because of their potential opposition, such as writers, teachers, churchmen, the military high command, or even high and low Communist party members themselves.

In fact, we have witnessed in the Soviet Union a true egalitarian social cleansing and flushing: no group or class escaped, for everyone and anyone could have had counterrevolutionary ancestors, class lineage, counterrevolutionary ideas or thought, or be susceptible to them. And thus, almost anyone was arrested, interrogated, tortured; and, after a forced confession to a plot to blow up the Kremlin or some such, they were shot or sentenced to the dry guillotine — slow death by exposure, malnutrition, and overwork in a forced labor camp.

Part of this mass killing was genocide, as in the wholesale murder of hundreds of thousands of Don Cossacks in 1919,[1] the intentional starving to death of about 5,000,000 Ukrainian peasants in 1932–33,[2] or the deportation to mass death of 50,000 to 60,000 Estonians in 1949.[3] Part was mass murder, as of the wholesale extermination of perhaps 6,500,000 kulaks (in effect, the better-off peasants and those resisting collectivization) from 1930 to 1937,[4] the execution of perhaps a million party members in the Great Terror of 1937–38,[5] and the massacre of all Trotskyites in the forced labor camps.[6]

Moreover, part of the killing was so random and idiosyncratic that journalists and social scientists have no concept for it, as in hundreds of thousands of people being executed according to preset government quotas. Says Vladimir Petrov (who in 1954 defected while a spy-chief in Australia and whose credibility and subsequent revelations were verified by a Royal (Australian) Commission on Espionage[7]) about his work during the years 1936 to 1938:

> I handled hundreds of signals to all parts of the Soviet Union which were couched in the following form:
> "To N.K.V.D., Frunze. You are charged with the task of exterminating 10,000 enemies of the people. Report results by signal. — Yezhov."
> And in due course the reply would come back:
> "In reply to yours of such-and-such date, the following enemies of the Soviet people have been shot."[8]

From time to time, in one period or another, quotas also were generally assigned for the numbers to be arrested throughout the length and breadth of Soviet territory. For example, Solzhenitsyn makes these quotas basic to the Great Terror of 1936 to 1938:

The real law underlying the arrests of those years was *the assignment of quotas*, the norms set, the planned allocations. Every city, every district, every military unit was assigned a specific quota of arrests to be carried out by a stipulated time. From then on everything else depended on the ingenuity of the Security operations personnel.[9]

But murder and arrest quotas did not work well.[10] Where to find the "enemies of the people" to shoot was a particularly acute problem for these local NKVD who had been diligent in uncovering "plots." They had to resort to shooting those arrested for the most minor civil crimes, those previously arrested and released, and even mothers and wives who appeared at NKVD headquarters for information about their arrested loved ones.

Westerners lack a concept for murder by quotas because they, not the journalist, historian, nor political scientist, have never before confronted the fact that a government can and has done this kind of thing. For the same reason, neither do they have a concept for the execution of starving peasants who fished in a stream without party permission (trying to steal state property), nor pinning a ten-year sentence on the first one to stop clapping after Salin's name was mentioned at a public meeting.[11] Nor for executing a fourteen-year-old because his father was purged; nor for the Red Army's not only permitting but encouraging mass rape and murder of civilians in virtually every country it newly occupied during World War II.

I call all this kind of killing, whether genocide or mass murder, *democide*. Throughout this book, democide will mean a government's concentrated, systematic, and serial murder of a large part of its population.

In sum, the Soviets have committed a democide of 61,911,000 people, 7,142,000 of them foreigners. This staggering total is beyond belief. But, as shown in figure 1.1, it is only the prudent, most probable tally, in a range from a highly unlikely low figure of 28,326,000 (4,263,000 foreigners); to an equally unlikely high of 126,891,000 (including 12,134,000 foreigners). This is a range of uncertainty in our democide estimates—an error range—of 97,808,000 human beings.

Just consider this error *range* in Soviet democide, as shown in figure 1.1. It is larger than the population of 96 percent of the world's nations and countries. Actually, if France, Belgium, the Netherlands, Norway,

FIGURE 1.1
Range in Soviet Democide Estimates*

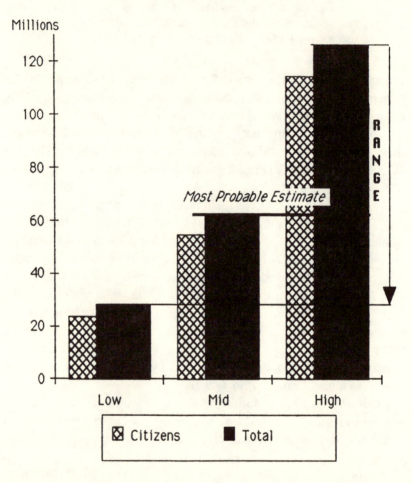

*From appendix 1.1

Sweden, Finland, Denmark and Switzerland were blasted clean of all human life in a nuclear war, the human toll would be less than just this range in the Soviet's probable democide—the range, and not even the total murdered.

Appendix 1.1 to this chapter provides the overall totals and comparisons of these totals to those estimated by others. Appendix 1.2 details various estimates of deathrates in labor camps or through deportations, and the overall deathrate estimates used throughout the appendixes. It also shows the effect of varying some assumptions underlying the totals.

All figures given in the text are taken from or based on one or more of these appendixes. Table 1.1 gives a breakdown of the most probable, central estimates of the various agents of murder developed in these appendixes for each historical period. The Soviet death toll from international and civil wars and rebellions is also shown for comparison. Figure 1.2 displays the relative contribution of the democide components to the overall 61,911,000; figure 1.3 shows the percentage contribution of these components and war to total violent deaths. Finally, figure 1.4 overlays the total democide per period by the annual democide rate.

It is impossible to fix in mind and digest this democide. Focusing on the most probable estimate of 61,911,000 murdered, as shown in table 1.2, it is more than *four* times the battle dead (15,000,000) for all nations in the Second World War.[12] Indeed, it exceeds the total deaths (35,654,000) from all this century's international, civil, guerrilla, and liberation wars, including the Russian Civil War itself.[13] Many other comparisons are given in table 1.2 and figure 1.5, the purpose of which is to communicate some feel for what the Soviet democide means in sheer numbers.

Another way of viewing the Soviet democide is in terms of the annual risk it posed to the Soviet citizen. Table 1.3 shows this risk of death from war and some commonplace risks, like smoking or cancer. Figure 1.6, following, graphs some of them.

Now consider just the low democide estimate of 24,063,000 citizens murdered. This is an absolute, rock bottom low. It is calculated from all the most conservative, lowest estimates for all kinds and sources and periods of democide, for 1917 to 1987. It is highly improbable that all these hundreds of very low estimates are correct. The low of 24,063,000 killed is over 20,000,000 dead below the 42-year average (1918–59) low estimate among experts or knowledgeable Soviets; more important, it is over 15,000,000 dead below the 42-year average of those low estimates based on census data (see appendix 1.1). Yet, this lower limit of 24,063,000 citizens murdered is itself much greater than the 15,000,000 battle dead of the largest, most lethal war of all time.

This absolute minimum is already so overwhelming that one's horror, shock, or disbelief hardly can be increased were the number five

TABLE 1.1
Overview of Soviet Democide
(Most Probable Estimates) [1]

PERIOD	FROM	DEMOCIDE (000)			COMPONENTS (000)				
		TOTAL	CITIZENS	RATE%[2]	TERROR	DEPORT.	CAMPS[3]	FAMINE[4]	WARS[5]
Civil War	1917	3,284	3,284	0.43	750	?	34	2,500	1,410
NEP	1923	2,200	2,200	0.25	?	?	232	0	?
Collectivization	1929	11,440	11,440	1.04	1,733	1,400	3,306	5,000	0.20
Great Terror	1936	4,345	4,345	0.89	1,000	65	3,280	0	1.20
Pre-WWII	1939	5,104	4,438	1.02	1,932	283	2,889	0	256
World War II	1941	13,053	10,000	1.21	1,257	1,036	10,761	0	19,625
Post-War...	1946	15,613	12,448	0.88	1,376	1,557	12,348	333	90
Post-Stalin	1954	6,872	6,613	0.08	250	8	6,613	0	22
TOTAL [6]	1917	61,911	54,769	0.45	>8,298	>4,349	39,464	7,833	>21,403

NOTES:

1. Mid-estimates of dead: most probable central values in a low-high range.
2. Annualized rates for mid-period populations. The total is the weighted average. For citizens only.
3. Camp totals include transit deaths.
4. Famine totals are only for those included as democide
5. Wars and rebellions; includes Nazi caused famine. Shown for comparison only.
6. Numbers may not add up to the total democide for each period due to rounding.

FIGURE 1.2
Democide Components and Soviet War/Rebellion Killed 1917–1987*

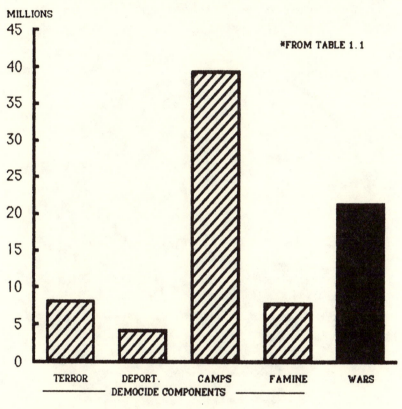

MILLIONS

*FROM TABLE 1.1

DEMOCIDE COMPONENTS

times higher, as is the high estimate; nor can any moral or practical conclusion that one would draw from this low be altered in the slightest by focusing on the more probable, middle estimate of 54,769,000 citizens killed.

Morally, we simply cannot distinguish a difference in evil between the murder of 20,000,000 from that of 60,000,000 human beings. Hitler's crimes against humanity, his mass murder of Jews, Gypsies, the handicapped, and so on, already take us to the limit of our moral discernment and we can only say of Stalin and Lenin that they—like Hitler—were absolutely evil. While for statistical and correlational analysis it is important to approximate the number murdered as closely

FIGURE 1.3
Democide Components and Soviet War/Rebellion Killed,
by Percent of Violent Deaths 1917–1987*

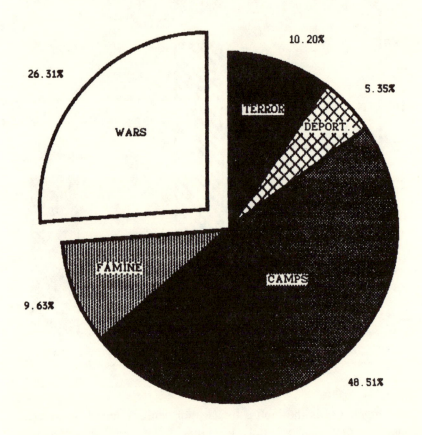

*From Table 1.1

as the data and prudence allow, for moral and policy purposes we well could focus on the low democide of more than 24,000,000 citizens or over 28,000,000 people in total.

Whether the actual democide is this low or higher, four points should be made. First, suicides are excluded. But given the pervasive fear and terror, the number of terror-related suicides must add significantly to the democide total. Second, in many cases the relatives of those murdered were also killed by virtue of this relationship, and the

FIGURE 1.4
Soviet Democide and Annual Rate by Period*

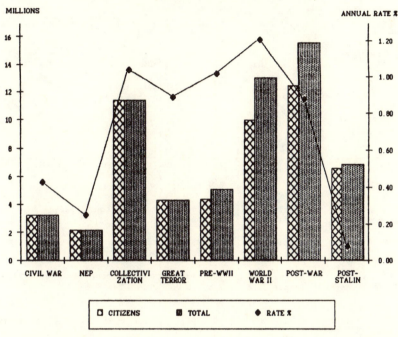

*From Table 1.1

democide figures take these into account. But these figures do not measure the misery among those loved ones left alive, the mothers and fathers, the husbands or wives, or the children, friends, and lovers of those killed. No accounting is made of those who died of heartbreak, who gave up on life and succumbed to disease or privation, or whose remaining years were full of anguish and bitterness.

Finally, there is the fact that tens of millions of people were intentionally and knowingly killed on a continental scale. Of course, this begs the most probing questions. What actually happened? When? Why? How are we to understand this democide? I will try to specifically answer these questions in the following chapters. But the key to it all can be disclosed here: *Marxism*.

In November 1917, Lenin led his small Bolshevik party in a very risky but ultimately successful coup against the provisional, democratic socialist government of Aleksandr Kerensky. This was not just

TABLE 1.2
Comparisons of Soviet Democide

COMPARISONS WHO/WHAT	UNITS	TOTAL	SOURCES/[NOTES]
Soviet Union	Democide	61,911,000	from Appendix 1.1 [1]
Other Democide			
Other 20th Century	Democide	57,489,000	Rummel (1987, p. 25; 1988) [2]
Nazi Germany	Democide	17,000,000	Ibid. [3]
Of Jews	Genocide	4,400,000	Reitlinger (1961, p. 501) [4]
Western Slavery 16th to 19th C.	Killed	37,500,000	Eckhardt & Köhler (1980, p.368) [5]
Wars			
Soviet WWI & WWII	War Dead	21,625,000	from Appendices 2.1 and 7.1
All U. S. Wars	War Killed	1,177,936	The World Almanac (1986, p.333) [6]
World War I	Battle Dead	9,000,000	Small & Singer (1982, p. 89)
World War II	Battle Dead	15,000,000	Ibid., p. 91
All 20th C. Wars	Battle Dead	35,654,000	Ibid., Tables 4.2, 13.2 [7]
	Civilian Dead	35,868,000	Sivard (1985, p. 11) [8]
Inter'al Wars	Battle Dead	29,683,000	Small & Singer (1982, Table 4.2) [7]
Domestic Wars	Battle Dead	5,970,000	Ibid., Table 13.2 [7]
All Major Wars 1740-1897	War Dead	20,000,000	Eckhardt & Köhler (1980, p.368) [9]
Worst Disasters			
Black Death 1347-51	Dead	75,000,000	McWhirter & McWhirter (1977, p.435)
Influenza 1918	Dead	21,640,000	Ibid.
China Famine 1877-8	Dead	9,500,000	Ibid.
China Flood 1931	Dead	3,700,000	Ibid.
Other			
U.S. Executions 1864-1982	Executed	5,753	Bowers (1984, p. 44)
In This Book	All Characters	350,000	[10]

NOTES
1. Most probable, mid-estimate of Soviet democide.
2. Provisional estimate; rounded off to nearest million;
   probably 10-20% under final estimate; excludes USSR.
3. Provisional estimate, probably within a million or so of the final estimate.
4. An average of an estimated range from 4.2 to 4.6 million murdered.
5. Of arrivals in the New World and during capture and transit;
   average of a range from 15 to 60 million killed.
6. U.S. military and civilian deaths; includes the Revolutionary and Civil Wars.
7. Of all wars with 1,000 or more killed.
8. The total is incomplete, since data are not available for some wars,
   but the estimate is probably a million or two under the actual number.
9. In 210 international and domestic wars.
10. An estimate of all the characters (letters,
    numbers, periods,, etc.) in this book.

FIGURE 1.5
Comparisons of Soviet Democide*

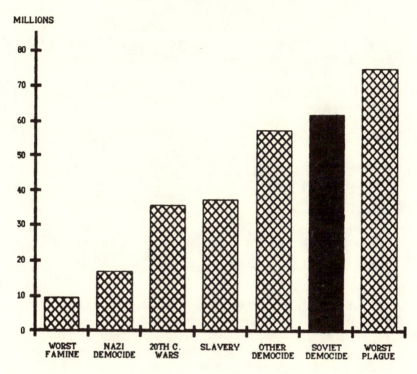

*From table 1

a seizure of power and change of leadership, but a revolutionary trans-
formation in the very nature and worldview of governance. It was the
creation of a unique reason-of-state; and the institution of an utterly
cold-blooded, social-engineering view of the state's power over its
people. This unparalleled, brand new Bolshevik government married a
fully self-contained, secular philosophy of nature and the Good to an
initially shaky, but eventually absolute, ahistorical political force—a
melding of an *idea* and *power*. It was then and has been since, *utopia
empowered*.[14]

The philosophy is a universal perspective, at once a theory about
reality (dialectical materialism), about man in society (historical materialism), about the best society (communism), about an implementing public policy (a socialist dictatorship of the proletariat), and about

TABLE 1.3

Comparison of Soviet Annual Democide Risk to War and Commonplace Risks

TYPE OF RISK	ANNUAL RISK DEATH RISK	ODDS OF DYING
Murdered by the Soviet government [1]	4.50E-03	1 out of 222
War Risk [2]		
Killed in any war	1.80E-04	1 out of 5,556
Killed in international war	1.50E-04	1 out of 6,667
Killed in domestic wars	3.00E-05	1 out of 33,333
Commonplace Risks [3]		
Cigarrette smoking a pack a day	3.60E-03	1 out of 278
All cancers	2.80E-03	1 out of 357
Mountaineering (mountaineers)	6.00E-04	1 out of 1,667
Motor vehicle accident (US) [4]	2.40E-04	1 out of 4,167
Police killed on duty (US) [5]	2.20E-04	1 out of 4,545
Of homocide (US) [5]	7.00E-05	1 out of 14,286

NOTES
   1. From the overall, annual democide rate (Table 1.1).
   2. Calculated from the battle-killed (see Table 1.2) and
      the sum of the populations involved in each 20th century
      war (see Small and Singer, 1982, Tables 4.2 and 13.2).
   3. Except for U.S. homocide, from Wilson &
      Crouch (1987,Table 2).
   4. Assumed specific to the U.S.; includes pedestrian risk.
   5. Average of the murder rates for each fifth year,
      1955 to 1980, and including 1984; from Homes and
      Burger (1988, p. 14).

political tactics (revolution, vanguard, party, etc.). And its praxis is to be absolute in scope, absolute in power, and absolute in technique. Quoting Lenin: "The scientific concept of dictatorship means nothing else but this: power without limit, resting directly upon force, restrained by no laws, absolutely unrestricted by rules."[15]

In sum, with its theory, attendant "factual" explanation of the past and present human condition, and vision of a better society, this ideology provides both answers to the whys and wherefores of political and economic life, and more important, it provides solutions: it defines

FIGURE 1.6
**Annual Risk of a Soviet Citizen Being Murdered by His Own
Government in Comparison to Some Other Risks***

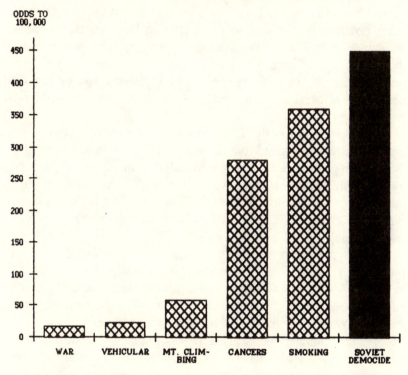

*From table 1

for the believer a way to peace and happiness, to equality and welfare,
and to freedom from hunger, poverty, and exploitation.

The theoretical part of this communist ideology was first developed
in the works of the nineteenth-century philosopher and political econ-
omist Karl Marx and his followers. Lenin, both a philosopher and a
political revolutionary, added a political program and tactics. Lenin's
peculiar brand of communism became known as Bolshevism before
and for decades after he successfully seized power in Russia. In our
time the ideology is called Marxism, or, more specifically, Marxism-
Leninism to denote the revisions introduced by Lenin. Henceforth, I
will simply refer to it as Marxism.

Marxism is thoroughly uncompromising. It knows the Truth, absolutely; it absolutely knows the Good (communism) and the Evil (capitalism, feudalism); it absolutely knows the Way (a socialist dictatorship of the proletariat). Once this ideology seized the authority and naked power of the Russian state—its army, police, courts, prisons—it moved to put its Marxist program into effect. And thus the history of the Soviet Union since the Bolshevik coup has been simply this: a protracted, total, engineering application of state power to demolish and then rebuild all social institutions—to create on earth the Marxist utopia.

Since Marxists know the Truth, ideological opponents could only be gravely mistaken and therefore be enemies of the people. Knowing the Way to Happiness, those who intentionally or unintentionally blocked the Way must be eliminated. Even at the level of tactics, even among those Marxists who had the correct vision, no one could be allowed to differ; for even at this level, at least until Mikhail Gorbachev, there was only one Truth.

Absolute ideas plus the absolute power of the state could mean only one thing: the state and its monopoly of force was the instrument of "progress," of utopian change. Thus, the Red Army would be used to suppress resistance to taking private property (being a source of evil), and a secret police force would be created to uncover enemies of the people and eliminate opponents. Law would become an instrument of terror and revolutionary change; court trials, if held, would be predetermined as the clergy of Marxism saw necessary. And all was permitted as a matter of course—governmental lies, deceit, robbery, beating, torture, and the murder of 61,911,000 people—all instrumental to the communist future.

Most important, in this ideology the living were to be sacrificed for the unborn. The living were objects, like mortar and bricks, lumber and nails, to be used, manipulated, piled on each other, to create the new social structure. Personal interests and desires, pain or pleasure, were of little moment, insignificant in the light of the new world to be created.[16] After all, how could one let, say, Ivan's desire to till the land of his father, Mikhail's to purchase better shoes, or Aleksandr's to store food to preserve his family through the winter, stand in the way of the greater good of future generations? This ideological imperative can be seen in Lenin's attitude toward the famine of 1891–92 on the Volga. As Russians, regardless of class and ideology, tried to help the victims,

Lenin opposed such aid, arguing that famine would radicalize the masses. Said Lenin, "Psychologically, this talk of feeding the starving is nothing but an expression of the saccharine-sweet sentimentality so characteristic of our intelligentsia."[17]

Ideology is the critical variable in Soviet democide. It explains how individual communists could beat, torture, and murder by the hundreds, and then sleep well at night. Grim tasks, to be sure, but after all, they were working for the greater good. It explains how Soviet rulers, particularly Lenin and Stalin, could knowingly command the death of hundreds of thousands and, as in the case of the Ukrainian famine of 1932–33, millions. On this, Solzhenitsyn says:

> Shakespeare's evildoers stopped short at a dozen corpses. Because they had no *ideology*.
>
> Ideology—that is what gives evildoing its long-sought justification and gives the evildoer the necessary steadfastness and determination. That is the social theory which helps to make his acts seem good instead of bad in his own and other's eyes, so that he won't hear reproaches and curses but will receive praise and honors. That was how the agents of the Inquisition fortified their wills: by invoking Christianity; the conquerors of foreign lands by extolling the grandeur of their Motherland; the colonizers, by civilization; the Nazis, by race; and the Jacobins (early and late), by equality, brotherhood, and the happiness of future generations.
>
> Thanks to *ideology*, the twentieth century was fated to experience evildoing on a scale calculated in the millions. . . .
>
> There was a rumor going the rounds between 1918 and 1920 that the Petrograd Cheka . . . did not shoot all those condemned to death but fed some of them alive to the animals in the city zoos. I do not know whether this is truth or calumny. . . . But I wouldn't set out to look for proof, either. Following the practice of the bluecaps [member of the Soviet secret police], I would propose that they prove to us that this was impossible. How else could they get food for the zoos in those famine years? Take it away from the working class? Those enemies were going to die anyway, so why couldn't their deaths support the zoo economy of the Republic and thereby assist our march into the future? Wasn't it *expedient*?
>
> That is the precise line the Shakespearean evildoer could not cross. But the evildoer with ideology does cross it and his eyes remain dry and clear.[18]

In human affairs, however, especially at the level of societies and nations, no ideology, religion, or policies are pure and simple. The practical articulation and implementation of Marxism has been swayed or refracted, hindered or aggravated, aided or abetted, by Russian tradition and racism, Russian imperialism, and Russian chauvinism.

Moreover, communists have not been immune to the lust for power for its own sake. Surely, the clichés of power—power aggrandizes itself, power can only be limited by power, and absolute power corrupts absolutely—apply no less to Marxists than other rulers. Was the unleashing of the Red Terror by Lenin in 1919 mainly to assure his power and rule? Was it simply the traditional reflex of a Russian ruler to political opposition? Was the famine Stalin knowingly imposed on the Ukraine an attempt to assure Russian national dominance over the Ukraine? Was it due to Stalin's fear that the assertive independence of Ukrainian communists would undermine his power? Doubtless such different factors played a role, but throughout this history, Marxism was mediating, channeling, directing. Communism was the Good, the state (read ruler) must have and use absolute power to create this better world, and anyone or anything that actually or *potentially* hindered this power or future must be eliminated.

In this light, the macrohistory of Soviet democide makes sense, although individual policies or campaigns may appear inexplicable, like quotas for shooting "enemies of the people." This history is long and complex, but if organized around the major ideological campaigns and events, it can be divided into eight periods: Civil War, National Economic Policy, collectivization, Great Terror, pre-World War II, World War II, postwar and Stalin's twilight, and post-Stalin. This study will discuss each period and try to provide some understanding of what democide occurred and why.

Appendix 1.1

Table 1A presents the overall democide and totals of those killed in terror, deportations, camps and transit, and democidal famine for the eight periods of Soviet history, 1917–87 (lines 18 to 23 in the table). From 28,326,000 to 126,891,000 people were killed during these years; a prudent estimate is 61,911,000 dead. Of these, 54,767,000 were Soviet citizens (line 8).

The totals for citizens and foreigners are given separately in the table (lines 2 to 15). Note that the democide figures for citizens, and thus the overall democide total, exceed the sum of the democide components

TABLE 1A
61,911,000 Soviet Victims: Totals, Estimates, and Comparisons

LINE	TOTALS/COMPARISONS	BEGIN YEAR M	END YEAR M	DEAD EST. (000) LOW	MID	HIGH	SOURCE	NOTES
	TOTALS 1917–1987							
	DEMOCIDE OF CITIZENS							
2,3	TERRORISM	1917 11	1987 11	>2,830	>6,515	>16,437		[for some periods estimates unavailable]
4,5	DEPORTATIONS	1917 11	1987 11	>1,470	>2,443	>4,677		[for some periods estimates unavailable]
6	CAMP/TRANSIT	1917 11	1987 11	14,059	36,010	76,714		
7	FAMINE	1917 11	1987 11	3,750	7,833	14,250		
8	SUM OF COMPONENTS	1917 11	1987 11	>22,109	>52,801	>112,079		[from Appendices 2.1–9.1]
9	DEMOCIDE	1917 11	1987 11	24,063	54,767	114,736		
	DEMOCIDE OF FOREIGNERS							
10,11	TERRORISM	1917 11	1987 11	1,372	1,783	2,496		
12	DEPORTATIONS	1917 11	1987 11	1,032	1,905	4,071		
13	CAMP/TRANSIT	1917 11	1987 11	1,860	3,453	5,567		
14	SUM OF COMPONENTS	1917 11	1987 11	4,263	7,142	12,134		[from Appendices 2.1–9.1]
15,16	DEMOCIDE	1917 11	1987 11	4,263	7,142	12,134		
	OVERALL DEMOCIDE							
17,18	TERRORISM	1917 11	1987 11	>4,202	>8,298	>18,934		[sum of lines 3 and 11]
19	DEPORTATIONS	1917 11	1987 11	>2,502	>4,349	>8,748		[sum of lines 4 and 12]
20	CAMP/TRANSIT	1917 11	1987 11	15,919	39,464	82,281		[sum of lines 5 and 13]
21	FAMINE	1917 11	1987 11	3,750	7,833	14,250		[from line 6]
22	SUM OF COMPONENTS	1917 11	1987 11	>26,372	>59,943	>124,213		[sum of lines 18 to 21]
23,24	DEMOCIDE	1917 11	1987 11	28,326	61,911	126,891		[from Appendices 2.1–9.1]
	OTHER DEAD							
25,26	INTER'L & CIVIL WAR/REBELLION	1917 11	1987 11	7,692	14,903	23,265		[excludes Nazi caused famine]
27	INTER'L & CIVIL WAR/REBELLION	1917 11	1987 11	12,692	21,403	30,765		[includes Nazi caused famine]
28,29	FAMINE/DISEASE	1917 11	1987 11	9,400	14,633	21,050		[includes Nazi caused famine]
30	**COMPARISONS OF DEMOCIDE TOTALS**							
31	**CAMP/FORCED LABOR DEAD**							
32	camps	1922	1953	32,600		60,00	Kosyk,62,79–80	low a total over 12 different periods, also includes 27 million foreigners (including 14 million Ukrainians); high is from calculations of others.
34	camps	1936	1950		12,000		Conquest,68,533	
35	forced labor camps	1918	1959		70,000		Solzhenitsyn,75,119	
36	forced labor camps	1918	1976c	12,000			Conquest,78,228	
37	forced labor camps	1918	1981c		66,700		Pipeline,82	presumed minimum
38	forced labor camps	1921	1939		8,000		Stewart-Smith,64,222	accepts est cited by Solzhenitsyn; interview with Michail Makarenko
39	forced labor camps	1930	1950		12,000		Elliot,72,223–5	
40	forced labor camps	1936	1950	12,000		16,000	Ramer,86,20	high is from Krushchev,
41	forced labor camps	1937	1953	16,000			Conquest,84,36	"cannot have been fewer than 1 million a year dying in the labor camps"
42	forced labor camps	1940	1960		11,000		Stewart-Smith,64,222	
43	forced labor camps	1930s	1950s	52,000			Pipeline,82	52–54 million a "conservative estimate," interview with M.Makarenko.

Table 1A (continued)

Line								Source	Notes
44	Stalin's camps		19287	1953		10,000		Nuclear Gulag,87	from the International Association of the victims of Communism
45			1918	1975		23,000		"The Current",79,4	reportedly Nikita Khrushchev's figure for the Stalin camps.
46			1928	1953		16,000		"The Current",79,3	low and high result by varying assumptions.
47	Kolyma camps		1930s	1950s		3,000	5,500	Conquest,78,227-8	
48	42 YEAR AVERAGE TOTAL		1918	1959	2,000	44,535	56,454		[average is of the estimates on lines 32-46 proportionated for 42 years]
49	70 YEAR AVERAGE TOTAL		1918	1987	32,861	74,226	94,090		[average is of the estimates on lines 32-46 proportionated for 70 years]
50	Cf. CAMP-TRANSIT DEAD		1917 11	1987	54,768 / 15,919	39,464	82,281		[from line 20, includes foreigners]
51									
52	DEPORTATION DEAD								
53	deported/exiled		?	1949 12		19,000		Kosyk,62,17	by 1949, Soviet citizens, from Spanish Communist El Campesino
54	foreigners deported/exiled		?	1949 12		4,000		Kosyk,62,17	by 1949, foreigners, from Spanish Communist El Campesino
55	national minorities		1936	1950	5,000			Ramoer,86,20	"non-Russian minorities"
56	Cf. DEPORTATION DEAD		1917 11	1987	>2,502	>4,349	>8,748	[from line 19]	
57									
58	STALIN PERIOD DEAD (CITIZENS)								
59	Stalin period		1928	1953	20,000	30,000		Legters,84,60	wholly due to Soviet penology and repression.
60	Stalin period		1930	1953	30,000			Conquest,68,533	
61	Stalin period		19287	1953	20,000		40,000	Antonov-Ovseyenko,81,126	
62			1930	1950				Elliot,72,223-4	may well be conservative; involves collectivization, man-made (famine, killing and privation, camps, and shot in prison
63									
64	Cf. DEMOCIDE (CITIZENS)		1929	1953	19,641	42,672	91,685	[from Appendices 41-6.1]	
65									
66	TOTAL SOVIET DEAD								
67	NONCENSUS BASED ESTIMATES								
68	civilians		1917	1953	57,000	60,000	69,500	Panin,76,93n	estimates of authors in the West.
69			1917	1953	45,000		80,000	Panin,76,93n	
70			1917	1950	27,500			Ramoer,86,20	
71			1917	1959		66,000		Solzhenitsyn,75a,10	from Kurganov, émigré Professor of Statistics.
72			1917	1960		44,000		Stewart-Smith,64,222	includes civil war and invasion of Poland, and famines of the 20 and 30s.
73			1917	1959		66,700		Dujrdin,78,150	cost of communism. excludes WWII, immigration and natural deaths
74			1918	1976	40,000			"The Current",79,4	from Vladimir Bukovsky interview; includes Civil War,
75									famines, collectivization, etc., but excludes WWII
76	42 YEAR AVERAGE TOTAL		1918	1959	44,557	62,134	84,851		[average is of the estimates on lines 68-75 proportionated for 42 years]
77	70 YEAR AVERAGE TOTAL		1918	1987	74,262	103,556	141,419		[average is of the estimates on lines 68-75 proportionated for 70 years]
78	Cf. DEMOCIDE (CITIZENS)		1917 11	1987	24,063	54,767	114,736	[from line 8]	
79									
80	CENSUS BASED								
81	uninatural deaths		1918	1953	22,000	23,000		Medvedev,79,140-1	from Soviet demographer M. Maksudov.
82	uninatural deaths		1926	1954	26,000	30,700	35,450	Dyadkin,83,41,48,55,60	population dead from repression [minus 20.2 million assumed for WWII and Soviet-Finnish Wars]
83									according to "demographic evidence."
84	uninatural deaths		1927	1958	66,000	50,000		Legters,84,60	"closely compatible" with census returns;
85			1918	1960				"The Current",79,4-5	from I.A. Kurganov; years covered assumed
86	population deficit		1926	1950		78,000		Dyadkin,83,59	population deficit, if no repression since 1926, includes unborn.
87	42 YEAR AVERAGE TOTAL		1918	1959	39,087	42,596	45,446		[average is of the estimates on lines 81-86 proportionated for 42 years]
88	70 YEAR AVERAGE TOTAL		1918	1987	65,146	75,743	111,407		[average is of the estimates on lines 81-86 proportionated for 70 years]
89	Cf. DEMOCIDE (CITIZENS)		1917 11	1987	24,063	54,767	114,736	[from line 8]	

Table 1A (continued)

	DEMOCIDE RATE			
92				
93	MID-PERIOD POPULATION 1952		184,780	Dyadkin,83,24
94	DEMOCIDE RATE (CITIZENS) 1917 11 1987	13.02%	29.64% 62.09%	[(line 8/line 93) X 100]
95	WEIGHTED ANNUAL DEMOCIDE RATE 1917 11 1987	0.20%	0.45% 0.94%	[(the sum of the products of the annual rates for a period and their duration in years)/70]

* NOTES, QUALIFICATIONS, PROCEDURES
1 Sources are defined by Author(s), year (last two digits), page(s), all sources are listed in the references.
   a All except small estimates are rounded off to nearest thousand for the USSR
   b If three estimates are shown, low and high are from others mentioned by the source and the mid-estimate is the source's.
2 Comments in brackets are the author's.
3 Cf means "compare to".
4 See Appendix A for additional procedures used in this and subsequent appendices.

(terror, deportations, etc.). This is due to the lack of estimates for some of these components for some of the periods, and the derivation of the democide total for these and some other periods from democide estimates available in the references.

Also given in the table is the total dead from international wars, battle dead from civil war and rebellions, and nondemocidal dead from famine and disease. Considering just the midestimates, 29,536,000 Soviet citizens have thus died (the sum of lines 26 and 28), or a little over half the democide among citizens.

Of course, this begs the question: how good are these democide figures? This will be answered, in part, through the appendixes to each of the following chapters, which will detail for the relevant period the various estimates, sources, qualifications, procedures, and calculations that accumulate across the periods to the democide totals given in table 1A.

However, some tests can also be applied here. But first, before considering them, some consideration must be given to the meaning of validity in this context. As pointed out in appendix A, the actual democide toll is beyond our grasp, were even Soviet archives open to us. At best, we can only find some high-low range that most probably brackets the true number, and estimate within that range a most likely, prudent estimate. At the beginning, therefore, we must accept that midestimates in table 1A are wrong, perhaps off by many millions. Even the lows and highs may not be low or high enough. Therefore, the validity of these results in the scientific sense of the term is already clear—they are undoubtedly invalid.

But there is a larger meaning of the term than being precisely true. That is, being *most probable* in the light of the experience of those involved, the knowledge of experts, the social and physical conditions, and the social context. For example, given what has been revealed about the gulag during the Second World War by former prisoners and Soviet officials (such as the near famine conditions imposed on the camps; the deadly camp regime, the heavy labor for possibly twelve to fourteen hours a day, often in a killing climate; the low value given prisoner's lives by the camp administration; the constant uncovering of "plots," with subsequent rounds of executions, by camp officials trying to justify their noncombat duties in wartime; and the assertions by prisoners and experts that many millions thus died), an estimate that the annual deathrate was from 10 percent to 28 percent seems likely.

That, consequently, more than 6,000,000 to nearly 18,000,000 camp prisoners were killed during the four and a half years out of an annual camp population ranging from 9,000,000 to 12,300,000 seems reasonable. And that within this range of killed the true number is around 11,000,000 dead appears most probable, given the detailed estimates in the references. On the other hand, given all the evidence, an estimate that, say, 500,000 prisoners (or 30,000,000), were killed during the war appears most improbable.

To establish validity here, therefore, is to make sure that a particular estimate is most consistent with all the evidence. This has been done in the subsequent chapters for each period, where the text establishes the social conditions and context for asserting particular estimates of democide, and the appendixes provide the detailed estimates, sources, and calculations. For each period, the validity of the democide totals, understood in these terms, has been established.

What remains here is to determine whether the democide components and overall totals of table 1A (lines 2 to 23) accumulated from these appendixes for each period are also consistent with the relevant, overall estimates of experts. If a democide low is at the lower end or below such estimates, the high is at their upper end or higher, and the midestimate—meant to be the prudent, most probable estimate—is near and perhaps somewhat below their central thrust, then (given also what has been done in the appendixes for each period) they will be considered valid.

With this in mind, table 1A presents a variety of estimates of the camp toll during all or a major part of Soviet history. Because these are so variable in the years they cover, all (except the estimates on line 47 specific to the Kolyma camp complex) were proportionated over forty-two-and seventy-year periods and averaged. In doing this, the one case (line 40) where there is a low and high estimate, but no midestimate, the midestimate is made from the average of the two. The formula for proportionating the estimates over 42 years is simply ([estimate/(1 + difference in years)] x 42), and the "c" and "s" are dropped from the years. Obviously, the seventy-year period covers the whole Soviet history considered here. But, after Stalin died in 1953, democide dropped sharply in the next decade and thereafter sloped down to very small numbers. Thus, proportionating the estimates only over the period up to 1960—forty-two years—may be more realistic.

The camp averages for both the forty-two-and seventy-year periods are shown in the table (lines 48 and 49), along with the component totals (line 50). Note that the component low of 15,919,000 dead in camps and transit is far below both the forty-two-and seventy-year average lows; also the high of 82,281,000 dead is higher than that for the forty-two-year average and closer to that for seventy years. That the seventy-year average high is higher is understandable, given the great reduction in the camp population and death rates after Stalin. The midestimate of 39,464,000 dead is below both average midestimates and, indeed, is slightly more than halfway between the low and the forty-two-year midaverage. Based on the references, therefore, these component totals seem to capture the variation in estimates of those killed in the camps, while the midtotal does appear prudent.

Next considered in the table are estimates of those citizens and foreigners who died in the deportations (lines 53 to 55). Since there are only three such estimates in the references, no proportionating need be done. For comparison, the component totals (line 56) are shown below the estimates. It is unclear from the sources whether these estimates include those among the deported who died in the camps. The component totals do exclude all such. Were they included, however, they would probably less than double the totals. Moreover, the totals given are underestimates, since there were no estimates available for some regions or periods where and when deportation must have taken place. In any case, as can be seen, the range and midtotal seem consistent with the estimates.

Next to compare is the total democide for the Stalin period itself. Four estimates are shown (lines 65 to 69) and below them are given for comparison the appropriate democide totals computed from the appendixes. It can be seen immediately that the low and high do bracket the estimates, but that the midtotal seems too high, even higher than one high estimate of 40,000,000. The most detailed of these estimates is that from Conquest, and we can get some insight into the reason for the high midtotal by considering his calculations.[19] Now, Conquest's estimate of 20,000,000 killed under Stalin is a minimum, "which is almost certainly too low and might require an increase of 50 per cent or so. . . ."[20] But even a 50 percent increase would only bring the total to 30,000,000, still under the midtotal of 42,672,000 given here. First, one source of the difference is that Conquest too conservatively estimates the death toll in the camps at 12,000,000 for the years 1936 to 1950, when for just the postwar period alone, 1946–53, the toll probably exceeded this (see appendix 8.1). The midtotal of those killed in the camps during the Stalin years is 32,584,000 (less than 2,000,000 of these foreigners); about 7,000,000 more were killed in other years.[21] It is significant here, therefore, that the overall midtotal of camp deaths based on these numbers already has been shown not to be excessive (lines 38 to 56).

Second, Conquest excludes the 5,000,000 intentionally starved to death in the Ukrainian famine (this intentionality and number Conquest establishes in a much later work),[22] and the perhaps 333,000 famine deaths Stalin was responsible for in the postwar period. Third, excluding those killed in collectivization and the camps, Conquest only allows for a million executions during the period, which he believes is "certainly a low estimate."[23] Indeed, a million executions is probably a safe estimate for the Great Terror period alone. Indeed, I get from the Appendixes (4.1-8.1) a total of 4,565,000 more killed in Stalin's terror throughout his twenty-five-year reign. Finally, Conquest ignores the millions that died in deportations after the collectivization period (in a much later work Conquest himself calculates that 530,000 died in the deportation of eight nations during the war alone;[24] this excludes the death toll among Ukrainians, non-Volga German-Soviets, Greek-Soviets, Korean-Soviets, etc.—see appendix 7.1).

When all these differences are added to Conquest's minimum figure, the result is consistent with the midtotal of 42,672,000 citizens dead under Stalin's regime that is given here.

The number killed by Stalin, however, is just part of the larger democide totals for Soviet history. The most important question, then, is how these totals compare to estimates of the total democide. The table (lines 68 to 75) gives noncensus-based estimates of the overall democide. As was done for the camp death estimates, these are proportionated and averaged for forty-two and seventy years (lines 76 to 77), and compared to the democide totals (citizens) determined here (line 78). This shows that the democide low is well below that of the estimates; the high is midway between the forty-two-and seventy-year averages, and the midtotal is appropriately prudent. This also lends support to the total for the Stalin years discussed above.

Finally, there is the census-based estimates. Too much can be made of unnatural death estimates based on supposed "census results." For one thing, census figures, particularly in the 1930s, were politically manipulated to show a greater population growth than actually occurred (thus understating total deaths—see the introduction to appendix 6.1). For another, the calculations of unnatural deaths are very sensitive to birth and death rate assumptions. Indeed, one can look at these census-based estimates as, like the democide totals here, having no more than a more or less reasonable probability of being true. In any case, five such estimates are shown in the table (lines 81 to 86). Four of them are proportionated as above (the population deficit includes the number that would have been born, had there not been a certain number of deaths, and therefore should not enter into an average of unnatural deaths, especially if it is to be compared to democide totals), and compared to the democide of citizens. The democide low and high do bracket the results, while the democide midtotal lies between the forty-two-and seventy-year averages (line 90).

Overall, the democide components and grand totals do reflect the diverse estimates of experts and in this sense are warranted. Moreover, similar assessments for each period also show that the subtotals are consistent with the references. Finally, actual Soviet democidal institutions, processes, and events that are outlined in subsequent chapters provide justification for these totals. In sum, probably somewhere between 28,326,000 and 126,891,000 people were killed by the Communist Party of the Soviet Union from 1917 to 1987; and a most prudent estimate of this number is 61,911,000.

The democide rates over the three generations of Soviet history are shown in the table (line 94). Clearly, an infant born in 1917 had a good chance of being killed by the party sometime in his or her future. A more precise statement of this is given by the average of the democide rates for each period, weighted by the number of years involved (line 95). Focusing on the most probable midrisk of 0.45 percent throughout Soviet history, including the relatively safe years after the 1950s, the odds of the average citizen being killed by his own government (party) have been about 45 to 10,000; or to turn this around, 222 to 1 of surviving terror, deportations, the camps, or an intentional famine. As pointed out in the text, this is almost twenty times the risk of an American dying in a vehicular accident.

Appendix 1.2

One problem in determining Soviet democide is that there are often—for one period or another or one year or another—only estimates of the number deported or in forced labor camps, but no estimates of the resulting dead. Were some deathrate statistics available, then, the number killed in deportations or the camps could be calculated. Accordingly, estimates of these rates were sought in the references and are given in table 1B. From them, a range of relevant deathrates and a prudent midrate were calculated.

The table first lists various deathrate estimates for the camps and special settlements (lines 2 to 16). These are consolidated into one set of rates by first making the low the lowest of all the estimates, the high the average among all rates higher than the low (excluding Solzhenitsyn's extremely high rate—line 5—and the higher of the two extremely high rates for the Kolyma camps—line 11), and the midestimate the average of all the estimated rates between the low and high. The result is a conservatively low 10 percent per annum deathrate; a moderate, midestimate of 20 percent, lower than more than half the estimated rates; and a high of 28 percent, modest enough considering some of the higher estimates in the table.

I could find no deathrates for the prisoners in transit to the camps, but four were available for the deportations. These are shown in the table (lines 20 to 24). Consolidating these as was done for the camp death rates gives a range of 10 to 26 percent killed during deportation. Now, the deportations involved whole families, including pregnant women, infants and young children, the aged, the sick and infirm. The death toll among the deported from lack of food and water, cold or heat, and disease in overcrowded railway freight cars was understandably high. By comparison, the transit to the camps involved mostly able, adult males. The death toll must have been much lower as a result, perhaps by around two-thirds. Accordingly, the transit deathrates were reduced to a range of 3 to 9 percent to get reasonable rates for transit to the camps (line 27).

Finally, there is need for overall deportation deathrates as well. Estimates of these rates or those calculated from estimates of deportation numbers and dead are shown in the table (beginning on line 31). These are subdivided in terms of the deportation of classes, minority nations, POWs, and foreign civilians. Deportation deaths and death rates normally also include transit deaths. POWs are included here, although most were deported to camps. A major reason is that estimates of their losses also cover transit deaths, which in many cases were high.

A consolidated range of deathrates was determined for each classi-

TABLE 1B
Soviet Transit, Camp, and Deportation Death Rates*

LINE	EVENT/PROCESS/STRUCTURE	(% or 000)			SOURCE	NOTES
		LOW	MID	HIGH		
	CAMPS-FORCED LABOR ANNUAL DEATH RATE (%)(11)					
2	camps			10	Conquest,68,365	from P.J de la F Wiles
3	camps			20	Conquest,68,365	from P.J de la F Wiles
4	camps	24		37	Conquest,68,532-3	not less than 40-50% of Polish camp inmates died during an avg incarceration of 2-25 years.
5	camps			98	Solzhenitsyn,75a,98	death rate of 1% per day "commonplace and common knowledge"
6	camps	20		25	Wiles,53,App.II,3	over a long period
7	camps	10			Conquest,68,532	in general, up to 1950.
8	camps (labor)			22	Wiles,53,App.II,2	timber camps, official rate from G. Kitchin
9	camps (labor)			12	Andics,69,111	based on 14,000 sworn statements
10	camps/prisons	30		35	Kusnierz,49,81	among Poles deported, high based on Vice-Commissar Vyshinsky declaration
11	Kolyma	75		80	Conquest,78,219	among Poles.
12	Kolyma	30		35	Conquest,78,220	among miners
13	Kolyma				Conquest,78,220	among miners
14	prisoners	21		29	Beck and Godin,51,76	overall rough average
15	special settlements	10		15	Kusnierz,49,34	"it took at most between two and three years for death to reduce a batch of prisoners by half."
16	special settlements?				Grudzinska-Gross,81,xxiv	among Poles deported
17		10	20	20		Polish children
18	CONSOLIDATED (ANNUM)	10		28		[low % is the lowest of all, high is the average of all figures greater than the low, mid-estimate is the average of all figures between the low and average high, the high on line 11 and line 5 were excluded]
19	TRANSIT DEATH RATE (%)					
20	deportation			50	Conquest,70a,103	Winter deportation in cattle cars for several weeks; death reported as high as 50%.
21	deportation	15		20	Conquest,86,285	high proportion were children; from Pigido-Pravoberezny
22	deportation				Kusnierz,49,74	among Poles deported
23	deported ethnic Germans	15		30	Fleischhauer & Pinkus,86,101	of 200,000 Soviet-Germans evacuated with German army and overtaken by Red Army and deported, 15-30% died during transit.
25	CONSOLIDATED TRANSIT	10	17	26		[low % is the lowest of all, high is the average of all figures greater than the low, mid-estimate is the average of all figures between the low and average high]
27	ESTIMATED CAMP TRANSIT	3	5	9		[line 25 adjusted downward to compensate for camp transit prisoners being mainly young or middle aged males]
	DEPORTED/DEAD/DEATH RATE (12)					
30	CLASSES					
31	Kulak dead	400		500	Maksudov,86,30	dead from transit and living conditions of 1.5 million deported; from data supplied by N. A. Ivnitskii.
32	% dead	27	30	33		[mid-% is the average between low and high %]
34	MINORITY NATIONS					
35	Balkars deported	43			Conquest,70a,64	[based on 1939 population, and thus an underestimate of the number probably deported]
36	% dead	27			Nekrich,78,138	net losses, after allowance for wartime losses, percent closer to minimal than maximal
38	Chechens deported	408			Conquest,70a,64	[based on 1939 population, and thus an underestimate of the number probably deported]
39	% dead	22			Nekrich,78,138	net losses, after allowance for wartime losses, percent closer to minimal than maximal
41	Crimean Tatars deported	200		250	Sheehy and Nahaylo,80,8	
42	% dead	22		46	Sheehy and Nahaylo,80,8	low from Soviet official estimate, which omits transit deaths, high from Tatar census.

Table 1B (continued)

#	Category	Measure			Source	Notes
43						
44	Ingushi deported	% dead	92		Conquest,70a,64	[based on 1939 population, and thus an underestimate of the number probably deported]
45			9		Nekrich,78,138	net loses, after allowance for wartime losses; percent closer to minimal than maximal
46						
47	Georgian Meskhetians deported		200		Sheehy and Nahaylo,80,24	includes local Turkmans, Turkic Karapapakh Azerbaydzhanis, Turkicized Kurds, and Khemshili Armenians
48		Dead	30	50	Sheehy and Nahaylo,80,24	died from hunger and cold in Uzbekistan to which deported
49		Dead	50		Conquest,70a,109	excludes transit deaths and therefore a low figure.
50		% dead	15	25		
51						
52						
53	Kalmyks	% Dead	134		Conquest,70a,64	[based on 1939 population, and thus an underestimate of the number probably deported]
54			15		Nekrich,78,138	net loses, after allowance for wartime losses; percent closer to minimal than maximal
55						
56	Karachai	% dead	76		Conquest,70a,64	[1939 population, and thus an underestimate of the number probably deported]
57			30		Nekrich,78,138	net loses, after allowance for wartime losses; percent closer to minimal than maximal.
58						
59	nations deported overall	Dead	1,850		Conquest,70a,65-6	8 nations; includes 200,000 Germans from outside the Volga Republic.
60			530		Conquest,70b,162	of 8 entire nations, including Meskhetians; supported by census data
61		% dead	29			
62						
63	nations deported death rate		40	45	Glaser & Possony,79,280	of 8 nations deported; in the 18 months after departure
64	*OVERALL % DEAD*		9	21	29	[low % is the lowest of all, high is the average of all figures greater than the low;
65						mid-estimate is the average of all figures between the low and average high]
66						
67	POWS [3]					
68	(German POWs		3,000	4,000	Dallin & Nicolaevsky,47,277	of an estimated 3-4 million POWs, Molotov claimed in 1947 that 1,003,974
69		Dead	1,105	2,105	Dallin & Nicolaevsky,47,277	were repatriated and 890,532 were still in the USSR
70		% dead	28	70		[see previous note]
71						
72	Italian POWs	Dead	60		Dallin & Nicolaevsky,47,280	Italian government claimed in 1947 that 12,513 POWs returned out of 60,000.
73			47		Dallin & Nicolaevsky,47,280	[see previous note]
74		% dead	78			
75						
76	Japanese POWs	Dead	900	300	Dallin & Nicolaevsky,47,277-	POWs transferred from Manchuria to Siberia
77			200		Elliott,82,233	never released and presumed dead
78		% dead	22	33		
79						
80	*OVERALL POW % DEAD*		22	70		[low % is the lowest of all, high is from line 71;
81						mid-estimate is the average of all figures between the low and average high]
82						
83	FOREIGNERS					
84	Balts deported	dead	200	456	Shtromas,86,212n33	from diverse estimates.
85			100		Misiunas & Taagepera,83,100	deported that died of cold and hunger.
86		%	22	50		
87						
88	Germans deported	dead	100	700	Swianiewicz,65,42	from Germany and Danumbian countries; from German Federal government in 1952
89				125	de Zayas,79,70,204	among deported Reich-Germans, 100,000-125,000 dead a conservative estimate.
90		%		18		
91						

Table 1B (continued)

Line	Item					Source	Note
92	Germans deported	dead			150	Dushnyck, 75,405	of 150,000 alledged former Nazis sent to camps. [see previous note]
93		%			80	Dushnyck, 75,405	
94							
95					53		
96	Romanians deported	dead			420		in 1948 Romania declared as dead all those who disappeared during the war. [see previous note]
97				230		Herling, 51, 103-5	
98		%		55		Herling, 51, 103-5	
99	Poles deported	dead	1,250			Gross, 88, 146	includes POWs
100		dead	709			Kusnierz, 49, 86	of deported; excludes forced labor camp dead, from Vyshinsky.
101		dead	270			Tolstoy, 81, 102	of deported and POWs
102		%	22		57		
103	Poles deported	dead			1,500	Gross, 88, 229	if accept from Norman Davies a deportation total of 1.5 million.
104		dead			750	Gross, 88, 229	[see previous note]
105		%			50		
106							
107	*OVERALL FOREIGNERS % DEAD*		14	21	41		[low % is the lowest of all, high is the average of all figures greater than the low, mid-estimate is the average of all figures between the low and average high]
108							
109							
110	*AVERAGE DEPORTED % DEAD*		18	26	43		[average of lines 32, 65, 81, 107]
111							
112	*SUMMARY %*						
113	*CAMP/FOR.LAB. DEATH RATE*		10	20	28		[from line 17]
114	*TRANSIT DEATH RATE*		3	5	9		[from line 27]
115	*DEPORTATION DEATH RATE*		18	26	43		[from line 110]

NOTES:

* See notes Table 1A.

1. Note that some inmates were in camps in which no one survived, therefore the death rates are from camps in which there were some survivors.(Conquest, 78, 219)
2. Deported death rates generally include transit deaths.
3. POWs is included under deported, since the death toll also includes transit dead.

fication, usually as was done for the camp estimates. Thus, for example, among nations deported (lines 35 to 63) the overall range in the death rates consolidated from them is 9 to 29 percent (line 65). These consolidations for each classification of deported were then averaged to get one set of rates (line 110): 18 to 43 percent killed by deportation, with a midestimate of 26 percent.

The table concludes by presenting together the death rates that were determined for the camps, transit, and deportations. These are the basic rates, then, used when necessary to calculating these deaths for each period.

An important question is how sensitive the democide totals are to using these rates. If the results hang on them, then this means that table 1B is the most important in this book and the rates developed there entail the most critical assumptions.

This question is particularly pertinent to the number of those killed in the camps. In total, probably 39,467,000 people died in the camps or in transit to them (table 1A, line 20)—about 64 percent of the likely overall democide. This number was found by consolidating or averaging (a) the result of calculating the death toll by applying camp and transit death rates determined in table 1B to annual estimates of the camp population, and (b) estimates of camp deaths given in the references.

Table 1C presents a sensitivity analysis of the effects of altering the death rates on the democide totals. Although it accounts for a small percentage of the deaths, deportation death rates are also included. First shown are the base deathrate estimates used for each period and the resulting overall democide figures. Then seven cases are given, each involving a zeroing or reduction in the transit, camp, or deportation death rates. The cases are rank ordered, Case I showing the least effect on the democide range, Case VII the most. The former involves eliminating transit deaths altogether by making transit death rates zero, while keeping camp and deportation deaths the same; the latter involves cutting all three death rates by three-fourths.

I should note that the effect of reducing the death rates for camps or deportations by, say, one-half, is not a matter of simply halving the total killed for the component. This is because, as mentioned above, the totals not only involve the computation of the number of deaths by use of the death rates, but also the consolidation or averaging of the results of these computations with the estimates of the number of dead

TABLE 1C
Democide Totals Under Different Camp/Transit and Deportation Death Rates

CASES CONDITIONS	RATES(%)/DEAD EST.(000)		
	LOW	MID	HIGH
BASE DEMOCIDE ESTIMATE			
transit death rate	0.03	0.05	0.09
camp death rate	0.1	0.2	0.28
deportation death rate	0.18	0.26	0.43
DEMOCIDE	28,326	61,911	126,891
CASE I			
no transit deaths	0	0	0
unchanged camp death rate	0.1	0.2	0.28
unchanged deportation death rate	0.18	0.26	0.43
DEMOCIDE	27,893	60,803	122,646
CASE II			
unchanged transit death rate	0.03	0.05	0.09
unchanged camp death rate	0.1	0.2	0.28
deportation rate cut 3/4ths	0.045	0.065	0.1075
DEMOCIDE	27,389	60,069	122,878
CASE III			
transit death rate cut 1/2	0.015	0.025	0.045
camp death rates cut 1/2	0.05	0.1	0.14
unchanged deportation death rate	0.18	0.26	0.43
DEMOCIDE	23,952	49,540	96,829
CASE IV			
one transit death rate at .01	0.01	0.01	0.01
one camp death rate at .05	0.05	0.05	0.05
unchanged deportation death rate	0.18	0.26	0.43
DEMOCIDE	23,887	43,363	77,727
CASE V			
transit death rate cut 1/2	0.015	0.025	0.045
camp death rates cut 1/2	0.05	0.1	0.14
deportation rate cut 1/2	0.045	0.065	0.1075
DEMOCIDE	23,014	47,698	92,816
CASE VI			
transit death rate cut 3/4ths	0.0075	0.0125	0.0225
camp death rates cut 3/4ths	0.025	0.05	0.07
unchanged deportation death rate	0.18	0.26	0.43
DEMOCIDE	21,782	43,408	82,100
CASE VII			
transit death rate cut 3/4ths	0.0075	0.0125	0.0225
camp death rates cut 3/4ths	0.025	0.05	0.07
deportation death rate cut 3/4ths	0.045	0.065	0.1075
DEMOCIDE	20,844	41,567	78,087
RANGE OF RESULTS			
transit death rate	0.0075		0.09
camp death rate	0.025		0.28
deportation death rate	0.01125		0.43
DEMOCIDE	20,844		126,891

given in the literature. Thus, reducing the death rate does not proportionally reduce the democide figures.

Now, given the estimates in table 1B, it is hardly likely that the death rates used here are four times too high—that the low for the camp death rate is 2.5 percent, rather than 10; or the high should be 7 percent, and not 28. Indeed, in the references no estimate of a camp, transit, or deportation death rate lower than 9 percent could be found (see table 1B). Yet, using these unrealistically reduced rates still gives in Case VII a total democide range of 20,844,000 to 78,087,000 killed, with a midestimate of 41,567,000. While this is a reduction of nearly 20,000,000 dead in the midestimate, this total killed still remains a demographic catastrophe greater than the civilian and military death toll of World War II. In other words, were the death rates used here much too high, the resulting democide totals would still be terribly significant.

There is another way of validating the death rates determined in table 1B. Are the resulting camp, deportation, and overall democide totals consistent with estimates in the literature? Appendix 1.1 shows that they are. We might conclude, therefore, that while these rates cannot be exact, they at least appear to reflect the actual death toll in the camps, transit, and deportations.

Epigraphs quoted in Conquest (1968, p. 544) and Antonov-Ovseyenko (1981, pp. 104–5).

Notes

1. "The suppression of the Don Cossack revolt . . . of 1919 took the form of genocide. One historian has estimated that approximately 70 percent . . . were physically eliminated" (Heller and Nekrich, 1986, p. 87). Around 1900, the Don region had a population of about 1,000,000 Cossacks (p. 78).
2. Conquest (1986, p. 306). "It certainly appears that a charge of genocide lies against the Soviet Union for its actions in the Ukraine. Such, at least, was the view of Professor Rafael Lemkin who drafted the [Genocide] Convention" (p. 272). The "Ukrainian famine was a deliberate act of genocide of roughly the same order of magnitude as the Jewish Holocaust of the Second World War, both in the number of its victims and in the human suffering it produced" (Mace, 1986, p. 11).
3. "The swath cut by deportation was so wide that the issue of genocide ought to be considered. . . . Most Estonian deportees never returned, having largely perished. In the case of 'kulaks', all members of a pop-

ulation group, identified through *past* socio-economic status, were deported, regardless of their individual *present* behavior. There was no legal way to leave the condemned social group. In the case of children, the guilt was hereditary. If destroying a social group entirely, with no consideration of personal behavior, is genocide, then the March 1949 deportation would seem to qualify" (Taagepera, 1980, p. 394).

4. Conquest (1986, p. 306). "The genocide against the peasants . . . was unique not only for its monstrous scale; it was directed against an indigenous population by a government of the same nationality, and in time of peace" (Heller and Nekrich, 1986, p. 236).

The Soviets now appear to admit to this genocide. In the *Moscow News*, a Moscow-published, English language newspaper, was recently written: "In what amounted to genocide, between five and ten million people died during the forced collectivization of farming in the early thirties" (Ambartsumov, 1988).

5. Hingley (1974, p. 284); Medvedev (1979, p. 102).
6. Medvedev (1979, p. 117).
7. Petrov (1956, pp. 9–10).
8. Ibid., p. 73–74. One such telegram to Sverdlovsk ordered that 15,000 "enemies of the people" be shot (p. 74).
9. Solzhenitsyn (1973, p. 71).
10. "NKVD cadres themselves were terrorized into 'production' frenzies by surprise visits from NKVD headquarters officials. In an unannounced visit to the Rostov NKVD office, Genrikh Lyushkov, a high-ranking state security officer, charged the gathered officials with laxness in pursuing enemies and immediately fingered three of their own number as enemies; the intimidated district chief quickly prepared the charges and had his own accused men shot" (Dziak, 1988, p. 68).
11. Solzhenitsyn (1973, pp. 69-70).
12. Small and Singer (1982, p. 91).
13. Calculated from ibid., tables 4.2 and 13.2.
14. This is a paraphrase of the title of Heller and Nekrich's (1986) history of the Soviet Union, *Utopia in Power*.
15. Leggett (1981, p. 186).
16. See Heller (1988).
17. Conquest (1986, p. 234).
18. Solzhenitsyn (1973, p. 174).
19. (1968, appendix A). Elliot (1972, pp. 223–24) accepts Conquest's total of 20,000,000, but arrives at it by a different breakdown of the agents of death.
20. Conquest (1968, p. 533).
21. From Appendixes 4.1–8.1.
22. (1986).
23. Conquest (1968, p. 533).
24. (1970a, p. 165).

2

3,284,000 Victims: The Civil War Period, 1917–1922

> *Steinberg (Commissar for Justice), seeing that his opposition to the introduction of a harsh police measure with far-reaching implications of terror was making no headway with Lenin, exclaimed in exasperation, "Then why do we bother with a Commissariat of Justice? Let's call it frankly the Commissariat for Social Extermination and be done with it!" At which Lenin's face brightened and he replied: "Well put . . . that's exactly what it should be. . . . but we can't say that."*

In March 1917, the Russian czar abdicated in the face of general strikes, huge demonstrations, and revolts among his troops. A First Provisional Government had been formed the day before under Prince Georgy Lvov. This government and that of Aleksandr Kerensky, a democratic socialist who took over as prime minister in July, were faced with economic and political chaos: a near total breakdown in government authority and military morale, frequent strikes, plots, and the active opposition of diverse, radical revolutionary groups, not the least of which were the Bolsheviks (who already in July had organized an unsuccessful uprising in Petrograd). The government itself was disorganized, feared a coup from the right, and was quite unable to move against those openly plotting to seize power from the left.

Originally the left wing of the Russian Social Democratic Labor Party, the Bolsheviks (cleverly meaning "majority" in Russian) were a very small, uncompromising, and militant group of dedicated Marxist communists. In the first all-Russian Congress of Soviets in June, for example, only 105 out of 1,090 delegates declared themselves Bolsheviks.[1]

On 7 November (25 October in the old calendar) 1917, with the powerful Petrograd garrison remaining neutral, the Bolsheviks seized the Winter Palace in Petrograd. Since this was the seat of Kerensky's shaky Provisional Government—and he had only 1,500 to 2,000 defenders to match the 6,000 to 7,000 soldiers, sailors, and Red Guards of the Bolsheviks—the government was easily overthrown.[2] Widely unpopular, however, and faced with strong political opposition, the Bolsheviks at first made common cause with the Left Social Revolutionaries (a militant socialist group) in their new government in an effort to survive, centralize power, and consolidate the communist revolution. In March 1919, they changed their name to the Communist Party (with Bolshevik in parentheses).

A rapidly developing problem for the Bolsheviks was the formation throughout former Russia of whole armies (Whites) to oppose Bolshevik (Red) power. Some armies were anti-Russian and nationalist, some anti-communist, some for the monarchy or authoritarian rule, some for democracy. Moreover, in the areas the Bolsheviks controlled they were opposed by the clergy, bougeoisie and professionals. The urban workers, who had been their allies at first, soon turned against them when they saw that the Bolsheviks had taken over the soviets (elected governing councils) and would not yield power to worker unions or representatives. And peasants, who also were especially supportive when the soviets began to divide among them land taken from the aristocrats' estates and rich land owners, turned to outright rebellion when the Bolsheviks began to forcibly requisition their grain and produce.

In the first year-and-a-half of Soviet rule there were 344 peasant rebellions[3] in twenty provinces alone. Up to early 1921, there were about fifty anti-Soviet rebel armies. For example, in August 1920, the starving peasants of the Kirsanov District, Tambov Province, rebelled against the further extortion of grain by the Bolsheviks. The rebellion soon spread to adjoining districts and destroyed Soviet authority in five of them. Under the command of Aleksandr Stepanovich Antonov, the rebellion became a full-scale armed insurrection. He created two armies consisting of Red Army deserters and peasants in revolt, and by February 1921 he had as many as 50,000 men under arms, including even

internal guard units. Until defeated in August 1921, he controlled
Tambov Province and parts of the provinces of Penza and Saratov.[4]

Numerous such rebellions broke out throughout the Soviet Union,
although few were as dangerous to Soviet control. Even in 1921, the
Cheka (secret police) admitted to 118 uprisings.[5] This Bread War
continued even after the White armies were defeated. It was so serious
that even in 1921 one Soviet historian noted that the "center of the
RSFSR is almost totally encircled by peasant insurrection, from Mak-
no on the Dnieper to Antonov on the Volga.1"[6]

White armies and peasant rebellions aside, even in the urban industrial areas Soviet control was precarious at best. What saved them was
the Red Terror. By 1918, terror was already being employed widely,
including inciting workers to murder their "class enemies." According
to *Pravda*, the party organ, workers and the poor should take up arms
and act against those "who agitate against the Soviet Power, ten bullets
for every man who raises a hand against it. . . . The rule of Capital
will never be extinguished until the last capitalist, nobleman, Chris-
tian, and officer draws his last breath.[7] Understandably, there was a
wave of arbitrary murders of civil servants, engineers, factory man-
agers, and priests throughout the country. Mass shootings, arrests, and
torture were an integral part of covert Soviet policy and not simply a
reaction to the formation of the White armies. Indeed, this terror
preceded the start of the civil war.[8]

With the assassination attempt on Lenin in August 1918, however,
the terror was legalized—it now became an overt, state-sponsored and
state-directed Red Terror against "enemies of the people" and "counterrevolutionaries," defined primarily by social group and class membership: bourgeoisie, aristocrats, "rich" landowners (kulaks), and clergy.
In inaugurating the Red Terror, *Pravda*'s cry for blood was even shriller:

> Workers, the time has come when either you must destroy the bour-
> geoisie, or it will destroy you. Prepare for a mass merciless onslaught
> upon the enemies of the revolution. The towns must be cleansed of this
> bourgeois putrefaction. All the bourgeois gentlemen must be registered,
> as has happened with the officer gentlemen, and all who are dangerous
> to the cause of revolution must be exterminated. . . . Henceforth the
> hymn of the working class will be a hymn of hatred and revenge.[9]

The Red Terror operated through a variety of government organs,
including the People's Courts for "crimes" against the individual, the
Revolutionary Courts, and the various local Chekas for "crimes" against

the state.[10] Then there was the right of execution given to or assumed by the Military Revolutionary Tribunals, Transport Cheka, Punitive Columns, and the like.[11] Actual or ideologically defined opponents were jailed, many tortured barbarously and forced to sign false confessions. Many were executed. Often, "enemies of the people" were arrested en masse and shot in batches. As Martyn Latzis, founding member of the NKVD Coellgium and top Cheka official, wrote:

> We are out to destroy the *bourgeoisie* as a class. Hence, whenever a *bourgeois* is under examination the first step should be, not to endeavor to discover material of proof that the accused has opposed the Soviet Government, whether verbally or actually, but to put to the witness the three questions: "To what class does the accused belong?" "What is his origin?" and "Describe his upbringing, education, and profession." Solely in accordance with the answers to these three questions should his fate be decided. For this is what "Red Terror" means, and what it implies.[12]

But that was the terror program; the application was far more general and idiosyncratic. Like executing a butcher in Moscow for "insulting" the images of Marx and Lenin by calling them scarecrows (a clear "enemy of the people"); or the party officials of Ivanovo-Vornesensk threatening to shoot anyone who did not register their sewing machines (obvious "counterrevolutionaries"); or the "commissary of posts and telegraphs at Baku issu[ing] an order that any telephone girl found guilty of tardy response to a call, or of response to a call 'in an uncivil manner,' should be shot within twenty-four hours. . . ."[13] (doubtless "sabotage"). Or like the Odessa Cheka, who, having information that an Aaron Chonsir was engaging in "counterrevolutionary activities," looked through the street directories to find his address. Locating eleven people with the same name, they arrested all, interrogated and tortured each several times, narrowed it down to the two most likely "counterrevolutionaries," and, since they could not make up their mind between them, had both shot to ensure getting the right one.[14] Obviously, the revolution was still immature—in the late 1930s under Stalin, all eleven would have been shot.

Now perhaps this all seems immoral, inhumane. But to the Marxist, such feelings would only reflect exploitive, bourgeois sensitivities and blindness toward true humanism. The first issue of *The Red Sword*, a Cheka periodical, tries to set this straight:

> For us there do not, and can not, exist the old systems of morality and

"humanity" invented by the bourgeoisie for the purpose of oppressing and exploiting the "lower classes." Our morality is new, our humanity is absolute, for it rests on the bright ideal of destroying all oppression and coercion. To us all is permitted, for we are the first in the world to raise the sword not in the name of enslaving and oppressing anyone, but in the name of freeing all from bondage. . . . Blood? Let there be blood, if it alone can turn the grey-white-and-black banner of the old piratical world to a scarlet hue, for only the complete and final death of that world will save us from the return of the old jackals.[15]

And moral teaching must begin with the children. The revolution demanded that they be taught to enthusiastically apply terror, to accept murdering class enemies. It is thus easy to understand this problem that appeared in a book on educational extension work of the libraries, published in 1920:

A girl of 12 years old, is afraid of blood; the father is a prominent Menshevik. To make up a list of books, the reading of which would overcome the girl's instinctive aversion to red terror. . . .[16]

And so vast numbers of men and women were shot out of hand: 200 in this jail, 450 in that prison yard, 320 in the woods outside of town.[17] Even in small outlying areas, such as in the small Siberian town of Ossa Ochansk in 1919, 3,000 men were massacred.[18] And this went on and on. As late as 1922, 8,100 priests, monks, and nuns were executed.[19] This alone is equivalent to one modern, jumbo passenger jet crashing, with no survivors, each day for 32 days.

Prisoners taken in clashes with the White armies were often executed. Even the relatives of defecting officers were shot. For instance, when the 86th Infantry Regiment went over to the Whites in March 1919, the relatives of all the officers were killed.[20] Places reoccupied after the defeat of one White army or another suffered systematic blood baths as the Cheka screened through the population for aristocrats, bourgeoisie, and supporters of the Whites. When Riga was captured in January 1919, for example, over 1,500 were executed in the city and more than 2,000 in the country districts.[21] When defeated White General Wrangel finally fled with his remaining officers and men from the Crimea, the Reds may have slaughtered from 50,000 to 150,000 people during reoccupation.[22] As the Red Army advanced into Cossack settlements, encountering the resistance of Cossack troops, the Central Committee of the Communist Party sent to the Kamensky Executive Committee this secret order:

> Institute a wholesale terror against the wealthy Cossacks and peasants, and having destroyed them altogether, carry out a pitiless mass terror against the Cossacks in general who took any direct or indirect part in the fight against the Soviet government.[23]

Undeniably, the Whites themselves carried out massacres, killed prisoners, and were guilty of numerous atrocities. But according to some observers, such "terror in the White-occupied areas was always a matter of individual acts by sadistic or fanatical generals, such as Mai-Maevsky or Slashchov. The Red Terror was sponsored by the state. It was not directed against individuals or even political parties but against entire social groups, entire classes, and in some phases of the civil war against the majority of the population."[24]

Then quite apart from the civil war, there were those captured in the hundreds of peasant rebellions. Predictably, since they had shown themselves to be "enemies of the people," they would be generally shot. While this Bread War tends to be ignored in the history books, it was no less vicious than the civil war.

> Authority to requisition food was taken as license to plunder. In count-less villages in the provinces under soviet rule savage struggles erupted. Men were burnt alive, cut up with scythes, and beaten to death. Armed bands clashed and fought pitched battles. . . . [There were] twenty-six major uprisings in July [1918], forty-seven in August, and thirty-five in September.[25]

As calculated in appendix 2.1, the total killed in the civil war itself was likely about 1,100,000, to which probably must be added about 250,000 killed in the Bread War. All these were combat deaths and not part of the democide. Although a fantastic toll by normal standards, this number was but a small fraction of the total killed during this period, as will be seen.

As the growing strength and generalship of the Red Army—and lack of unity and a common strategy and program among the Whites and peasant rebels—surely won the civil war for the Bolsheviks by 1920, the Red Terror secured their home front. It eliminated or cowed the opposition and enabled Lenin to stabilize the Bolshevik government and assure its continuity and authority. Above all, this killing saved the revolution—the ideology. The success of the Bolsheviks and their consolidation of power during this period surely justifies thereafter applying the contemporary label to them—"Soviets." And "Soviet Union" for the Marxist, communist-governed state they created.

The success of the Red Terror was bought at a huge cost in lives. Not only were political opponents, class "enemies," "enemies of the people," former rebels, and criminals shot, but even those poor citizens guilty of nothing, fitting under no label but hostage, were shot. For example, in 1919 the Defense Council commanded the arrest of members of the Soviet executive committees and Committees of the Poor in areas where snow clearance of railway lines was unsatisfactory. These peasant hostages were to be shot if the snow clearance was left undone.[26]

The number killed throughout Soviet territory by the Red Terror, the execution of prisoners, and revenge against former Whites or their supporters possibly involved the murder of between 250,000 and 3,650,000 people; *most probably about 500,000, including at least 200,000 people officially executed.*[27] Among all the conflicting figures, 500,000 seems the most prudent estimate. Yet, as large as it is, it may be overly conservative (and this is what makes it prudent).

For example, according to Pitirim Sorokin, who was exiled from the Soviet Union during these years and subsequently became an esteemed Harvard sociologist, the "most conservative estimate, which certainly understates the real number," is at least 600,000 executions during 1917 to 1922.[28] Also, a Special Judiciary Commission of Inquiry, set up by the White General Denikine, concluded that there were 1,700,000 victims,[29] possibly in the southern provinces alone.[30]

Independently, an even higher number of victims can be estimated by an apparently sensible series of calculations. In 1920 there were fifty-two provinces in the RSFSR, and therefore fifty-two provincial Chekas, fifty-two special branches, and 52 provincial Revolutionary Tribunals. Then there were many regional-transport Chekas, railway tribunals, tribunals of "internal defense," and circuit sessional courts (commissions sent out to supervise local mass shootings). Finally, there were the special branches and special tribunals of the sixteen armies and the special branches and tribunals attached to the several divisions of these armies. Now, also taking into account the many district Chekas, there thus should have existed more than 1,000 torture chambers. Therefore, using the Soviet's own data, we get a modest average of five persons per day shot per torture chamber, or at least 5,000 per day for over 1,000 torture chambers, or more than 1,825,000 just for 1920.[31]

Incidentally, the Cheka itself officially admitted to only 12,733 executions between 1918 and 1921, excluding those of local authorities.[32] Still, this incredibly low number for four years is by itself almost equal to the total number of those executed in the United States under state and local authority for the 119 years from 1864 through 1982—13,630 criminals.[33]

Lest all those Soviet executions during these years be dismissed as the traditional Russian way of handling opposition, czarist Russia executed an average of seventeen people per year in the eighty years preceding the Revolution—seventeen![34] From 1860 to 1900, Soviet sources give only ninety-four executions, although during these years there were dozens of assassinations.[35] And in 1912, after years of attempted revolts, assassinations of high officials, bombings and anti-government terrorism, there was a maximum of 183,949 imprisoned, including criminals,[36] less than half the number executed by the Soviets during the civil war period.

Whether the Soviets murdered 50,000, 500,000, or some higher toll yet, they did not shrink from this carnage. They not only accepted such a body count, they proclaimed the necessity for one many times higher. Consider the September 1918 speech by Grigory Zinoviev, Lenin's lieutenant in Petrograd:

> To overcome our enemies we must have our own socialist militarism. We must carry along with us 90 million out of the 100 million of Soviet Russia's population. As for the rest, we have nothing to say to them. They must be annihilated.[37]

To the estimated 500,000 murdered in the Red Terror must be added a probable 250,000 killed in the Bread War (apart from battle dead), but certainly no less than 70,000 (see appendix 2.1). No mercy was shown the peasant rebels taken captive. Moreover, those who had helped the rebels, provided food and shelter, or simply showed sympathy were massacred. Some villages "infected within rebellion" were leveled, inhabitants slaughtered. Other such villagers were deported north,[38] and many probably died in the process. Keeping in mind that this Bread War was fiercely fought over the full length and breadth of the Soviet Union from 1918 through 1922, and that at any one time there were apparently over a hundred rebellions, involving thousands of peasant fighters, a nonbattle toll of 250,000 is reasonable.

Consider the aforementioned figure of 344 rebellions in only the first year-and-a-half of Bolshevik rule. Make this 400 rebellions for the whole civil war period, a clear underestimate. Then aside from battle, an average of 625 wounded peasants, prisoners, supporters, or alleged sympathizers were murdered per rebellion. This surely seems sensible in light of this Cheka order circulated in 1920:

> In case of a mass uprising on the part of any town or village we shall be compelled to use *mass terror* in respect to those localities, the life of every soviet activist will be paid for with the lives of *hundreds* of residents of those towns and villages.[39]

That an average of 625 people would be killed per rebellion is not only consistent with this order, but also with the shooting, frequently reported, from one city, town or district to another, of batches of prisoners in the dozens and hundreds.[40]

When those probably killed in cold blood in the Bread War are added to the number murdered in the terror, we get a toll of 750,000 people. To this also must be added the 34,000 who likely died from the brutal regime in the new concentration and labor camps or in transit to them.

These camps were legally sanctioned in July 1918, with the decree that inmates capable of labor must be compelled to do physical work. This was the beginning of the deadly Soviet forced labor system, which could as well be called a slave labor system. In the next year decrees established forced labor camps in each provincial capitol and a lower limit of 300 prisioners in each camp.[41] The first large camps were established on the far north Solivetsky Islands. In August 1919, Lenin made the party view clear in a telegram: "Lock up all the doubtful ones in *a concentration camp* outside the city."[42] As Solzhenitsyn notes, these people are not even "guilty" ones, but only "doubtful."

From the beginning, the conditions in some of these camps were so atrocious, often calculatingly so, that prisoners could not expect to survive for more than several years. One at Kholmogori near Archangel was so perilous to prisoners that it became known as a death camp.[43] I should mention that prisoners were sent to these camps, often to die, not after a court trial but by a simple administrative decision.[44]

By the end of 1920, official figures admitted to eighty-four camps in forty-three provinces of the Russian Republic alone, with almost 50,000 inmates (including civil war POWs).[45] By October 1922, there were 132 camps with about 60,000 inmates.[46] That among all these prisoners during this whole period, 34,000 are estimated to have died is prudent. This can be seen in the light of the frequent camp executions; the not uncommon deaths of prisoners from beatings, disease, exposure, and fatigue; and the occasional emptying of camps by loading inmates on barges and then sinking them (such as on the River Dvina, near the two camps Kholmogori and Pertominsk in Archangel Province).[47]

Adding these camp deaths to those murdered in the terror and Bread War does not end the accounting. The agricultural economy was severely disrupted by the civil war and peasant insurrections, and especially by the Soviet's socialist agricultural policies. Moreover, peasants were encouraged to seize large estates by a Decree on Land, thus depriving the cities of essential produce.[48] And the committees of poor peasants that were established in the villages to "assume the responsibility for repression . . ."[49] created much local disorder. So did Lenin's decree that in all small, grain-producing districts, twenty-five to thirty "wealthy" hostages should be selected, all of whom would be killed if the peasants did not deliver their "excess" grain.[50] But in practice, excess grain often turned out to be any grain, and even the peasants' reserve and seed grain were expropriated by detachments of workers ignorant of farming but nonetheless sent in the tens of thousands from the cities to uncover the "excess" (and be yet another source of disarray hardly conducive to good harvests). As Lenin himself confessed: "Practically, we took all the surplus grain—and sometimes even not only surplus grain but part of the grain the peasant required for food."[51]

In 1919, some 15 to 20 percent of what the peasant produced was requisitioned; in 1920, this rose to 30 percent. This seizure of the peasant's produce is sometimes called "War Communism." But it was not dictated by the civil war, which had "not really started at the time of the original decrees. . . ."[52] The purpose of the requisitioning was to move from a capitalist free market to a socialist one, as Lenin declared.[53] It was an attempt to *nationalize* the peasant.

Nationalization and its attendant forced requisitions was a solution to the problem of getting the peasant's grain without paying for it and of preventing the peasant from keeping his grain and other crops from the state. And new Soviet laws tried to assure that the peasant would play his proper role in the Marxist state. Laws set low prices for his produce, banned private trade and established a system of rationing.[54] These laws alone provided little motivation to produce, notwithstanding the likelihood of new detachments of workers coming through to expropriate or loot whatever was in field or house. Understandably, the harvest of 1921 was only 40 percent that of 1913.[55] And the sown area had shrunk to 70 percent of the five-year average preceding World War I, even more in the Volga region.[56]

This disastrous harvest, in conjunction with the peasant having lost or by necessity eaten the reserve food supplies needed to survive the periodic droughts, had human costs far beyond the hundreds of rebellions this all caused. In 1921, a drought, which in some Russian provinces in the past would have at most caused a minor famine, triggered one of the worst famines in modern times: starvation faced by over 30,000,000 people.

Even the most religious who believed that God was punishing them realized that the famine that followed the loss of their crop "was in some measure the fault of human authority. Men in power far from the fertile plains of the Volga made decisions that left the peasant with little or no reserve grain to sustain life if the rains failed."[57] It may be that the Soviets' requisition policy alone must bear the primary responsibility for this disastrous famine.[58] After all, some places, such as the Saratov region, were virtually stripped of all their food."[59]

Confronted with a calamity that could again threaten their survival, with seventeen provinces affected by famine,[60] the Soviets began to provide some aid while requesting urgent international help. International relief, particularly from the United States, was soon forthcoming. But even in the face of this historical disaster, aid and food were wielded as a socialist weapon. Said Lenin,

> it is necessary to supply with food out of the state funds only those employees who are actually needed under conditions of maximum productivity of labor, and to distribute the food provisions by making the whole matter an *instrumentality of politics*, used with the view of cutting down on the number of those who are not absolutely necessary and to spur on those who are really needed.[61]

Also, for political reasons, the counterpart famine in the Ukraine was ignored at first. Soviet officials must have known as early as August 1921 that the southern Ukraine was verging on famine, but they refused to allow a transfer of food from the north to the south. This was to pacify Ukrainian nationalism and defeat the numerous rebellions there—to crush peasant resistance.[62] Requests for foreign aid were for the Russian Republic. Nothing was mentioned about famine in the Ukraine,[63] and nothing was done initially for the Ukraine. Indeed, the Soviets tried to feed Russia with Ukrainian grain, justifying this by exaggerating the amount of its grain production.[64] "Starving Ukrainians were forced to sacrifice their own lives to save hungry Russians. . . "[65] No aid was allowed from the outside until American relief officers forced the issue, and even then the Soviets hindered the aid effort.

Then, in the summer of 1922, irrationally—unless one has firmly in mind their Marxist obsession with building socialism—the Soviets resumed large scale grain exports. This, in spite of having to starve a part of the population to get the grain. But the Soviets wanted capital for industrial heavy equipment. To feed some of these people the American Relief Administration (ARA) was asked to continue aid. Thus:

> In January 1923, inhabitants of Odessa could witness the bizarre spectacle of the *SS Manitowac* discharging a cargo of ARA relief supplies in their port while alongside the *SS Vladimir* was at the same moment loading a cargo of Ukrainian grain destined for Hamburg.[66]

With about $45 million in Federal and private funds,[67] the ARA kept alive more than 10,000,000 people, a figure reluctantly verified and acknowledged by the Soviets.[68] Years later the Soviets would derogate the ARA's relief effort, if they admitted it at all, and claim that it was a capitalist plot to subvert the revolution. Nonetheless, it is "no exaggeration to conclude that the major outcome of the American relief mission was the defeat of what the League of Nations called the worst famine in the history of modern Europe."[69]

Regardless of such international aid, the Soviet Central Statistical Office itself estimated that overall some 5,000,000 people were lost.[70] Maximoff claims that according to official data, 5,200,000 died.[71] Others also give figures close to 5,000,000,[72] and there are also estimates that from 1,000,000 to 10,000,000 perished.[73]

As though the devil had this country in its hand, disease and epidemics also ravaged the land. From 1918 to 1923, 2,000,000 to possibly 3,000,000 people may have died in epidemics, especially typhus.[74] Probably the total was around 2,000,000. Many of these deaths were due to the famine conditions, others to the disruption of public services and sanitation by the civil and Bread wars. Although a case can be made for blaming the party for at least half of these deaths, *none* will be labeled democide here.

Moreover, neither should all who died in the famine be added to the Soviet account. The disruption of the countryside caused by marauding and clashing armies also must be given some weight. But we should keep in mind as well that about 1,500,000 to 2,000,000 starved to death in the Ukraine alone,[75] many of whom were allowed to die in order to feed Russians or export grain. It will be surely a conservative approach, then, to blame only *half* of the probable 5,000,000 famine deaths on Soviet policies.

Overall, in the Red Terror, the Bread War, the new concentration and labor camps, and famine, Lenin and party probably murdered 3,284,000 people (apart from battle deaths), but surely no less than an absolute low of 832,000. Given the sheer size of the USSR, its large population of over 150,000,000, and the widespread mass killing, the toll could have been as high as 8,122,000. This range of possible error in the democide estimate is shown in figure 2.1. (Appendix 2.1 gives the derivation of all these figures and the sources.) Some believe a figure so huge is impossible, but Soviet mass graves, smuggled secret documents, and defecting high officials have often shown our worst case estimates to be conservative.

But also consider that an official Soviet figure, reported in 1969, for deaths during World War I and the Civil War period is 14,000,000;[76] and that using data from the census of 1926 and assuming a normal population growth, 28,000,000 people "had disappeared" in the years from 1914 to 1925.[77] Now, subtract from this loss a high of 4,000,000 Russian /Soviet dead for World War I and a democide high of 3,000,000 for the years from 1923 to 1925 (see appendix 3.1). Moreover, subtract a high of 2,000,000 who fled or were exiled from the Soviet Union during the civil war years.[78] Subtract also 2,500,000 who died from famine not ascribable to democide, and another high of 3,000,000 who died from disease. And finally, subtract a maximum of 2,000,000 civilian and military battle dead from the Bread War (the nondemocide half—see appendix 2.1). This still leaves 10,850,000 census-based, unnatural, nonbattle deaths to account for during the civil war period. Since this census-based accounting, in which mainly high estimates

FIGURE 2.1
Range in Civil War
Democide Estimates*

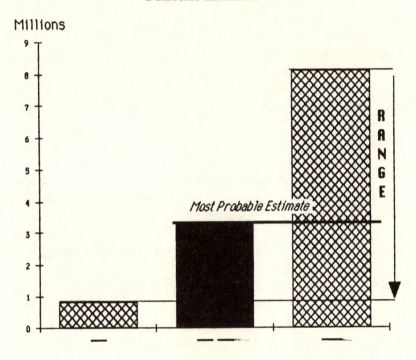

*From appendix 2.1

were *subtracted* along the way, ends up with 1,910,000 *more* than my probable democide high of nearly 8,122,000 people killed, this figure should now seem more credible.

In any case, I believe 3,284,000 to be the most prudent estimate of the human sacrifice to Marxism during these years. Table 2.1 presents the most pertinent data from appendix 2.1; figure 2.2 gives a bar graph of the sources of this huge total and compares them to the number of battle-killed in the civil war and rebellions.

Except for those who died in the famine, all those killed in the democide were intentionally killed. It was murder. But for the famine-dead for which the Soviets are held responsible (half the total famine-dead, be it recalled), the intention is mixed. Those who died because

TABLE 2.1
Civil War Period
Democide and Other Killed*

FACTORS	DEAD ESTIMATES (000)		
	LOW	MID EST.	HIGH
DEMOCIDE	832	3,284	8,122
PERIOD RATE	0.54%	2.13%	5.26%
ANNUAL RATE	0.11%	0.43%	1.05%
FOREIGNERS		?	
DEMOCIDE COMPONENTS			
TERROR	320	750	4,300
DEPORTATIONS		?	
CAMP/TRANSIT	12	34	72
FAMINE	500	2,500	3,750
OTHER KILLED	3,430	6,210	9,460
WAR/REBELLION	930	1,410	2,710
FAMINE/DISEASE	2,500	4,800	6,750

*From appendix 2.1

aid was withheld or their food was taken to feed others or to be exported were also murdered. Then some died because of forcibly and recklessly implemented socialist agricultural policies, a barbarous endangerment of human life with little apparent regard for the consequences. Recall that even peasant food reserves and seed grain were taken by force. The Soviets thus precipitantly imposed policies on the peasant that must lead to starvation. Consistent with Western legal practice, I also will call such wanton endangerment of human life murder.

With a democide of most probably 3,284,000 people and a Soviet midperiod population of 154,500,000, the Soviets murdered 2.13 percent of their subjects during the civil war period. This democide rate alone is much higher than the total population losses from all causes in the Spanish and American civil wars (1.8 and 1.6 percent respectively).[79]

The annual democide rate itself was 0.426 percent, or 426 killed per 100,000 people per year. As is clear from table 1.3, this means that during the civil war period the average Soviet citizen had a 52 percent higher risk of being murdered by the Soviet government than he would

FIGURE 2.2
Democide Components and Soviet
War/Rebellion Killed 1917–1922*

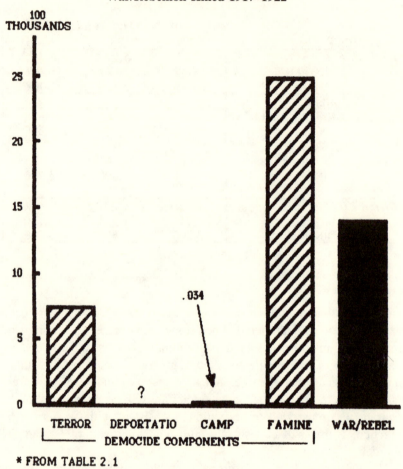

* FROM TABLE 2.1

of dying from any cancer, more than *seven times* the risk of dying as were he to climb a mountain, and about *eighteen times* the risk of a present-day American dying in an auto accident or from being hit by a car.

Moreover, to get another perspective on this democide total of 3,284,000 victims, note that for all nations who fought in World War I, 9,000,000 people died from battle, including 1,700,000 for Russia/

USSR.[80] In just this one country in five years, the Soviets likely murdered more than one-third the number who died fighting World War I for all nations combined. But for the Soviets, all these killed were *non*combatants.

To those who know the subsequent history of this country, however, 3,284,000 was small stuff—a little democide (see figure 1.4). Soviet Marxism was still in its infancy, the power structure still embryonic, the party still subject to defeat by workers and peasants, as evidenced in the retreat to be described below. Only under Stalin in the 1930s and 1940s would Marxist adulthood and full power be achieved. Whole nations could then be liquidated.

Appendix 2.1

Following in table 2A is the detailed table of estimates and calculations involved in determining Soviet democide for the civil war period. Untangling the sources of death during this period was no easy task. There was World War I, a civil war against the White armies, the Bread War against peasant rebels, the official Red Terror, the shooting of prisoners of war and hostages, and the purging of actual or potential "enemies of the people" from territories newly occupied or reoccupied by the Bolsheviks. And there were the newly organized camps. The table has been so organized as to provide as much discrimination among these agents as available estimates allow.

Soviet democide only includes those helpless people killed by the government of de facto authorities, such as Communist party organs. Thus, those who died in World War I, the Soviet-Polish War, civil war battles, or battles during rebellions are excluded. Prisoners of war or rebellion who were executed are included, as is mass killing resulting from rebellion or reoccupation of territory formerly held by White armies or rebels.

Although not included in democide, for comparison table 2.A also gives estimates for World War I, the Soviet-Polish War, and civil war dead. A midestimate of Russian World War I losses is 2,000,000 (line 10 in the table). Probably the Bolsheviks are responsible for some of these deaths, but the number must be relatively small, since the Bolsheviks took control of the government on 7 November 1917, and on the twentieth of the next month they signed the Brest-Litovsk Armistice with the Central Powers. No World War I war dead are added to Soviet war totals here or in the overall table in appendix 1.1.

TABLE 2A

3,284,000 Victims during the Civil War Period: Sources, Calculations, and Estimates*

LINE	EVENT/PROCESS/STRUCTURE	BEGIN YEAR	M	END YEAR	M	DEAD ESTIMATES (000) LOW	MID EST	HIGH	SOURCE	NOTES
1	*WWI DEAD*									
2	losses	1914		1917	?		1,665		Antonov-Ovseyenko,81,278	excluding 3,748,600 wounded.
3	military						2,000		Kulischer,48,71	
4	military	1914		1917			1,700		Wright,65,664	soldiers killed or died of wounds
5	military						1,700		Small and Singer,82,89	battle deaths.
6	military					1,000		2,000	Elliot,72,220	
7							4,000		Sorlin,68,78	"victims."
8							2,000		Conquest,86,53	
9	CONSOLIDATION (MILITARY)	1914		1917		1,000	1,700	2,000		
10	*CONSOLIDATION (LOSSES)*	1914		1917		1,000	2,000	4,000		
11										
12	*SOVIET-POLISH WAR DEAD*									
13	military	1919	2	1920	10		60		Small and Singer,82,89	battle deaths.
14										
15	*CIVIL WAR DEAD*									
16	civilian	1914		1921			14,000		Timasheff,48,155	from F. Lorimer.
17	military	1914		1921			2,000		Timasheff,48,155	from F. Lorimer.
18	military	1917		1920			1,000		Kulischer,48,61	both sides, Red Army lost 632,000 (including Polish campaign).
19	military	1917		1921			1,000		Elliot,72,221-2	battle killed
20	military	1917		1920			502		Small and Singer,82,227	battle deaths.
21	military	?					300		Conquest,86,54	from B.T.Urlanis, a "leading Soviet authority;" includes Poles and Finns.
22	military	?					500		Elliot,72,29	military deaths.
23	military/civilian	1918		1920				1,000	Conquest,72,103	violent deaths.
24	military/civilians	?					1,500		Kulischer,48,71	
25	mili./massacres/killing pris/etc	?						1,000	Conquest,86,54	presumably involves 300,000 killed on both sides in battle.
26	Ukraine	1918		1920			70		Sorlin,68,70	in area between Kiev and Odessa
27		1917		1921			1,000		Elliot,72,221-2	"mixed demographics."
28		?					1,764		Melgounov,25,111	from Saroléa.
29		?					1,000		Sorlin,68,81	"dead"
30	CONSOLIDATION (MILITARY)	1917		1921		500	600	1,000	[sum lines 30 and 31]	
31	CONSOLIDATION (CIVILIAN)	1917		1921		300	500	1,000		
32	*SUM WAR DEAD*	1917		1921		800	1,100	2,000		
33										
34	*REBELLIONS (BREAD WAR) DEAD*									
35	suppression of insurrections	1918		1921		140			Leggett,81,360	killed by Cheka/Internal Security troops suppressing insurrections.
36	suppression of insurrections	1917	12	1922	2		140		Leggett,81,467	
37	Bread War	1918	6		11		1,000		Elliot,72,32-4	
38	civil/guerrilla violence	?					300		Elliot,72,33	includes deaths caused by peasant guerrilla bands, independent terrorist groups, and criminal gangs.
39										
40	*CONSOLIDATION*	1918		1921		140	500	1,300		

TABLE 2A (continued)

Line	Item	Begin	End				Source	Notes
41	**RED TERROR DEAD**							
42	**BY GROUP/LOCALITY**							
43	Crimea	1920 7		50		150	Melgounov,25,76	shot after the defeat of Wrangel.
44	Don Cossack "genocide"	1919				700	Heller & Nekrich,86,87	from historian M. Bernshtam
45	pogroms	?				100	Heller & Nekrich,86,153	possibly both Reds and Whites
46	upper classes	?				350	Liebman,75,351	"lost their lives in the slaughter."
47	aristocrats/middle class	1918	1920			350	Sorlin,68,79	
48	bourgeoisie	1917	1923	2,000		2,000	Ramzer,86,20	
49	bourgeoisie/professionals	1918	1921			2,000	Stewart-Smith,64,73,222	
50	CONSOLIDATION	1917	1922	1,800	2,100	2,400		
51	**IN GENERAL**							
52	Cheka	1917	1922	250		300	Leggett,81,467	from Vladimir Brunovskii, a senior Soviet official; covers executions and deaths in insurrections.
53								a "most conservative estimate."
54	executions	1917	1922	600			Sorokin,37,601	by Cheka; excludes camp and prison deaths.
55	executions	1917	1923			200	Pilon,88,286	achieved annual rate of 12,000 executions.
56	executions	1918 6	1919 10			17	Glaser and Possony,79,477	include 12,733 executions officially reported by the Cheka
57	executions	1918	1921			18	Andics,69,55	acts of terror by Cheka and the armed forces.
58	public terrorism	?		100		200	Elliot,72,33	Cheka only; these are "rather conservative estimates."
59	shot	1919	1919	23		25	Maximoff,40,111	
60	shot	1920				30	Maximoff,40,143	executions, shot out of hand, dying from prison/camp conditions.
61	victims	1917	1923	500			Conquest,70,11	
62	victims	1918	1919			1,700	Denikine,73,292	from The Special Judiciary Commission of Inquiry into Bolshevist atrocities.
63	executed	1917 12	1922 2			140	Leggett,81,467	"opposants" russes massacrés
64		1917	1923			1,862	Dujardin,78,50	low is official and excludes local Cheka units;
65		1918	1919	70		1,700	Stewart,33,59	high is from Denikin's commission of investigation and is for South Russia
66								from official Soviet statistics.
67		1918	1919			10	McCauley,75,187	those put to death; excludes battle killed
68		1918	1919	200			Maximoff,40,240	or those killed by mobs or uncontrolled military bands
69		1918	1920	500			Conquest,72,103	source corrected for multiplication error; 18 million
70		1918	?	50			Chamberlin,35,75	per annum; generalized from local and partial Cheka statistics.
71								
72		1919	1920	3,650		3,650	Melgounov,25,110-1	includes prison and camps dead during year;
73								
74		1921		70			Maximoff,40,199	and a "most conservative" 30,000–40,000 executed;
75								
76		?		50			Grey,67,158	"possibly too moderate", from W. H. Chamberlin"
77	CONSOLIDATION (GENERAL TERROR)	1917 11	1922	250		3,650	[from line 50]	
78	CONSOLIDATION (GROUP/LOCALITY)	1917 11	1922	1,800	2,100	2,400		
79								
80	**CONSOLIDATED RED TERROR DEAD**	1917 11	1922	250		3,650	[of lines 77 and 78]	
81								
82	**CAMP/FORCED LABOR POPULATION/DEAD**							
83	camps/prisons	1918		42		47	Dziek,88,174	Official: from Latsis; includes hostages.
84	CONSOLIDATED CAMP POPULATION	1918		5	7	9		
85	CALCULATED CAMP DEAD	1918		0	1	3		
86								
87	prison/camps	1919		45		81	Dziek,88,174	official: from Latsis; includes hostages.
88	CALCULATED CAMP DEAD	1919		0		3		[assumed the same as for the previous year]
89								

TABLE 2A (continued)

Line	Item	Year				Source	Note
90	camps/prisons (NKtu RSFSR)	1920	48		60	Leggett,81,182	low from official sources, high an estimate from Commissar for Justice.
91	forced labor camps	1920 1		9		Leggett,81,178	NKVD RSFSR.
92		1920 12	50			Solzhenitsyn,75e,20-1	official statistics, includes civil war POWs.
93	CONSOLIDATED CAMP POPULATION	1920	13	20	27		
94	CALCULATED CAMP DEAD	1920	1	4	7		
95							
96	forced labor	1921			100	Forced Labor,52,6	
97	forced labor camps	1921 1		51		Leggett,81,178	NKVD RSFSR.
98	forced labor camps	1921 12		41		Leggett,81,178	NKVD RSFSR.
99	forced labor camps	1921 12		60		Leggett,81,178	NKVD RSFSR.
100	prisons	1921 12	73			Leggett,81,182	NKVD RSFSR
101	CONSOLIDATED CAMP POPULATION	1921	41	60	100		
102	CALCULATED CAMP DEAD	1921	4	12	28		
103							
104	forced labor camps	1922		60		Gerson,76,149	NKVD RSFSR.
105	forced labor camps	1922 10	6	60		Leggett,81,178	from Alexander Ouralov
106	prisons	1922				Kosyk,62,16	
107	CONSOLIDATED CAMP POPULATION	1922	40	60	80		
108	CALCULATED CAMP DEAD	1922	4	12	22		
109							
110	OVERALL CAMP DEAD						
111	MAXIMUM CAMP POPULATION	1918 1922	41	60	100		
112	CALCULATED TRANSIT DEAD	1918 1922	1	3	9		
113	SUM CAMP/TRANSIT DEAD	1918 1922	12	34	72		[sum of lines 85, 88, 94, 102, 108, and 112]
114							
115	FAMINE/DISEASE DEAD						
116	DISEASE DEAD 1918-1923						
117	epidemic diseases	1918	2,000		2,000	Kulischer,48,64,71	low an "official estimate".
118	epidemic diseases	1921	1,000			Kulischer,48,70	half due to typhus.
119	typhus	1918	1,500		2,500	Kulischer,48,64,70,79	mid-estimate agrees with that of the Health Commissariat.
120		1923	3,000		3,000	Conquest,86,53	mainly typhus.
121	CONSOLIDATION	1918	2,000	2,300	3,000		
122							
123	FAMINE 1921-1922						
124	Ukraine	1921			1,100	Dujardin,78,50	
125	Ukraine	1921				Serbyn,86,169-70	
126	Volga Region/Elsewhere	1922			2,000	Ramaer,86,20	from Soviet Central Statistical Bureau.
127		1933			13,000	Heller & Nekrich,86,120	low from a soviet report; high from Central Statistical Office.
128		1923	1,500		5,053	Kulischer,48,70-1	
129		1917	7,500		3,000	Conquest,86,53	from the Large Soviet Encyclopedia (First Edition), Vol 5, p. 463.
130		1921	5,000		5,000	Current Death,79,2-3	
131		1921			5,000	Conquest,72,104	
132		1921			5,000	Stewart-Smith,64,222	
133		1921			4,000	Elliot,72,36	
134		1921				Elliot,72,221	
135		1919	3,000			Stewart-Smith,64,79	
136		1921	3,000		5,000	Elliot,72,220-2	"officially reckoned."
137		1921	2,000		5,200	Maximoff,40,185	from official sources
138							

TABLE 2A (continued)

Line	Category	From	To	Low	Mid	High	Source	Notes
139		1921		1,000		10,000	Serbyn,86,169	from different sources.
140		1921	1923	4,000		5,000	Serbyn,86,169	this range "seems fairly accurate."
141	CONSOLIDATION	1921	1922	1,000	5,000	7,500		
142								
143	**DISEASE/FAMINE 1917–1923**							
144	famine/epidemics	1921		3,000			Sorlin,68,86	civilians
145	famine/epidemics/cold	1918 12	1920 12	7,500		8,000	Sorlin,68,78,81	includes famine, influenza, and typhus deaths.
146	privation	1917	1921	6,000			Elliot,72,34-6,221-2	largely from Typhus and famine
147	famine/disease	1918	1920		9,000		Conquest,72,103	from the League of Nations.
148	famine/disease	1921		1,000		3,000	Weissman,74,6	
149	CONSOLIDATED FAMINE	1921	1922	1,000	5,000	7,500	[from line 141]	
150	CONSOLIDATED DISEASE	1918	1923	2,000	2,300	3,000	[from line 121]	
151								
152	SUP FAMINE/DISEASE DEAD	1917 11	1923	3,000	7,300	10,500	[sum of lines 149 and 150]	
153								
154	**REFUGEES**							
155	emigration	1914	1921	1,000		2,000	Timasheff,48,155	from F. Lorimer.
156		1918	1920?	1,000			Conquest,86,53	range of estimates; low from Nansen.
157		?	?				Stewart,33,430	
158		?	?	1,000			Elliot,72,221	
159	CONSOLIDATION	1918		1,000	1,200	2,000		
160								
161	**TOTAL DEAD FOR CIVIL WAR PERIOD**							
162	civil war/famine	1917	1922			16,000	Antonov-Ovseyenko,81,213	
163	civil war/repression/famine	1921	1922			18,000	Antonov-Ovseyenko,81,307	
164	civilian/military dead	1914	1926			16,000	Glaser and Possony,79,526	
165	shot/tortured	1917	1921	6,000		12,000	Panin,76,93n	from Frank Lorimer, military deaths were 2 million.
166	prison	1917	1923	500			Ramzer,86,20	
167	unnatural deaths	1914	1923		12,000		Kulischer,48,71	
168	unnatural deaths	1914	1926		16,000		Kulischer,48,71	
169	unnatural deaths	1914	?		27,000		Grey,67,181	
170		1917	1920		14,000		Elliot,72,220	from Lorimer.
171		1917	1921	10,000	10,000		Stewart-Smith,64,73	based on 1926 census and "normal population growth"
172		1917	?				Elliot,72,220...	"official Soviet view"; excludes military dead and 1922 famine casualties.
173		1918	1920	9,000			Conquest,86,53-4	for period.
174		1918	1920		10,180		Heller & Nekrich,86,120	from official soviet data; omits WWI dead and refugees
175		?				14,000	Pearson,83,192	excluding 1921-2 famine
176	CONSOLIDATED	1918	1922	9,000	14,000	18,000		including disease and famine.
177								
178	**OVERALL DEAD**							
179	INTERNATIONAL WAR DEAD	1919	1920	60	60	60	[from line 13]	
180	CIVIL WAR DEAD	1917 11	1921	800	1,100	2,000	[from line 32, no democide]	
181	REBELLIONS DEAD	1918	1921	140	500	1,300	[from line 39, 50% democide]	
182	RED TERROR DEAD	1917 11	1922	250	500	3,650	[from line 80, democide]	
183	CAMP/TRANSIT DEAD	1918	1922	12	34	72	[from line 113, democide]	
184	DEPORTATIONS	1918	1922		?		[no estimates available]	

TABLE 2A (continued)

Line								Note
185	FAMINE	1921	1922	1,000	5,000	7,500		[from line 141; 50% democide]
186	DISEASE	1918	1923	2,000	2,300	3,000		[from line 121; no democide]
187	TOTAL DEAD	1917 11	1922	4,262	9,494	17,582		[sum of lines 179 to 186]
188								
189	COMPONENTS OF DEMOCIDE							
190	TERROR	1917 11	1922	320	750	4,300		[sum of line 182 and half of line 181]
191	DEPORTATIONS	1917 11	1922		?			
192	CAMP/TRANSIT	1918	1922	12	34	72		[from line 183]
193	FAMINE	1921	1922	500	2,500	3,750		[half of line 185]
194	*DEMOCIDE*	1917 11	1922	832	3,284	8,122		[sum of lines 190 to 193]
195	*DEMOCIDE (CIVILIANS)*	1917 11	1922	832	3,284	8,122		[from line 194]
196	*DEMOCIDE (FOREIGNERS)*	1917 11	1922		?			[no estimates available]
197								
198	WAR AND REBELLION DEAD	1917 11	1922	930	1,410	2,710		[sum of lines 179, 180, and half of line 181]
199								
200	DEMOCIDE RATE							
201	population	1914				140,000		Timasheff,48,155
202	population	1914				174,000		Sorlin,68,97
203	population	1917				142,000		Kulischer,48,79
204	population	1922	1923			135,000		Kulischer,48,79
205	MID-PERIOD POP	1917	1922			154,500		
206	*DEMOCIDE RATE*	1917 11	1922	0.54%	2.13%	5.26%		[(line 195/line 205)x100]
207	*ANNUAL DEMOCIDE RATE*	1918	1922	0.11%	0.43%	1.05%		[line 206/5]

from F. Lorimer. includes subsequent WWI territorial losses with 35 m. inhabitants.

*See notes to Table 1 A of Appendix 1.1.

In 1919, however, the Bolsheviks did get involved in their own war with Poland and lost about 60,000 battle-dead (line 13).

A number of estimates of civil war military and civilian killed are shown in the table (lines 16 to 29). The consolidated range of these estimates is from 800,000 to 2,000,000 dead, with a midestimate of 1,100,000 (line 32). A little more than half of these are probably military.

Thus, there were from the beginning of the World War in 1914 through the civil war period probably 2,160,000 war deaths. While huge by normal standards, it appears small in comparison to census-based estimates of 12,000,000 to 16,000,000 unnatural deaths.[81] The Soviet civil war actually accounted for less than 10 percent of this number; peasant rebellions, famine, disease, and democide account for all the rest.

Not many estimates of those killed in the peasant rebellions are available, but the few that could be found (lines 35 to 38) yield a midestimate of 500,000 dead (line 39). Perhaps much less than half of these were killed in battle (the peasants had few light weapons and no heavy equipment with which to oppose the Red Army). The great majority were probably killed as hostages, prisoners, or in repression after the rebels were defeated. Nonetheless, to be conservative, only half of those killed in the rebellions will be counted as democide.

As described in the text, however, the Red Terror was wholly democide. The many estimates of the Red Terror are divided into those focused on a group or locality (lines 43 to 49) and those generally concerned with the terror (lines 52 to 76). These provide two different, but overlapping, ways of determining the Red Terror and give two different ranges of estimates (lines 77 and 78). The low and midestimates of those murdered by groups and localities are over four times higher than are the general estimates, even though the groups and localities covered are incomplete. Nonetheless, the much lower general estimate, with its midestimate of 500,000 killed, will be accepted here (line 80).

Now, the midestimate of 500,000 dead includes those killed in the official Red Terror, such as bourgeoise, clergy, landlords, civil war prisoners, White supporters in reoccupied regions formerly controlled by the White armies, and hostages. I believe a toll of 500,000 is therefore very conservative, especially considering that the genocide of the Don Cossacks alone may have far exceeded this number.[82]

Nevertheless, I have taken this low as the most probable midestimate, since it generally far exceeds the separate estimates of the terror's victims usually made by historians. For example, Chamberlin estimates that there were 50,000 victims;[83] Grey estimates a "possibly too moderate" 50,000;[84] Leggett estimates that 140,000 were executed and mentions estimates in top party circles that overall, 250,000 to 300,000 were killed by the Cheka;[85] and Maximoff estimates that at a minimum, 200,000 were shot.[86] To "certainly be erring on the side of underestimation," Conquest does estimate that there were 500,000 victims,[87] but this also includes those massacred in the rebellions, which are counted separately here. There are much higher estimates, as given in table 2A, but these are usually considered by Western historians as too extreme or highly exaggerated.

I have been able to give some estimates of the newly formed concentration and labor camp populations for each year of this period but could find no estimates of overall camp or transit deaths, although I was able to calculate these for each year from the estimated camp populations in the table (beginning with line 83) and camp deathrates determined in appendix 1.2. These calculations summed for the period gave a range of total camp/transit dead of 12,000 to 72,000 with a midestimate of 34,000 (line 113)—surely a prudent number. From the writings of Solzhenitsyn[88] and others on these early camps, it seems that the death toll may have been much higher than the midestimate, especially in the camps of the northern Solovetski Islands.[89]

The greatest source of unnatural deaths during this period was from famine and disease. There are many estimates of both, together and separately, and these are listed in the table. Just looking at the consolidated midestimates of these, that for disease is 2,300,000 dead (line 121) and for famine 5,000,000 (line 141). Their sum is 7,300,000 dead from disease and famine (line 152), which in the table may be compared to estimates of this toll given in the references (lines 144 to 148). Regarding the famine itself, a strong case can be made that it was wholly due to the reckless Soviet policies outlined in the text. But the Soviets did try to help the victims and encouraged international aid (to regions outside of the Ukraine). Therefore, only 50 percent of famine deaths are considered democide. This may or may not be conservative, depending on which historical study is consulted. Therefore, to push the democide estimates toward the conservative side, none of the probable 2,300,000 famine-related disease deaths are considered democide. This means that the democide total includes about one-third of famine and disease deaths.

Regarding other components of democide, I could find no estimates on deportations—those dying from forced deportation to Siberia or other remote and inhospitable regions. This will be a large component of democide in the 1930s and 1940s, and must have occurred to a limited extent during the civil war period. I cannot say, however, whether including estimates of deportation killed would have raised the democide total significantly, since those who died during or from deportation may have been included in the terrorism total.

Moreover, I could find no estimate of foreigners killed, specifically during the occupation of Poland by Soviet forces during the Soviet-Polish War. During the occupation, Soviet forces and the Cheka exercised widespread terrorism, killing bourgeoisie, clergy, and landlords. The numbers killed must be at least five digits long and might have added 1 or 2 percent to total Soviet democide.

Turning now to the totals, there are in the references a large number of estimates of those killed during this period, including estimates based on census data. These are listed in the table (lines 162 to 175), and will be discussed below.

These figures provide a nice check on the totals derived from the different sources of death estimated previously—wars, rebellions, famine/disease, terror, and camps. These are tallied in the table (lines 179 to 187) and give a midestimate of 9,494,000 dead. Of this total, the democide components themselves sum (lines 190 to 194) to a midestimated 3,284,000 killed.

That this estimate of the total killed and democide is indeed conservative now can be seen in the table. The overall estimates among experts of the this period's dead is around 14,000,000 (line 176), or more than 4,000,000 dead higher than the final midestimates separately developed here (line 187). Even if one focuses on the low and high estimates, those finally given here are conservative. The lows and highs in the references for those killed or the census-derived unnatural dead during this period range from 9,000,000 to 18,000,000 (line 176). I estimate 4,262,000 to 17,582,000 total dead from war, famine, terror, etc. (line 187), of which the democide range is from 832,000 to 8,122,000 (line 194). If future revisions in these estimates are made, I think it likely that they will be increased.

A final note. In comparing census-based estimates of unnatural deaths to the totals given in the table, an accounting of the decrease in the population due to emigration and refugees has to be made. This is done in the table (lines 155 to 159), with a midestimate that 1,200,000 citizens left the country during the period.

Epigraph quoted in Leggett (1981, p. 56).

Notes

1. Grey (1967, p. 94).
2. Heller and Nekrich (1986, p. 42).
3. Solzhenitsyn (1973, p. 303).
4. Leggett (1981, pp. 330–31).
5. Ibid., p. 329.
6. Quoted in Conquest (1986, p. 50).
7. Levytsky (1972, p. 30).
8. Dziak (1988, p. 28).
9. Quoted in Leggett (1981, p. 113–14).
10. Ibid., p. 174.
11. Maximoff (1940, p. 112).
12. Quoted in Melgounov (1925, p. 39–40).
13. Ibid., p. 153.
14. Ibid., p. 155.
15. Quoted in Leggett (1981, p. 203).
16. Quoted in Maximoff (1940, pp. 128–29).
17. See Melgounov (1925) for a detailed accounting of many such executions and massacres.
18. Stewart (1933, p. 289).
19. Heller and Nekrich (1986, p. 137).
20. Melgounov (1925, p. 17).
21. Stewart (1933, p. 215).
22. Melgounov (1925, p. 76).
23. McCauley (1975, p. 189).
24. Heller and Nekrich (1986, p. 87).
25. Grey (1967, p. 148).
26. Leggett (1981, p. 148).
27. Conquest (1970, p. 11). Conquest includes those executed in the Bread War.
28. Sorokin (1937, vol. 2, p. 601).

29. Denikine (1973, p. 292).
30. Stewart (1933, p. 60).
31. From Egeny Komnin, quoted in Melgounov (1925, pp. 110–11). Melgounov quotes the total of these calculations as 2,500,000. But 5,000 per day is 1,825,000 for the year, not 2,500,000.
32. Andics (1969, p. 55).
33. Bowers (1984, pp. 395–96).
34. Dziak (1988, p. 173).
35. Conquest (1978, p. 229).
36. Dziak (1988, p. 173).
37. Quoted in Leggett (1981, p. 114).
38. Heller and Nekrich (1986, p. 105).
39. Maximoff (1940, p. 123).
40. See Melgounov (1925) and Maximoff (1940) for frequent listing of such executions.
41. Solzhenitsyn (1975a, pp. 14–15).
42. Quoted in ibid., p. 17.
43. Conquest (1968, p. 334).
44. Leggett (1981, p. 179).
45. Solzhenitsyn (1975a, p. 21).
46. Leggett (1981, p. 178).
47. Ibid., p. 464.
48. Ulam (1976, p. 27).
49. Ibid.
50. Leggett (1981, p. 148).
51. Quoted in Conquest (1986, pp. 46–47).
52. Ibid., p. 47.
53. Ibid., p. 48.
54. Ulam (1976, p. 27).
55. Stewart-Smith (1964, p. 79).
56. Weissman (1974, p. 6).
57. Ibid., p. 1.
58. "The main cause of the famine . . . was the requisitioning policy, the policy of an immediate leap into communism" (Heller and Nekrich, 1986, p. 118). The famine "resulted from the grain requisitions, when special detachments roamed the villages, stripping them bare. Particularly affected was the Volga Region. . . ." (Panin, 1976, p. 67–32). "Agriculture was ruined by anarchy and civil war, but even more by the Soviet order established after their definite triumph" (Kulischer, 1948, pp. 69–70). "We see thus that by his policy of terror, by the destruction of the peasant economy, by exiling thousands of peasants from the native places, by the policy of grain requisitions, etc., Lenin prepared one of the ghastliest famines in the history of Russia. . . ." (Maximoff, 1940, p. 88).
59. Sorlin (1968, p. 74).
60. Weissman (1974, p. 5).

61. Quoted in Maximoff (1940, pp. 149).
62. Serbyn (1986, pp. 153–54).
63. Ibid., p. 155.
64. Ibid., p. 157.
65. Ibid., p. 159.
66. Ibid., p. 168.
67. Conquest (1986, p. 55).
68. Weissman (1974, p. 199).
69. Ibid.
70. Kulischer (1948, p. 70).
71. Maximoff (1940, p. 185).
72. Conquest (1986, p. 53); Heller and Nekrich (1986, p. 120); Stewart-Smith (1964, p. 79).
73. Serbyn (1986, p. 169).
74. Kulischer (1948, pp. 70–71); Conquest (1986, p. 53).
75. Serbyn (1986, p. 170).
76. Elliott (1972, pp. 220–22).
77. Grey (1967, p. 181).
78. Timasheff (1948, p. 155).
79. Heller and Nekrich (1986, p. 120).
80. Small and Singer (1982, p. 89).
81. Kulischer (1948, p. 71).
82. Heller and Nekrich (1986, p. 87). The population of Don Cossacks is given on page 78.
83. Chamberlin (1935, p. 75).
84. Grey (1967, p. 158).
85. Leggett (1981, p. 467).
86. Maximoff (1940, p. 240).
87. Conquest (1970, p. 11; 1972, p. 103).
88. Solzhenitsyn (1973).
89. For example, see Dallin and Nicolaevsky (1947, chap. 8).

3

2,200,000 Victims: The NEP Period, 1923–1928

> *The history of this sewage system [labor camps] is the history of an endless swallow and flow; flood alternating with ebb and ebb again with flood; waves pouring in, some big, some small; brooks and rivulets flowing in from all sides; trickles oozing in through gutters; and then just plain individually scooped-up droplets.*
> —Alexandr Solzhenitsyn

Of all the rebellions and setbacks during the civil war period, perhaps the one that most shocked the Soviets was the 1921 mutiny of the Kronstadt naval base sailors. They had been the "cream of the revolution,"[1] a crucial support in its early, shaky years. Now, they openly declared their opposition to the revolution and support of the peasant rebellions. "In exchange for almost totally requisitioned grain, and confiscated cows and horses, they got Cheka raids and firing squads," the sailors wrote in their newspaper.[2] Trotsky himself declared that at Kronstadt "the middle peasant talked with the Soviet Government through naval guns."[3] It took almost a month, and nearly 50,000 troops launched against 3,000 to 5,500 defenders of Kronstadt, to defeat the rebellion, with much bloodshed and slaughter of prisoners and sympathizers afterward.[4]

This mutiny, together with the growing opposition of workers, the severe economic crises, the agricultural disruption, the human cost of the Bread War, and the resulting famine, defeated Soviet social engineering. In other words, the peasants had won. The party realized that it faced ruin if it continued to try to nationalize the agricultural market.[5]

To party ideologists there was still nothing wrong with socialism, with the vision. Only a mistake about the timing had been made. It soon was realized that socialism could not be created in seven days, that people had to be prepared beforehand and a proper infrastructure of cadre and communist institutions put in place. So the party tactically retreated from socialism. Like Gorbachev of our day, when faced with economic disaster, Lenin instituted his own perestroika. Private enterprise was encouraged (under socialist guidance), and peasants were assured of an end to forced requisitions and of a relatively free market. Approved in March 1921, this New Economic Policy (NEP) gradually improved and stabilized the economy. Food and goods became more plentiful.

But while the worst excesses of the Red Terror were ended, selective terror continued. In fact, Lenin wanted to institutionalize terror. In 1922, he ordered the Commissar for Justice to assume in his work "the justification of terror and its indispensability . . . the court must not abolish terror . . . but must substantiate it and legalize it in principle."[6] What this meant is clear from a secret letter Lenin wrote to members of the Politburo after the adoption of NEP. Reacting to the faithful in the small town of Shuya resisting the confiscation of religious articles from their churches, Lenin demanded that a "very large number" of them be arrested and executed. "Now is the time to teach these people such a lesson that for decades to come they will not dare even to think of such opposition."[7]

And in the party there still was much purifying to be done after the civil war and famine. For example, the many Russian staff members of the American famine relief effort, who from the party's perspective had to be involved in or were ripe for anti-Soviet espionage, were arrested after the ARA (American Relief Administration) mission closed down in the summer of 1923. Moreover, the OGPU (successor to the GPU, itself successor to the Cheka) were suspicious that ARA officials might themselves carry home to the United States vital Soviet secrets. In order to steal their documents, therefore, a bandit raid on the train carrying these officials from Moscow to Batum was cleverly staged.[8]

Still, between the bad days of the Red Terror and the years prior to Stalin's death in 1953, terror during the NEP period was minimal. "Hardly noticeable," by earlier and later standards, says Conquest.[9] But this was widely assumed in the party to be but an intermission. As a top secret OGPU circular put it in 1925: "That this situation is only temporary is clear to every one of us. The OGPU should therefore not lose a good opportunity to unmask our enemies, in order to deal them a crushing blow when the time comes."[10] For this reason, good record keeping on "suspected" enemies of the people was emphasized.

Moreover, while retreating at the macroeconomic level, the party could not allow poisons to accumulate in the system—only social prophylaxis could protect the future against this present. Peasants and workers, scientists and doctors, engineers and writers, and especially, church leaders and goers, were arrested, tried for spying, sabotaging state property, counterrevolutionary activity, or simply being enemies of the people. Many were shot. Many were sent to rapidly swelling prison or labor camps.

The concentration or forced labor camp population had now grown to possibly around 60,000 in 1922.[11] In these years the party laid the legal framework for expanding it beyond imagination. Among other decrees, a new criminal code provided for forced labor for political crimes and political opponents.[12] The camp system then multiplied rapidly during the "peaceful, productive" NEP period. By the end of the period in 1928, prisoner totals reached 240,000,[13] of which at least 140,000 may have been in camps.[14] However, there is one difficulty in comprehending such numbers, even during this immature stage in this "sewage disposal system"[15] that in a decade would be a multimillion-prisoner slave empire. The number of prisoners at any one time was a dynamic, a snapshot of this swirling "sewage" as new refuse poured in from various pipes and old waste was flushed out the bottom.

In his three-volume work, *The Gulag Archipelago*,[16] Solzhenitsyn has made vividly stark the life among these prisoners of the Gulag, as the labor camp system became known.[17] As dictated by Lenin, the party had made clear that these camps were not simply to isolate enemies of the people and criminals, but to work them for the revolution. As this imperative was developed by the party, it was the most work at the least cost. The prisoners were expendable; other state resources were not. They were forced to labor usually twelve, thirteen, fourteen hours a day, seven days a week, in excavating mines, felling timber, digging canals. They were worked in snow and ice, at temperatures sometimes at thirty or forty degrees below zero Fahrenheit, often without adequate clothing and sometimes in the clothes they wore when arrested. They were fed a diet hardy adequate in calories to maintain the life of an inactive person, and surely deficient in those nutrients required to avoid scurvy and other such diseases.

For example, in the 1937 regulations of the Ukhta-Pechora labor camp located above the Arctic Circle (the only such regulations known outside the USSR), the daily allotment of calories for hard labor was 1,292 (American standards call for 3,000 for similar work). By the time the rations reached the prisoner, however, much of his allotment had been taken (by cooks, porters, guards, etc.). Moreover, including an allotted 400 grams of meat (that seldom reached the prisoner), the guard dogs were fed better.[18] But the resulting hunger was not sheer brutality or bureaucratic malfeasance. Hunger became planned.

> Hunger is sovereign. Hunger is the master of the stomach, master of one's thought, the dictator of all one's acts. How well the MVD [the successor to the NKVD, itself the successor to the OGPU in 1926] knows this: King Hunger is their best aid and ally. That is why people are starved in prison. This provides an excellent point of departure for work, work till you drop dead in the camps of the MVD. He who does not work, neither shall he eat. . . .
>
> A prisoner will exhaust himself, wringing the last bit of strength from his muscles, in order to get those extra few ounces of bread, never realizing that his body will burn it up without replenishing his reserves. No one thought about his body any more, nor about falling hair, teeth that dropped out, shoulders rubbed raw, broken feet. We were all motivated by only one thing—to go to sleep with a full belly.[19]

This, not to mention the beatings, arbitrary shootings, disciplinary starvation and exposure in solitary cells, and permitted violence and atrocities of the true criminals against the far more numerous political prisoners.

In the gulag's maturity, more than 30 percent of new inmates might die in a year from exposure, disease, malnutrition, and overwork (a table of death rates is given in appendix 1.2), especially in the 1930s. Among miners in the infamous death camps of Kolyma, 30 to 35 percent died per year.[20] Prisoners calculated that in the mines generally there were "two dead men for every yard dug underground."[21] Among Poles sent to these camps in 1940 and 1941, the toll was 75 to 80 percent in less than two years.[22] But over the whole camp system and up to the death of Stalin, the deathrate was most likely between 10 and 28 percent a year, most probably 20 percent (see appendix 1.2).

This means that even those sentenced to a lucky five years would probably not survive; those sentenced to the numerous "tenners" or, in the late 1930s and throughout the 1940s, the commonplace twenty-five years, in effect received a sentence of death by hard labor. Survivors were usually those who were transferred to less deadly work, especially an administrative job in a camp, and in a position to make "deals" for life-preserving food and clothing.

But survival was even more an individual odyssey, a bet of one's life on a long series of sevens on the dice, than so far appears. Camp was only the final stage of a three-stage deadly obstacle course that life had to run.

First, a person was arrested, secretely or otherwise. And for those common folk who lived during the first forty-two years of Soviet history, the chances were very high of undergoing at least one arrest. In fact, just during the Great Terror of 1936 to 1938, 5 to 10 percent of the population probably was arrested.[23] Some lucky ones were released after an initial interrogation, perhaps after promising to spy on their associates or neighbors. But tens of millions were subjected to a savage interrogation, and often torture, of which the invariable aim was a written confession of guilt and the naming of accomplices. Since arrest was prima facie evidence of guilt, screaming claims of innocence only provoked the interrogator. One fingered others, signed the confession, or died.

Most prisoners probably signed almost immediately. Yes, they were plotting to kill Lenin or Stalin or to provide maps for German paratroopers to drop on the Kremlin. Better to die quickly with a bullet in the back of the head than slowly under the interrogator's twisting knife. The problem was that they also had to incriminate others. It was no good just to contrive some plot involving, say, top communists, for there had to be plausible evidence (meetings, letters, etc.) of a relationship. Often, the interrogator suggested the names of associates or friends that they were after and one only needed to fill in some details ("Yes, we did meet and we talked about . . .").

How many died in interrogation, and how many were subsequently executed overall, can only be a wild guess; I can find no overall estimates in the references. Surely, over the thirty years during which this system was developed and functioned to chew up tens of millions of people, several million must have died in interrogation or by execution. While no general figures are available, we can estimate for one period, that of the Great Terror, that from 500,000 to 2,000,000 were executed, most likely 1,000,000.[24] A report that the Politburo requested of its organs in 1956 claimed that 7,000,000 were shot in prison from 1935 to 1940.[25] Some credibility is given this figure in considering that of those who escaped execution at this stage, the pipeline would carry at least 32,600,000 to their death in the camps.[26] Some experts say 60,000,000.[27] A Soviet scientist gives a research estimate of 52,000,000 to 54,000,000 for just the 1930s to 1950s.[28] Solzhenitsyn claims 70,000,000.[29] I calculate a most probable estimate of 39,464,000 killed in the camps and in transit to or between them (see table 1.1).

If one managed to survive interrogation, then came the dangerous second stage: transportation to one's final camp. Although there was some variation in means, transport, and mortality between the transportation of prisoners and that of deportees, which highlighted subsequent periods, there were important similarities.

Prisoners (or deportees) were crowded, even sometimes stacked without room to all lie down or sit, in cattle cars or cars converted and partitioned for the purpose, and possibly for some of their transport, in the holds of ships and barges (or even on rafts, as when conveyed by river to some desolate spot where prisoners were told to build their new camp). Generally, the cars were unheated and often unventilated; toilet facilities were hardly adequate and sometimes were simply holes in the floor boards. Some food and water might have been given, sometimes just water, sometimes nothing at all—but never enough. For political prisoners being transported to camps, there was an added danger from the criminals being transported with them. In gangs, these criminals robbed the politicals, beat and even killed them on a bet or for the joy of it, if not for the best places in the cars, or for the politicals' food and water.

These transports may have lasted many weeks as cars were pulled from one siding to another, in fits and lurches to finally reach some dispersal camp (with its own dangers and mortality). And then again another transport, this time to some remote camp in, say, Siberia.

How many died on these trips? The only hard estimates we have are from deportations. In come cases the deathrate reached 50 percent, especially for those crowded in cattle cars for several weeks during winter.[30] In the February 1940 deportations of Poles, the number who died reached 10 percent.[31] In many other deportations, it may have been between 15 and 30 percent.[32] Those in the camps calculated one death per railway sleeper.[33] A prudent overall estimate is probably 17 percent for deportees, and 5 percent for prisoners transported to camp (who were generally males in the early or middle years). Working backwards from the most likely maximum camp population of the NEP period, which was 200,000, the number that died in transit was likely around 9,000. For the forty-two years to Stalin's death in 1953, the transit toll among those being sent to camp alone was likely about 1,798,000, possibly as high as 5,895,000.

If these figures seem irresponsibly exaggerated, at least one must keep in mind that these dead accumulated over two generations during which at least probably 37,666,000 prisoners were killed in the camps, and possibly more than 76,386,000 (the high estimate of camp deaths) must have safely made the trip to gulag. Also consider, then, some of the historic death tolls en route or otherwise in transit between camps. In 1933, the transit ship Dzhurma sailed too late in the season and was caught in the ice near Wrangel Island—all prisoners died, perhaps as many as 12,000. In 1949, a transit ship carrying prisoners northward to the Kolyma camps from Vladivostok was wrecked and 5,000 prisoners died.[34] Compare these virtually unknown fatalities (not even Ripley had recorded them) to the immortalized sinking of the Titanic, which cost 1,503 lives.

Aside from transit deaths, how many died in the new forced labor camps during the NEP period? An estimated low of 43,000 to a high of 298,000 people were killed—probably about 223,000. Note that these deaths in the camps were not fast and easy, not like an execution. Death was usually slow, miserable, often an aching death by inches. And for many, death must have been a welcome relief.

Why all these deaths? For reasons of ideology, of Marxism. To remove potential, if not actual opponents, to create a new society, a new Soviet man. Valuable state resources could not be wasted on coddling these enemies. It was enough that they were permitted to survive, to contribute to socialism by working, to be reformed through labor. And another, more positive element in all this became more evident in the late 1930s and 40s. That is, the party wanted cheap labor to industrialize and move posthaste toward the communist future. Workers were needed to labor where few would volunteer to log in the wilderness, mine in the remote arctic, dig canals across frozen land. And the enemies of the people provided an available, cheap pool of

FIGURE 3.1
Range in NEP
Democide Estimates*

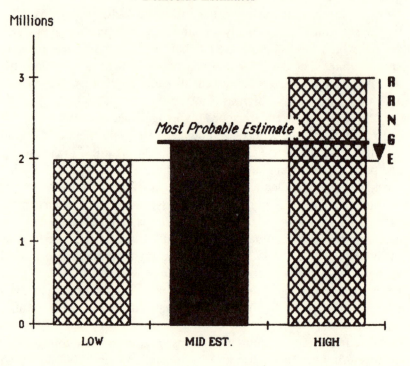

*From appendix 3.1

workers; they could be made to work at no wages and less than bare
subsistence, then ultimately to die when their last reserves of energy
and health had been finally exploited. Perhaps in two months. Perhaps
in two years. In any case, two birds were killed with one stone.

Although in the references and Western perception the NEP period
was one of Soviet economic and political progress and of relative
peace and harmony after the civil war years, well over a hundred
rebellions still took place. One of the more serious ones occurred in
Georgia. In 1924 Mensheviks, Georgian nationalists, and Basmatchi
revolted against Soviet rule. Perhaps 3,000 were killed in battle, and
thousands were probably killed in the resulting Soviet purge in Georgia, including even those in prison at the time of the rebellion.[35]

TABLE 3.1
NEP Period Democide

FACTORS	DEAD ESTIMATES (000)		
	LOW	MID EST.	HIGH
DEMOCIDE	2,000	2,200	3,000
PERIOD RATE	1.37%	1.50%	2.05%
ANNUAL RATE	0.23%	0.25%	0.34%
FOREIGNERS		?	
DEMOCIDE COMPONENTS			
TERROR		?	
DEPORTATIONS		?	
CAMP/TRANSIT	46	237	321
FAMINE		0	
OTHER KILLED	>650	>1,000	>1,300
WAR/REBELLION		?	
FAMINE/DISEASE	650	1,000	1,300

*From appendix 3.1

Moreover, under the surface calm during the NEP, the currents of Soviet repression flowed along. Overall, based on census statistics, there were probably about 3,840,000 unnatural deaths during this period. Much of this is due to various forms of repression, including individual level terrorism, brutal interrogation and torture, executions of those associated with the still frequent rebellions, and mass killing in the camps and prisons aside from the normally high deathrate. While we may not be able to pin numbers on each of these agents of death, their combined effect on Soviet population statistics for this period gives us some measure of the democide.[36] Adjusting downward the estimate of unnatural deaths for a possible famine, possible census error, and causes of death other than repression, a prudent estimate is that the democide during the NEP period likely amounted to 2,200,000 people. A low estimate is 2,000,000; a high is 3,000,000 (see appendix 3.1).

Figure 3.1 shows the range involved in this democide. Table 3.1 provides the basic data. Figures 3.2 and 3.3 compare the democide and its components to that for the civil war period. It is clear that democide

FIGURE 3.2
Democide Components for
Civil War and NEP Periods*

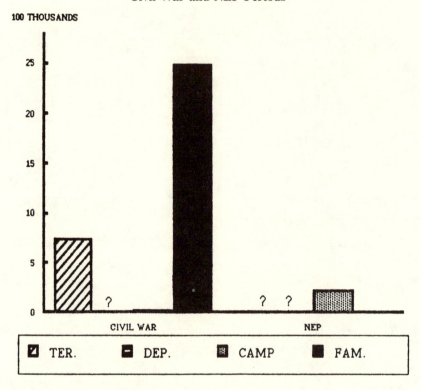

*From Tables 2.1 and 3.1

was not as little during the NEP period as scholars have believed. But it was less than that during the civil war period, and one will find that by comaprison to the collectivization period to come, it was minor, indeed.

That the democide of 2,200,000 people during the NEP was murder is obvious in the case of executions and death from life-threatening torture during interrogation. But what about those who died in transit or forced labor? Are these not more like (unintentional) involuntary manslaughter? I do not accept this. If we imprison a man in our home, force him to do exhausting work fourteen hours a day, not even min-

FIGURE 3.3
Soviet Democide and
Annual Rate by Period*

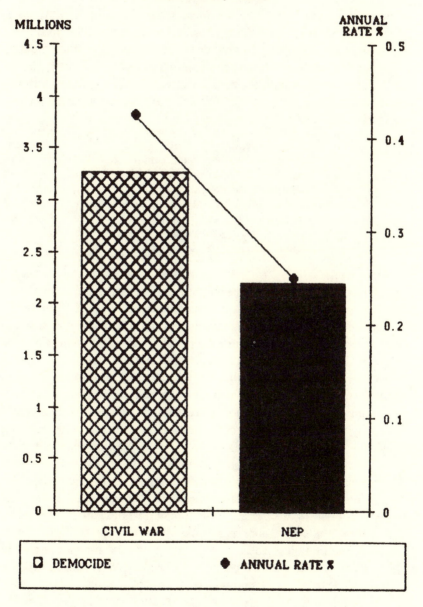

*From tables 2.1 and 3.1

imally feed and clothe him, and watch him gradually die a little each day without helping him, then his inevitable death is not only our fault, but our *practical* intention. It is murder.

In spite of this democide, as will be seen better in the next period, the NEP was a breather for the party, a time to prepare the ground for again moving to the next stage towards communism, to plan the total socialization of the economy, to again try to nationalize the peasant. Of course, arrests (and thus potential forced laborers) in the millions were anticipated, and so in March 1928, the Council of People's Commissars decreed that

> harsh measures of repression should be applied to class enemies and hostile-class elements, that the camp regime should be made more severe . . . [and that] forced labor should be set up in such a way that the prisoner should not earn anything from his work but that the state should derive economic profit from it. "And to consider it necessary from now on *to expand the capacity* of labor colonies." In other words, putting it simply, it was proposed that more camps be prepared in anticipation of the abundant arrests planned.[37]

Moreover, in 1928, in what might as well have been a test run for collectivization, Stalin ordered extraordinary emergency measures against the peasants to forcibly overcome a shortage of grain.[38] This turned out to be a mass confiscation of grain, and a victory that had two serious consequences. For the party, it showed that confiscation was successful; for the peasant, it showed that the party had not changed from the Bread War days—that it could and did take what it wanted when it wanted. This only weakened the peasant's incentive to produce, since the party could not be trusted to leave the market alone.[39]

In any case, a return to confiscating grain was only one of many ways the party was again beginning to squeeze the peasant and to anticipate the firestorm to come. By 1928, it was clear that whatever harmony NEP had promoted was fast disappearing. In the first half of 1928 alone, according to Nikolai Burkharin (the chief ideologist of the NEP), the secret police had to quell about 150 peasant rebellions.[40]

Moreover, in 1928 the NEP was clearly being superseded by a new approach: comprehensive central planning on a continental scale. In 1928 the First Five-Year Plan was announced. Its emphasis was on massive industrializtion, but entailed in the plan was a dynamic that itself would have lead inexorably to collectivization in the following years. The plan did not allow market conditions and decisions to dictate production and consumption. That would have ruined the precise, scientific calculations of the central planners. The days of the free peasant farming his own plot, making his own decisions, were ended.

And 1928 marked the resumption of the campaign to eradicate religion by force, which reached fever pitch in 1930 when religion was believed to be an obstacle to collectivization. Then, 80 percent of village churches were closed and a "large number" of priests were deported.[41]

However, what was most significant about 1928 was party leadership. Lenin had died of a stroke in January 1924, leaving no clear inheritor of his power. The main contestants were Joseph Stalin, general secretary of the Central Committee of the party (a great position for putting people he wanted in control of the party's gates and levers) and Leon Trotsky, commissar for war and Lenin's heir apparent, at least to outsiders. The struggle for power between these two men was titanic and momentous; a battle not only for incredible power, but also of party strategy. Trotsky believed in world revolution, without which he thought that communism in the Soviet Union would fail. Stalin, however, thought that socialism should be built up in the Soviet Union first—that revolution in one country could be successful. Trotsky had the brillance and charisma; Stalin effectively controlled the party.

In 1927, Trotsky lost the final battle; he was expelled from the Central Committee and subsequently deported to Kazakhstan, and in a few years from the country altogether. Seventy-five other leading members of the opposition were also expelled from the party. Through these expulsions and by having gradually placed supporters in virtually all important party positions during the NEP, Stalin finally established almost complete dominance over the Communist party and its policies. This was manifest in September 1928, when the Sixth Comintern Congress fully accepted Stalin's views, especially that the Soviet Union was "the main basis of world communism."[42] In the following decade, Stalin would turn this party leadership into the most absolute rule—a rule so complete and arbitrary that all Soviet policy was virtually his alone, obeying no law or custom but that which he deemed expedient.

Appendix 3.1

There are few works in English on the NEP period itself and little historical attention has been given to the amount and varieties of terrorism during this period. The only specific total for terror-related killing is that of Dimitri Panin, a mechanical engineer who spent over a dozen years in the gulag. From a variety of sources, including former officials in the camps, he estimated that 2,000,000 to 3,000,000 of the old social classes, clergy, and believers were killed during 1922 to 1928.[43] To evaluate this total, consider first that experts are agreed that terrorism reached a minimum during these years and that the secret police were held in check. It was a time of comparative moderation in Soviet history—a calm between the storms of civil war, rebellion, Red Terror, and the collectivization, dekulakization, and Great Terror to follow. Then consider that Panin estimates that during this period over 2.6 times the democide during the civil war period occurred (excluding the famine). On its face, therefore, this seems a gross exaggeration, unacceptable even as a high, and should be ignored.

But then there are Dyadkin's census-based estimates. Iosif Dyadkin was professor of geophysics at the All-Union Geophysical Research Institute, Kalinin, USSR, when he wrote a work estimating from census "returns" and birth and death statistics the number of unnatural deaths in the USSR from repression, terror, and camps.[44] Some of the best Western demographic work on the Soviet Union was unavailable to him, and he used only those statistics available to all Soviet citizens. Doubtless, his calculations suffer from this. His work was circulated in the underground (as a samizdat), for which he was subsequently arrested and sentenced to three years in the gulag. Of the major thrust of this work, Nick Eberstadt (of Harvard University's Center for Population Studies) says that "Dr. Dyadkin's manipulation of data affords the reader a reasonable, and probably conservative, first approximation of the magnitude of unnatural mortality under Stalin. It is worth mentioning that Dyadkin's own estimates for fertility and mortality in the 1930s correspond closely with those reconstructed by a leading soviet Demographer. . . ."[45]

Some respect, therefore, should be given to Dyadkin's estimate of 450,000 to 750,000 unnatural deaths during 1926, and 540,000 to 820,000 during 1928. If extrapolated over the NEP period, this amounts to 2,970,000 to 4,710,000 unnatural deaths—even higher than Panin's estimate. Clearly, if Panin and Dyadkin are correct, much killing had gone on.

Now, an indication of one cause of some of these deaths is given by G. P. Maximoff.[46] In a surprisingly brief account, he says that "we should add to [estimates of those imprisoned and exiled in 1924] the

1,040,000 victims of the famine who died from starvation. Like the famine of 1921–1922, the one of 1924 was the result not only of natural forces but—to a very great extent—of the terrorizing grain policy of the government." I found no mention of this famine in any other source.

All this is thin stuff upon which to build a prudent estimate. To try to be conservative, but at the same time to give some value to Dyadkin's work and Panin's estimates, I have done this. I give no specific estimates for those killed in terror, deportations, mass killing in the camps, or as a result of rebellions. The alleged famine I have included in table 2A (line 51) is only for the record, and I do not count it into the period's democide. It is not mentioned in the text. Based on the annual estimated camp population in the table and a calculation of the likely camp (lines 3 to 36) and transit dead (line 40), I estimate that probably 232,000 died from transit and camp conditions (line 43). Now, lacking estimates of terror, etc., I cannot derive an overall democide estimate by addition. But the midestimate of 3,840,000 unnatural deaths from Dyadkin does give an initial estimate (line 66). To derive a final estimate, I subtracted 1,000,000 possibly dead in the alleged 1924 famine (line 51), and another approximate 20 percent for possible error in the unnatural deaths total. Rounded downwards, this gives a democide of 2,200,000 people (line 67). The counterpart low is 2,000,000. The high is treated differently. It is taken directly from Panin's high of 3,000,000 (line 54), which is still far under Dyadkin's high of 4,710,000 unnatural deaths (line 67).

As best as I can estimate, therefore, 2,200,000 people probably were killed. What contributed to all this killing during these "calm" years? One source is uncounted rebellions, especially numerous in 1923 and 1928, but which continued through this period and must have cost many lives (the Georgian uprising of 1924 alone may have cost at least 4,000 lives—see lines 46 to 47). Another source is unsystematic, individual level terrorism. While prisoners may no longer have been killed in large batches, and wealthy landowners, bourgeoisie, and Whites may no longer have been killed as such, there was still the eradication of "counterrevolutionaries," "enemies of the people," "spies," and what became later known as "wreckers," those believed to be sabotaging the economy. Social prophylaxis took its toll. Moreover, religious believers and church officials were particularly subject to terrorism. Working with a population of about 146,000,000 (line

TABLE 3A
2,200,000 Victims During the NEP Period:
Sources, Calculations, and Estimates

LINE	EVENT/PROCESS/STRUCTURE	BEGIN YEAR	M	END YEAR	ESTIMATES (000) LOW	MID	HIGH	SOURCE	NOTES
1	*CAMP/FORCED LABOR*								
2	POPULATION/DEAD								
3	camps	1923	10				68	Solzhenitsyn,75a,20-1	official statistics, includes civil war POWs
4	camps/prisons/isolators	1923					84	Wiles,53,35	politicals/criminals.
5	prisoners	1923					65	Antonov-Ovseyenko,81,210	From Yevsei Shirvindt, former head, GULAG's research department.
6	CONSOLIDATED CAMP POPULATION	1923			34	50	68		
7	CALCULATED CAMP DEAD	1923			3	10	19		
8									
9	prisoners	1924					86	Antonov-Ovseyenko,81,210	From Yevsei Shirvindt, former head, GULAG's research department
10	prisons	1924					88	Dallin & Nicolaevsky,47,160	exclusive of camps and special prisons
11	CONSOLIDATED CAMP POPULATION	1924			54	80	106		
12	CALCULATED CAMP DEAD	1924			5	16	30		
13									
14	camps/prisons/isolators	1925	9				159	Wiles,53,35	politicals/criminals.
15	prisoners	1925					98	Antonov-Ovseyenko,81,210	From Yevsei Shirvindt, former head, GULAG's research department.
16	prisons	1925					148	Dallin & Nicolaevsky,47,160	exclusive of camps and special prisons
17	CONSOLIDATED CAMP POPULATION	1925			66	98	159		
18	CALCULATED CAMP DEAD	1925			7	20	45		
19									
20	prisoners	1926					104	Antonov-Ovseyenko,81,210	From Yevsei Shirvindt, former head, GULAG's research department
21	prisons	1926					155	Dallin & Nicolaevsky,47,160	exclusive of camps and special prisons
22	CONSOLIDATED CAMP POPULATION	1926			100	150	200		
23	CALCULATED CAMP DEAD	1926			10	30	56		
24									
25	forced labor	1927					140	Swianiewicz,65,37	from Abdurakhman Avtorkhanov
26	prisoners	1927					122	Antonov-Ovseyenko,81,210	from Yevsei Shirvindt, former head, GULAG's research department.
27	prisons	1927					198	Dallin & Nicolaevsky,47,160	exclusive of camps and special prisons
28	prisons	1927			140	200	200	Kosyk,62,16,79	low from Alexander Ouralov, mid-estimate for camps
29	CONSOLIDATED CAMP POPULATION	1927			140	200	266		
30	CALCULATED CAMP DEAD	1927			14	40	74		
31									
32	camps/prisons/isolators	1928			200		240	Wiles,53,35	politicals/criminals.
33	prisons	1928					30	Dallin & Nicolaevsky,47,160	assumed from Dallin and Nicolaevsky's series
34	camps	1928					266	Dallin & Nicolaevsky,47,52	from former GPU official in the northern camps.
35	CONSOLIDATED CAMP POPULATION	1928			30	200	266		
36	CALCULATED CAMP DEAD	1928			3	40	74		
37									
38	OVERALL CAMP DEAD								
39	MAXIMUM POPULATION	1923		1928	140	200	266		
40	TRANSIT DEAD	1923		1928	3	9	23		
41	SUM CAMP/TRANSIT DEAD	1923		1928	46	165	321	[sum of lines 7, 12, 18, 23, 30, 36, 40]	
42	camp dead	1922		1927	46	300		Kosyk,62,79	
43	*CONSOLIDATED CAMP/TRAIN DEAD*	1923		1928	46	232	321	[consolidation of lines 41-42, mid-estimate an average of these lines]	

TABLE 3A (continued)

Line	Category	Year	Year	Year	4	3			Source	Notes
44										
45	REBELLIONS									
46	Georgian uprising	1924								"dead"
47	Georgian uprising	1924							Stewart-Smith,64,81 / Maximoff,40,295	"official soviet data"; shot in crushing rebellion
48										
49	FAMINE									
50	famine	1924								due "to a very great extent" to grain policy of government
51	CONSOLIDATED FAMINE	1924			650	1,040	1,000	1,300	Maximoff,40,297	
52										
53	TERRORISM									
54	old social classes, clergy, believer	1922			2,000		3,000		Panin,76,93n	
55										
56	OVERALL DEAD									
57	COMPONENTS OF DEMOCIDE									
58	TERRORISM	1928				?				
59	DEPORTATIONS	1928				?				
60	CAMP/TRANSIT DEAD	1928			46	232	321		[from line 43, 100% democide]	
61	FAMINE	1928				0				
62										
63	CENSUS BASED ESTIMATES									
64	unnatural deaths	1926			450	600	750		Dyadkin,83,41	based on census
65	unnatural deaths	1928			540	680	820		Dyadkin,83,41	from census
66	CONSOLIDATED	1923			2,970	3,840	4,710		[annual average: ((line 64+line 65)/2)x6]	
67	DEMOCIDE	1928			2,000	2,200	3,000		[line 66 adjusted downward for famine deaths on line 56; further adjustments downward made to be conservative, high from line 54]	
68										
69	DEMOCIDE (CIVILIANS)	1923			2,000	2,200	3,000		[same as line 67]	
70	DEMOCIDE (FOREIGNERS)	1923				?			[in Mongolia, no estimates available]	
71										
72	OTHER DEAD									
73	REBELLION	1928				?			[no estimates available]	
74	FAMINE	1928			650	1,000	1,300		[from line 51, no democide]	
75										
76	DEMOCIDE RATE									
77	population	1922			135,000				Kulischer,48,79	
78	population	1925			140,000				Dyadkin,83,59	census based
79	population	1926			147,000				Sorlin,68,97	from census
80	population	1926			148,800				Antonov-Ovseyenko,81,207	from census
81	MID-PERIOD POP	1928			146,500					
82	DEMOCIDE RATE	1923			1.37%	1.50%	2.05%		[(line 69/line 81)x100]	
83	ANNUAL DEMOCIDE RATE	1923			0.23%	0.25%	0.34%		[line 82/6]	

81) over an empire of diverse nations for a period of six years, the number of terror victims may well add up to a bloodbath few scholars would have suspected without the big picture given by Soviet demographic statistics. Moreover, many more may have died in the camps and transit to them than counted here. Camp deaths are particularly difficult to estimate, even when based on fairly solid camp population figures. This is because camp populations may have been flushed out and renewed several times during this period. Whole camps may have been nearly emptied, say by inmates dying in months due to especially severe conditions, being all killed in retaliation for unrecorded rebellions, or killed outright by, say, being sunk in barges (a favored technique). While for this period I give a midestimate of 232,000 people who died in the camps or in transit, it is not inconceivable that this is too low by 1,000,000.

Also, there must have been some foreign democide during this period. The Soviets were fully involved in Mongolia; the Red Army had established dominance over the country and the Soviets directly controlled the Mongolian army and intelligence service and supervised the secret police.[47] The Mongolian People's Republic was established in 1924 and became the Soviets' first satellite. With Soviet involvement, the Mongolian party struggled to overcome the great power of the Lamaist Buddhist Church and to expropriate the land and capital of the church and aristocracy. Many were executed and otherwise killed; rebellions were brutally suppressed. No doubt the Soviets permitted and probably were involved in much of this, but no estimates are available for either the total killed or those for which the Soviets are responsible. Consequently, Soviet foreign democide must be left as a question mark in the table.

Notes

1. Prpic (1967, p. 38).
2. Quoted in Conquest (1986, p. 53).
3. Quoted in ibid., p. 53.
4. Heller and Nekrich (1986, pp. 109–10).
5. Conquest (1986, p. 57).
6. Conquest (1970, p. 12).
7. Heller (1988, p. 36).
8. Leggett (1981, p. 292).
9. Conquest (1986, p. 70).
10. Quoted in ibid., p. 71.

11. Gerson (1976, p. 149).
12. Herling (1951, p. 11).
13. Wiles (1953, p. 35).
14. The camp figure is from a former high party official (Abdurakhman Avtorkhanov) and for 1927 (Swianiewicz, 1965, p. 37).
15. This is Solzhenitsyn's term. See the opening quote to this chapter.
16. Solzhenitsyn (1973, 1975a, 1978).
17. *Gulag* is derived from the Russian acronym for the labor camp administration, which translated is the "Main Directorate of Corrective Labor Camps."
18. Herling (1951, p. 218).
19. Krasnov (1960, p. 119).
20. Conquest (1978, p. 220).
21. Roeder (1958, p. 16).
22. Conquest (1978, p. 219).
23. Beck and Godin (1951, p. 67).
24. Ulam (1976, p. 130); Hingley (1974, p. 284); Solzhenitsyn (1973, p. 438–39).
25. Antonov-Ovseyenko (1982, p. 212).
26. Kosyk (1962, pp. 79–80).
27. Ibid., p. 79.
28. "Pipeline. . . ." (1982).
29. Solzhenitsyn (1975, p. 119).
30. Conquest (1970a, p. 103).
31. Kusnierz (1949, p. 74).
32. Fleischauer and Pinkus (1986, p. 101).
33. Roeder (1958, p. 16).
34. Conquest (1978, pp. 25–26).
35. Stewart-Smith (1964, p. 81); Maximoff (1940, pp. 294).
36. Dyadkin (1983, p. 41).
37. Solzhenitsyn (1975a, pp. 71–72).
38. Heller and Nekrich (1986, p. 737).
39. Conquest (1986, pp. 89–90).
40. Swianiewicz (1965, p. 120).
41. Medvedev (1979, pp. 70–72).
42. Prpic (1967, p. 48).
43. Panin (1976, p. 93n).
44. Dyadkin (1983).
45. Eberstadt (1983, p. 7).
46. Maximoff (1940, p. 297).
47. Bawden (1968, pp. 264,); Rupin (1979, p. 44).

4

11,440,000 Victims: The Collectivization Period, 1928–1935

You [party activists] must assume your duties with a feeling of the strictest Party responsibility, without whimpering, without any rotten liberalism. Throw your bourgeois humanitarianism out of the window and act like Bolsheviks worthy of Comrade Stalin. Beat down the kulak agent wherever he raises his head. It's war—it's them or us! The last decayed remnant of capitalist farming must be wiped out at any cost! . . .
Through you, the Party brigades, the villages must learn the meaning of Bolshevik firmness. You must find the grain and you will find it. It's a challenge to the last shred of your initiative and to your Chekist spirit. Don't be afraid of taking extreme measures. *The Party stands foursquare behind you. Comrade Stalin expects it of you. It's a life-and-death struggle; better to do too much than not enough.*

—Hatayevich
(Central Committee member)

By 1929, the party was the complete master of all Soviet territory and institutions. And Stalin controlled the party. But to be its absolute dictator, he still had to tidy up a few things. First, he was strong enough to have his major rival, Trotsky, exiled abroad (in 1940, one of Stalin's assassins would finally succeed in murdering him). Then with the expulsion of Bukharin and his followers from the party in 1929,

Stalin became the unquestioned ruler. Controlling the party and through it all aspects and institutions of Soviet society and politics, he began implementing his brand of Marxist utopia.

All he needed was encouragement, and this was given by the "victorious" grain confiscation of 1928 mentioned in the last chapter. It showed that the command communist infrastructure was in place. He renewed the war against the peasants and, this time, with no retreat. It was launched in 1929.

Like the Bread War of the civil war period, on the one side were the unorganized, poor, ignorant peasants. Their only weapons were sullen obstinacy, sabotage, the back road assassination of local party organizers, mass disobedience and rebellion. And large-scale armed rebellions there were, some spreading beyond single villages; one estimate is of 40,000 Ukrainian rebels in 1930 alone.[1] Against them was arrayed the full might of the state: its army and air force, its now fully developed secret police forces (now called the OGPU), its phalanxes of eager communist activists, its propaganda machine, its full control over all transportation and communication, and its tight subordination of local economies—even dictating whether peasants could buy soap. The war aims were to socialize (nationalize) the countryside by consolidating (without compensation) formerly independent farms, their livestock and land, into huge farm factories run by the party, with each farmer an employee earning a daily wage for his work. That is, total collectivization of the peasantry, including nomads.

Abstractly, the idea has a certain appeal: turn "inefficient" small plots for which modern farming equipment could not be afforded or used efficiently into large factory-like farms, each with its own tractors, each efficiently allocating workers (farmers) to specialized tasks. To be sure, this required persuading farmers to give their lands, animals, implements, and often their homes to the communes and become workers with regular wages, hours, and tasks.

Yet, those "dull witted" peasants simply failed to understand the party's wisdom in all this or appreciate their contribution to the greater good, the better future, the collective. They killed their livestock rather then give them up, burned down their homes, fled to the cities, shot at the troops who came to enforce the party's commands, and committed suicide. Whole villages were destroyed and depopulated in this Peasant War. Even nomadic herdsmen were not exempt, as the party decreed that they also must be settled into communes and their wandering herds collectivized. From 1 June 1929 to 1 March 1930, the number of peasant holdings collectivized throughout the Soviet Union increased from 1,003,000 to 14,264,300,[2] surely a satisfying measure of success to the party.

As it turned out, once forced into "voluntarily" turning all he owned to a collective farm, the peasant found it "closer to a penal colony whose inmates' work, cooperation, indeed the entire manner of life was prescribed from above and run by outsiders, often people quite ignorant of both agriculture and the local conditions."[3] As a former member wrote:

> In the collective farm, our personal existence became completely dependent upon the dictates of the Communist Party, and on the whims of the local officials. Every detail of our life was supervised. Our daily routine was subject to the strictest regimentation. We had to obey orders without any protest, and without giving any thought as to their sense or purpose. A vast system of secret police, spies, and *agents provocateurs* watched our every move.
>
> We were always suspected of treason. Even sadness or happiness were causes for suspicion. Sadness was thought of as an indication of dissatisfaction with our life, while happiness, regardless of how sporadic, spontaneous, or fleeting, was considered to be a dangerous phenomenon that could destroy the devotion to the Communist cause. You had to be cautious about the display of feelings at all times, and in every place. We were all made to the understand that we would be allowed to live only as long as we followed the Party line, both in our private and social lives.[4]

The Peasant War was the largest and most deadly war fought in between the two world wars. Many millions were killed, and it was fought on three fronts. One was the attempt to "persuade" peasants to "voluntarily" join the communes through lies, false promises, peer pressure, coercion, and finally naked force. Secondly, on the home front a massive, coordinated propaganda barrage extolled the manifold virtues of collectivization and condemned those "rich" peasants—or kulaks—who were systematically and selfishly sabotaging this humanitarian party effort to spread the benefits of communism to the poor peasant. Indeed, as a new and critical front in the Peasant War, in a 1930 *Pravda* article, "Stalin formally declare[d] war on *kulaks*."[5]

Party activists and even everyday workers became convinced that these kulaks were wholly responsible for the resistance to collectivization and its associated violence. Party officials throughout the Soviet Union spewed forth hate propaganda, and consistently harangued activists on the kulaks' evildoing. Whipped into a frenzy of hostility, and upon being sent out to the countryside in waves of collectivization, activists unleashed their pent-up rage on any assumed kulaks. They were

> under a spell—they had sold themselves on the idea that the so-called "kulaks" were pariahs, untouchables, vermin. They would not sit down at a "parasite's" table; the "kulak" child was loathsome; the young "kulak" girl was lower than a louse. They looked on the so-called "kulaks" as cattle, swine, loathsome, repulsive: they had no souls; they stank; they all had venereal diseases; they were enemies of the people and exploited the labor of others. And, on the other hand, the poor peasants, the members of the Young Communist League, and the militia— they were all Chapayevs, heroes of the Civil War. Yet these activists were in reality ordinary people like all the rest; many of them were just plain whiners and cowards; and there were plenty of ordinary scoundrels as well.[6]

Kulaks were not only scapegoats, they were the focus of attack. The collectivization campaign was supplemented, complemented, and pursued through a campaign to eliminate the kulaks as a class. The party decreed the liquidation of all kulaks and their families, even extended relatives. This meant execution for many or the slow death of labor camps for lots more. Others were barely more fortunate to be deported to forced settlements in remote regions like Siberia—in some ways worse than the camps. "And there was no pity for them. They were not to be regarded as people; they were not human beings; one had a hard time making out what they were—vermin, evidently."[7]

And if a poor peasant were not a kulak? Well, he was not much better. Party activists were usually city-dwellers who often expressed "hatred and contempt" for the peasant. And as Khrushchev said, "for Stalin, peasants were scum."[8]

One small problem in thus cleansing the countryside: who was a kulak? All truly rich land owners had been exterminated during the civil war period. The party tried to settle this question by defining a kulak by income, land size, hired workers, etc. But few peasants met these criteria and those who did hardly matched the propaganda image of the hated kulak exploiter. In 1927, their better year, "most prosperous" peasants had two to three cows and up to twenty-five acres of sowing area, supporting an average family of about seven. The richest peasant got 50 to 56 percent more income per capita than the poorest. Also, these peasants, who were about 3 to 5 percent of peasant households, produced about 20 percent of the grain.[9] Their liquidation played no little role in the subsequent famine.

In practice, those liquidated "kulaks" were mainly the peasants who had been more successful farmers—they owned fatter cows, they built better houses or barns, and they earned more than their neighbors. In short, these were not the rich (the average kulak earned less than the average factory worker or the rural official persecuting him)[10] or the exploiting. They were simply the best farmers.

And they paid for their success. The Peasant War consumed their lives and their country. Stalin admitted to Churchill that it was worse than World War II, it "was a terrible struggle. . . . It was fearful." After saying that he had to deal with 10,000,000 kulaks, Stalin claimed that "the great bulk were very unpopular and were wiped out by their labourers."[11] Given the number of peasants involved over the whole expanse of the Soviet Union, Lewin says that "Churchill is, possibly, mistaken. Stalin probably said 100 million."[12]

How many peasants actually were killed outright or died in camps or desolate, frozen regions can be only roughly estimated, with a margin of error itself in the millions. From 1929 to 1935, possibly 10,000,000,[13] maybe even 15,000,000,[14] "kulaks" and families were deported to labor camps or resettlements, usually to a slow death. Even infants and children, the old and infirm. Even they apparently stood in the way of progress, of Stalin's agricultural "perestroika." A good party member had to keep his priorities straight, to know his Marxism, as Lenin said.[15]

From 1929 to 1935, in implementation of the party's collectivization and dekulakization campaigns, or as a consequence of them, as many as 10,000,000 peasants may have perished.[16] Even the Soviets now admit to this possibility. An English language Moscow-published newspaper reported that in "what amounted to genocide, between five and ten million people died during the forced collectivization of farming in the early thirties."[17] Note particularly the Soviet willingness to accept this as *genocide*.

Restricting ourselves only to those who were killed outside the labor camps to which millions of peasants and assumed kulaks were sent, and excluding famine deaths, the number of peasants slain probably ranges from 1,662,000 to 6,454,000—most likely 3,133,000 (see appendix 4.1). In Kazakhstan in central Asia, where the party tried to collectivize a nomadic culture, out of a population of over 4,000,000 at least 1,000,000 "must" have been killed or died from the resulting famine.[18] The 1939 census showed a 21.9 percent *drop* in the Soviet Kazakh population since 1926.[19]

For no other social experiment in history have so many been killed. And did collectivization work? No, this greatest of experiments in scientific social engineering utterly failed. It denied the laws of economics and human nature, and accordingly, the communes never did produce enough food for even the Soviet table. The party has had to turn to massive food imports and now to a counter restructuring (Gorbachev's perestroika) that would largely decollectivize, desocialize the countryside. Mistakes will happen, so says the party, but the Marxist vision of the future remains true.

Incredibly, our calculations for this period do not end here; this was only the beginning. As in the civil and Bread wars, this Peasant War totally disrupted the agricultural economy. By 1932, famine again threatened, but this time the response was different. It was wartime and aid could not be given to the enemy. Indeed, a famine was positive: it would encourage peasants to join the collectives, particularly if that were their only source of food.

But Stalin perceived another potential benefit from a famine. He could use it to squash Ukrainian nationalism. Ukrainians, even top communists, were becoming more assertive about strictly Ukrainian interest: music, language, Ukrainian history and literature were undergoing a renaissance. This could not be allowed to continue. Nationalism had no role, at least non-Russian nationalism, in the revolution. Indeed, inherently, it was an opposing force.

The peasant was at the heart of Ukrainian nationalism and tradition. Destroy this peasantry and Russian immigrants and collectivization would easily follow. So in the war against the peasants a new and differently fought front was opened in the Ukraine in 1932. This was launched in July when Stalin ordered an impossible grain delivery target of 7.7 million tons out of a harvest already reduced by a third from that of 1930. After much argument Ukrainian officials got this reduced to 6.6 million tons,[20] but when the quotas were apportioned among the villages, said one survivor, "our village was given a quota that it couldn't have fulfilled in ten years!"[21] Then this survivor asked:

Who was it who then signed the act which imposed mass murder? I often wonder whether it was really Stalin. I think there has never been such a decree in all the long history of Russia. Not the czars certainly, not the Tartars, nor even the German occupation forces had ever promulgated such a terrible decree. For the decree required that the peasants of the Ukraine, the Don, and the Kuban be put to death by starvation, put to death along with their tiny children.[22]

Stalin's war strategy on this front was simple yet imperial in scope. It was

not only to force collectivization upon the recalcitrant and stubborn peasants. . . . It was to destroy the spiritual and cultural backbone of the entire nation, as well as to terrorize the peasantry. Without this complete annihilation of spiritual resources and cultural achievements, Stalin's victory in the Ukraine could never be complete. Realizing this, he decided to unleash all the forces of devastation at his disposal against those who stood for an independent Ukrainian culture, tradition and consciousness, even though they were devoted Communists.[23]

This campaign was kept a secret; no word of the famine was mentioned in the press. In fact, until recently it was a crime to mention the famine at all.

No mercy was shown the starving peasants. During the famine, detachments of workers and activists were marshaled in the countryside to take every last bit of produce or grain. Activists and officials went through peasant homes with rods, pushing them into walls and ceilings, seeking hidden stores of food or grain; yards were dug up or poked with rods in the search; and dogs were brought in to sniff out food. For the party officials and activists, food must have been somewhere. After all, while whining about lack of food and their empty bellies, they were still alive. "That meant that we had to have food—but where? It had to be somewhere. The officials felt that they had failed in their duties to find the hidden treasure of food. This made them frustrated, angry, and all the more vicious and cruel to us."[24]

Baked bread was taken.[25] All reserves and the seed grain needed for planting were seized. The peasants were left with nothing. To isolate the victims, the Ukrainian borders were sealed off to block the importation of food. And some villages, with especially recalcitrant peasants, were blacklisted: they were completely cut off from the outside and all sale of food or other products forbidden—even soap.[26]

The peasants simply starved slowly to death throughout the Ukraine. Observed one witness:

> Hunger: a terrible soul-chilling word of darkness. Those who have never experienced it cannot imagine what suffering hunger causes. There is nothing worse for the man—the head of the family—than the sense of his own helplessness in the face of his wife's prayers, when she cannot find food for her hungry children. There is nothing more terrible for the mother than the sign of her emaciated, enfeebled children who through hunger have forgotten to smile.[27]

They ate their pets and farm animals, and then roots; they boiled bark and the soles of their boots for the broth. But at each grasp for food, the authorities stepped on their hands. When the peasants started eating dogs and cats, village officials were ordered to bag a "certain quota of dog and cat skins, and thus went through the village shooting these animals."[28] When the peasants tried to eat birds and their eggs, communist activists organized systematic bird hunts, shooting birds out of the trees with shotguns.[29] And they ate, as a peasant women said, horse manure. "We fight over it. Sometimes there are whole grains in it."[30] Finally, they sometimes ate their own children and those of their neighbors they could kidnap. And then they died by millions in the winter of 1932–33. No aid was given. Observed a former party activist:

> On a battlefield men die quickly, they fight back, they are sustained by fellowship and a sense of duty. Here I saw people dying in solitude by slow degrees, dying hideously, without the excuse of sacrifice for a cause. They had been trapped and left to starve, each in his home, by a political decision made in a far-off capital around conference and banquet tables. There was not even the consolation of inevitability to relieve the horror.
>
> The most terrifying sights were the little children with skeleton limbs dangling from balloon-like abdomens. Starvation had wiped every trace of youth from their faces, turning them into tortured gargoyles; only in their eyes still lingered the reminder of childhood. Everywhere we found men and women lying prone, their faces and bellies bloated, their eyes utterly expressionless.[31]

Nearby silos or graineries were full of grain. Guarded by troops, grain might have lain on the ground rotting at train stations.[32] From 1931 to 1933, more grain was exported than at anytime since the revolution—8,485,000 tons as compared to 178,000 tons for 1929 to

1930[33] —and near starving villages, plants had been processing milk into butter for export,[34] but the peasant was not fed. The war continued until Ukrainian nationalism was destroyed and collectivization successful.

Of course, party officials and activists were fed well, even on the front line. As a former Soviet Ukrainian admitted:

> Day and night [their food] was guarded by militia keeping the starving peasants and their children away from the [dining hall for party officials]; their terrible appearance alone could ruin the appetite of the "builders of socialism." In the dining room, at very low prices, white bread, meat, poultry, canned fruit and delicacies, wines and sweets were served to the district bosses. At the same time, the employees of the dining hall were issued the so-called Mikoyan ration, which contained 20 different articles of food. Around these oases famine and death were raging.[35]

About eighteen months of famine did it. With whole villages lifeless, highways and fields dotted with the dead, the survivors too weak to work, the Ukraine prostrate and even workers in the cities now threatened, with victory in hand, Stalin ended requisitions in March 1933. In April, some army grain reserves were released for distribution to the dying peasants.[36] What was left?

> [The] Ukraine and the Ukrainian, Cossack and other areas to its east—a great stretch of territory with some forty million inhabitants—was like one vast Belsen. A quarter of the rural population, men, women and children, lay dead or dying, the rest in various stages of debilitation with no strength to bury their families or neighbors. At the same time, (as at Belsen), well-fed squads of police or party officials supervised the victims.[37]

The war was over. Ukrainian nationalism received a blow from which it was not to recover until the 1980s. And the collective farm had taken over the countryside. Said Hatayevich, secretary of the Dniepropetrovsk Regional Committee, this "was a test of our strength and their endurance. It took a famine to show them who is master here. It has cost millions of lives, but the collective farm system is here to stay. We've won the war."[38]

Out of a farm population of 20,000,000 to 25,000,000,[39] 3,000,000[40] to 10,000,000[41] Ukrainians were starved to death; Stalin was handed an approximation of 8,000,000 to 9,000,000 dead.[42] Given the variation in estimates and subsequent census figures, most likely about 5,000,000 Ukrainians were murdered by hunger (see appendix 4.1). Another 2,000,000 probably starved to death elsewhere, such as 1,000,000 in the North Caucasus alone.[43] All these deaths were caused by the war on the peasants.

There was no particularly bad drought that caused the famine. Collectivization was the clear, general cause. But in the Ukraine (and neighboring Caucasus) the party was not only directly responsible due to collectivization, with starvation being the practical intention, it was the party's specific intention—the public *policy*. This became obvious to the survivors:

> Now it began to dawn on everyone why there wasn't any food left in the village; why there weren't any prospects of getting any more; why our expectation that the government would surely help us to avert starvation was naive and futile; why the Bread Procurement Commission still searched for "hidden" grain; and why the government strictly forbade us to look for means of existence elsewhere. It finally became clear to us that there was a conspiracy against us; that somebody wanted to annihilate us, not only as farmers but as people—as Ukrainians.[44]

Faced with such a monstrous crime that surely defies the laws of humanity, we should not mince words. Let us agree with Mace that "the Ukrainian famine was a deliberate act of genocide of roughly the same order of magnitude as the Jewish Holocaust of the Second World War, both in the number of its victims and in the human suffering it produced."[45] And with Conquest, the author of a well researched, book-length study of the Ukrainian famine: "It certainly appears that a charge of genocide lies against the Soviet Union for its actions in the Ukraine."[46]

But the world knows about Hitler's genocide, not many know about Stalin's in the Ukraine. Few now doubt what Hitler did, but not many readers will remain unskeptical about such a Ukrainian genocide by hunger. Of course, Hitler lost a war and his propagandist and sympathizers either died with him or were thoroughly discredited. Stalin won all his wars.

But the surving peasants remember. After World War II, a Harvard Project on the Soviet Social System interviewed Soviet refugees. They found that when asked "'whether or not it would be a good idea to drop an atom bomb on Moscow,' half the Ukrainian collective farmers answered yes, twice the proportion of the Russian collective farmers."[47]

Incidentally, the famine had been reported in some American news-papers in full detail, even as to its being starvation by policy.[48] But apparently it was not believed. As this murder of millions of souls was winding down, on 16 November 1933, the United States gave diplo-matic recognition to the Soviet Union.

One final note on the Ukraine. The party not only used starvation to subdue Ukrainian nationalism, but also tried to exterminate its culture-carriers. It had shot Ukrainian writers, historians, composers; Ukrai-nian party officials too considerate of the Ukraine; and even itinerant, blind folk singers. Those with "bourgeoisie sensitivities" might find the following from the memoirs of composer Dmitrii Shostakovich to have its own chilling horror.

> Since time immemorial, folk singers have wandered along the roads of the Ukraine. . . . [T]hey were always blind and defenseless people, but no one ever touched or hurt them. Hurting a blind man—what could be lower?
>
> And then in the mid thirties the First All-Ukrainian Congress of Lirniki and Banduristy [folk singers] was announced, and all the folk singers had to gather and discuss what to do in the future. "Life is better, life is merrier," Stalin had said. The blind men believed it. They came to the congress from all over the Ukraine, from tiny, forgotten villages. There were several hundred of them at the congress, they say. It was a living museum, the country's living history. All its songs, all its music and poetry. And they were almost all shot, almost all those pathetic blind men killed.
>
> Why was this done? . . . Here were these blind men, walking around singing songs of dubious content. The songs weren't passed by the censors. And what kind of censorship can you have with blind men? You can't hand a blind man a corrected and approved text and you can't write him an order either. You have to tell everything to a blind man. That takes too long. And you can't file away a piece of paper, and there's no time anyway. Collectivization. Mechanization. It was easier to shoot them. And so they did.[49]

Collectivization, dekulakization, and the denationalization of the Ukraine were not the only basis for murder during this period. Those who survived were killed for other reasons of the party. Just the enor-mity in the number of the homeless orphans produced by these cam-paigns, for example, was enough for their number to be reduced by shooting them, said one NKVD veteran,[50] or, in effect, poisoning them, or penning them up and starving them to death.[51] Moreover, scapegoats for the famine had to be punished. Thus, there was a "severe" purge and shooting of veterinarians for the death of live-stock, and the staff of the Meteorological Office was arrested for falsifying weather forecasts in order to damage the harvest.[52]

And day-by-day terror continued to operate and exact its victims. Capital punishment was applied liberally. One peasant was executed, for example, for stealing two sheaves of corn.[53] Then in 1934, Stalin began his purge of the opposition within and without the party, a purge that would reach its zenith with the Great Terror of 1936 to 1938 (to be discussed in the next chapter).

Moreover, not to be ignored was the selective killing associated with other policies or campaigns. In particular, the 1928 campaign to erad-icate religion by force reached high gear in 1930. In addition to the Marxist gut opposition to all religion, the party condemned religion as an obstacle to collectivization. A "large number" of priests were deported and, as mentioned in the last chapter, 80 percent of village churches were shut down.

One cannot forget the labor camps, either. They were flooded with kulaks and ordinary peasants. Hundreds of new camps were built, usually by prisoners in some grim, undeveloped area. By 1935, pos-sibly as many as 6,700,000 people were enslaved in the camps,[54] probably no fewer than 5,000,000.[55] Most of these people were chained to some form of life-endangering hard labor. For example, they were forced to build the Belomor Canal under such life-consuming condi-tions that at least 100,000 prisoners died.[56] (Praised as a monument to the achievements of socialist labor, the canal was little used after-wards.)

This forced-labor camp system—the gulag—was fully developed during this period. It became, in effect, a slave-labor system, with prisoners bought and sold and contracted for as though they were commodities. They were treated with the same consideration: they had absolutely no rights, no individuality, and could be and were killed at the whim of the owner (especially, nonessential intelligentsia—scientists, engineers, doctors, teachers—who were weeded out for life-threatening physical labor).[57] Ponder the impressions of the man-ager of a trust who was sent to Kem, the administration center for the Solovetzki camp, to *purchase* a squad of forced laborers.

Can you imagine that there . . . the following expressions are freely used: "We sell!" — "We discount for quantity!" — "First class merchandise!" — "The city of Archangel offers 800 roubles [*sic*] a month for X. and you offer only 600! . . . What merchandise! He gave a course in a university, is the author of a number of scientific works, was director of a large factory, in pre-war time was considered an outstanding engineer; now he's serving a ten-year sentence at hard labor for 'wrecking'; that means that he'll do any kind of work required of him, and yet you quibble over 200 roubles!" Nevertheless, I bargained and they finally agreed to reduce the price, because we purchased at wholesale fifteen engineers.[58]

A contract was signed, a lawyer checked and approved it, and the chief of the camp signed it.[59]

As the collectivization and dekulakization campaigns concluded, the rivers of prisoners emptying into the gulag began to dry up. In 1934 a shortage of slave labor developed, affecting NKVD production. Obviously, something had to be done and in a year plans for a new intake of prisoners were worked out. The NKVD subsequently assigned local agencies a fixed quota of arrests.[60] Perhaps this partially explains why NKVD agents were then going out of their way to entrap citizens into showing dissatisfaction or making negative comments on Stalin, the USSR, or the party.[61] The camps had to be filled.

While the horror of collectivization and the famine now starkly reveals itself to the historian, what the Soviet people then and through their subsequent history most identified with Stalin and Stalinism were these camps. "The Stalinist system was thoroughly understood by the Russian people, and particularly by us in the camp, for the basic principle of Stalinism *is* the camp: the camp as a new way and order of life, replacing the institutions that had developed as products of history."[62]

How many were killed in these camps? Kosyk estimates the number to be 1,300,000 from 1930 to 1933 and 1,900,000 from 1933 to 1936.[63] Wiles figures the toll to be a modest 2,600,000 from 1928 to 1939.[64] After proportionating various estimates so that they would cover the period 1929 to 1935, applying the general deathrate of 20 percent to the camp populations, and taking the transit deaths into account, the most probable estimate of the gulag's victims seems to be 3,306,000 (appendix 4.1). As high as this number is, it must be added to those who died in the process of collectivization and dekulakization, and the sum must then be added to those murdered by hunger, and this sum in turn must be added to the victims of the everyday terror and social prophylaxis.

FIGURE 4.1
Range of Collectivization Democide Estimates*

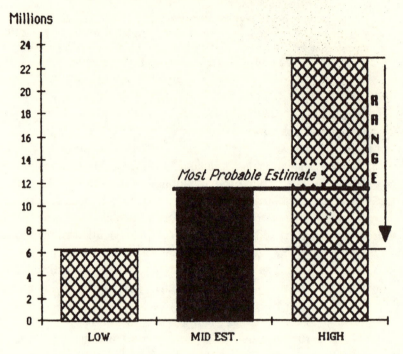

*From appendix 4.1

And what is this grand total? Just for 1930 to 1932, one estimate by Soviet statisticians is that 22,000,000 people were killed.[65] Another estimate for 1930 to 1937 and based on census data is of 14,500,000.[66] A variety of other estimates are given in appendix 4.1. I conservatively estimate the total democide as 11,440,000, with a possible range of 6,227,000 to 22,880,000 men, women, and children.

These estimates and this range in possible error are shown in figure 4.1. Table 4.1 gives the estimates and the democide components (note that the killing involved in collectivization and dekulakization is treated as a form of terrorism). And these components are shown in figure 4.2 and compared to those for previous years.

Overall, more than 7 percent of the population likely was murdered, or an annual democide rate of 1.04 percent (more than one out of each

TABLE 4.1
Collectivization Period Democide

FACTORS	DEAD ESTIMATES (000)		
	LOW	MID EST.	HIGH
DEMOCIDE	6,227	11,440	22,880
PERIOD RATE	3.97%	7.29%	14.57%
ANNUAL RATE	0.57%	1.04%	2.08%
FOREIGNERS	?		
DEMOCIDE COMPONENTS			
TERROR	677	1,733	3,592
DEPORTATIONS	985	1,400	2,863
CAMP/TRANSIT	1,566	3,306	6,426
FAMINE	3,000	5,000	10,000
OTHER KILLED	1,000	2,000	5,000
WAR/REBELLION		0.20	
FAMINE/DISEASE	1,000	2,000	5,000

*From appendix 4.1

hundred men, women, and children per year). Figure 4.3 compares this rate, as well as the totals, to those for previous periods. In sheer killing, this period dwarfs that for even the civil war years.

But to fully assimilate the incredible magnitude of this killing—over 11,000,000 people—just consider some simple comparisons. In this seven-year period, the Communist Party of the Soviet Union murdered over two-thirds the total killed from battle for all nations in World War II, more than the number killed in battle in World War I, and almost twice the number killed in all domestic revolutions, civil war, guerrilla wars, and the like, in the twentieth century so far (see table 1.2). To put this in terms of risks faced by a Soviet citizen, during this period his annual risk of being murdered by the party was almost fifty-eight times that of dying in any kind of international or domestic war, and almost four times the risk of dying from any cancer. He would have been over seventeen times safer climbing a mountain (see table 1.3).

Why, in this period, all this killing? The ideas had not changed. Marxism still provided the map, tactics, and justification, as before. But the party under the control of Joseph Stalin was monolithic; there

FIGURE 4.2
Democide Components for Three Periods*

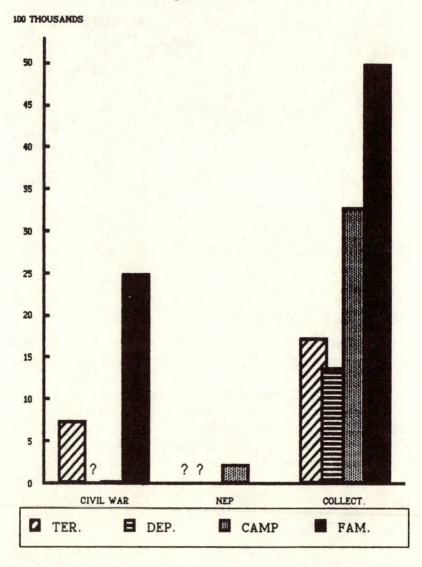

*From Tables 2.1, 3.1, 4.1

was no significant opposition. And it completely controlled the whole country: the Red Army, the secret police, the bureaucracy, the courts,

FIGURE 4.3
Soviet Democide and Annual Rate by Period*

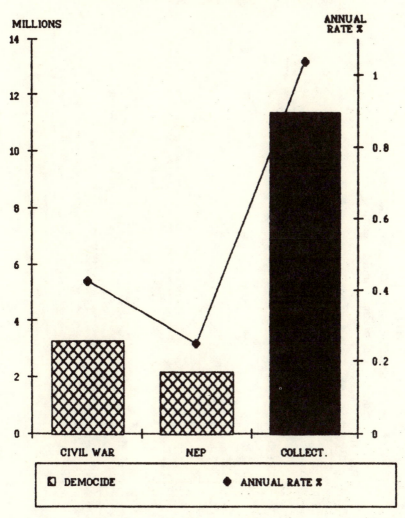

*From Tables 2.1, 3.1, 4.1

and all national, provincial, and local government. There was no countervailing power. Now, the society could be totally reformed for the Good. Now, collectivization—this great experiment in social scientific engineering—could be tried. And it was.

TABLE 4A
11,440,000 Victims during the Collectivization Period: Sources, Calculations, and Estimates*

LINE	EVENT/PROCESS/STRUCTURE	BEGIN YEAR M	END YEAR M	ESTIMATES (000)			SOURCE	NOTES
				LOW	MID	HIGH		
1	COLLECTIVIZATION/DEKULAKIZATION							
	OVERALL COLLECTIVIZATION DEAD							
2	collectivization	1929	?	10,000			Hingley,74,206	includes famine dead
3	collectivization	1929	1935?		3,000		Wiles,53,13	
4	collectivization	1932c		5,000		10,000	Ambartsumov,88	In a Soviet newspaper article
5	collectivization	?		5,000			Riasanovsky,77,551	one-million kulaks, plus families, disappeared; often to camps
6	collectivization	?		5,000			Roeder,58,196	peasants; estimate generally accepted in the camps
7	collectivization	?			10,000		Weissberg,52,320	
8								
9	CONSOLIDATION	1929	1936	3,000	5,000	10,000		
10								
11	DEKULAKIZATION DEAD							
12	dekulakization	1930	1937		6,500		Conquest,86,306	
13	dekulakization	1932	1938	1,000			Ramser,86,20	
14	dekulakization	1933			1,000		Stewart-Smith,64,222	
15	Ukraine dekulakization	1929	1932			500	Conquest,86,303	
16	CONSOLIDATION	1929	1936	1,000	3,000	6,500		
17								
18	DEPORTED							
19	NUMBERS							
20	Cossack villages	1932			200		Conquest,86,277	16 whole Cossack villages, based on Roy Medvedev (1972, p. 93).
21	German-Soviets	1935	1932			?	Fleischhauer & Pinkus,86,89	"from a band of territory 100 km. wide on the Volhynian frontier."
22	kulaks	1929	1932	10,000			Lewin,68,508	4 million from RSFSR.
23	kulaks	1929	1932c	10,000		15,000	Conquest,86,127	
24	kulaks	1929	1935?		1,000		Wiles,53,13	to forced laborer.
25	kulaks	1930	1931	2,500	2,000		Medvedev,79,74	from official data.
26	kulaks	1930	1931			5,000	Antonov-Ovseyenko,81,65-66	
27	kulaks/fugitives/ousted	1929	1931	1,000		5,000	Kulischer,48,93n22	total.
28	peasants	1935c		10,000			d'Encausse,81,20	during collectivization, from historian Moshe Lewin
29	peasants	?	1934	10,000	8,000		Antonov-Ovseyenko,81,104	
30	CONSOLIDATED DEPORTED	1929	1935	8,000	10,000	15,000		[50% assumed deported to camps/forced labor; 50% to resettlement]
31	CALCULATED DEPORTED DEAD	1929	1935	720	1,300	3,225		[from line 30; only for 50% assumed resettled]
32								other 50% assumed picked up by camp/forced labor figures, below]
33	DEAD							
34	kulaks	1929	1932	2,500	3,000	4,000	Conquest,86,127,142	of deported, high and low from general estimates
35	kulaks	1930	1940	400		500	Maksudov,86,30	of 1.5 million deported, from data supplied by H. A. Ivnitskii.
36	resettled	1935c		60		70	Solzhenitsyn,78,363	an example of one group
37	deportation dead	1929	?		3,000		Sorlin,68,153	

TABLE 4A (continued)

#	Category	Year	Year				Source	Note
38	deported peasant dead	?		5,000			d'Encausse,61,20	from Commissariat of Works' data given by H. Walpole
39		1931		4,000		5,000	Souvarine,39,523	
40	CONSOLIDATED DEAD (50%)	1929	1935	2,500	3,000	5,000		[except for low from Maksudov which excludes camps, 50% of line 40 assumed
41		1929	1935	1,250	1,500	2,500		died in resettlement and transit; rest of the dead picked up camp calculations, below]
42	CALCULATED DEPORTED DEAD	1929	1935	720	1,300	3,225		[from line 31]
43	OVERALL DEPORTED DEAD	1929	1935	985	1,400	2,863		[average of lines 41 and 43]
44								
45								
46	*OVERALL COLLECTIVIZATION/DEKULAKIZATION DEAD*							
47	COLLECTIVIZATION	1929	1935	3,000	5,000	10,000		[from line 9]
48	DEKULAKIZATION	1929	1935	1,000	3,000	6,500		[from line 16]
49	DEPORTED	1929	1935	985	1,400	2,863		[from line 44]
50	*AVERAGE OVERALL DEAD*	1929	1935	1,662	3,133	6,454		[average of lines 47–49]
51								
52	*CAMP/FORCED LABOR POPULATION/DEAD*							
53	POPULATION/DEAD							
54	forced labor camps	1928	1930	700			Chyz,62,95	number reached, deportees
55	forced labor camps	1929c			25		Leggett,81,178	NKVD RSFSR
56	camps	1929				350	Swianiewicz,65,14	
57	CONSOLIDATED CAMP POPULATION	1929		200	260	350		
58	CALCULATED CAMP DEAD	1929		20	52	98		
59								
60	camps	1930		600			Conquest,68,335	from a former GPU official in the northern camps
61	camps	1930		662		734	Dallin & Nicolaevsky,47,52	from David Dallin
62	camps	1930		910		980	Swianiewicz,65,123	politicals/criminals
63	camps/prisons/isolators	1930			1,500		Wiles,53,35	
64	forced labor	1930			900		Swianiewicz,65,37	from A. Avtorkhanov (pseud. for A. Ouralov).
65	GULAG	1930		1,500	2,500		Rosefielde,81,65	
66	prisons	1930			3,000		Kosyk,62,16,79	low from Alexander Ouralov, mid-estimate for camps
67	sent to camps	1930			1,500		Elliot,72,43	peasants sent to camp this year.
68							Dujardin,78,50	
69	CONSOLIDATED CAMP POPULATION	1930		600	1,500	3,000		
70	CALCULATED CAMP DEAD	1930		60	300	840		
71								
72	places of detention	1931	1932	2,000			Conquest,68,335	politicals/criminals.
73	camps/prisons/isolators	1931		2,000			Wiles,53,35	RSFSR, from Vyshinsky.
74	forced labor camps/prisons	1931		2,000			Swianiewicz,65,123	
75	GULAG	1931		2,000			Rosefielde,81,65	
76	places of detention	1931		2,000			Dallin & Nicolaevsky,47,54	from diverse estimates.
77	CONSOLIDATED CAMP POPULATION	1931		2,000	2,000	2,200		
78	CALCULATED CAMP DEAD	1931		200	400	616		
79								
80	forced labor	1932		2,500			Swianiewicz,65,37	from A. Avtorkhanov (pseud. for A. Ouralov).
81	GULAG	1932		3,400			Rosefielde,81,65	peasants, from Alexander Ouralov.
82	prisons	1932					Kosyk,62,16	from a condemned, important official of the GPU
83	arrests	1928				37,000	Souvarine,39,640	
84	CONSOLIDATED CAMP POPULATION	1932		2,500	2,500	3,400		
85	CALCULATED CAMP DEAD	1932		250	500	952		
86								

TABLE 4A (continued)

#	Category	Year	Year	(1)	(2)	(3)	Source	Note
87	camps	1933				4,500	Kosyk,62,16,79	
88	GULAG	1933				5,600	Rosefielde,81,65	
89		1933				3,500	Dujrdin,78,50	
90	CONSOLIDATED CAMP POPULATION	1933	1933	3,500	4,500	5,600		
91	CALCULATED CAMP DEAD	1933	1933	350	900	1,568		
92								
93	camps	1933				5,000	Conquest,68,335	from diverse estimates.
94	camps	1935		1,000		5,000	Dallin & Nicolaevsky,47,54-8	from David Dallin
95	camps	1935				5,000	Swianiewicz,65,123	peasant's only, based in part on David Dallin's figures.
96	forced labor camps	1935				3,500	Swianiewicz,65,123	number reached, deportees
97	forced labor camps	1935				2,000	Chyz,62,95	
98	GULAG	1934				6,200	Rosefielde,81,65	
99	CONSOLIDATED CAMP POPULATION	1934	1934	1,000	3,500	6,200	Kosyk,62,16-17	
100	CALCULATED CAMP DEAD	1934	1934	100	700	1,736		
101								
102	camps	1935		5,000		6,000	Kosyk,62,16-17	from Soviet authorities.
103	camps/prisons	1935				5,000	Conquest,86,127	from general estimates.
104	forced labor camps	1935				5,000	Chyz,62,95	deportees.
105	GULAG	1935				6,700	Rosefielde,81,65	
106	CONSOLIDATED CAMP POPULATION	1935	1935	5,000	5,000	6,700		
107	CALCULATED CAMP DEAD	1935	1935	500	1,000	1,876		
108								
109	OVERALL CAMP/FORCED LABOR DEAD						[for Collectivization Period]	
110	MAXIMUM CAMP POPULATION	1929	1935	5,000	5,000	6,700	[sums of lines 58, 70, 78, 85, 91, 100, 107, 111]	
111	CALCULATED TRANSIT DEAD	1929	1935	152	261	666		
112	SUM CAMP/TRANSIT DEAD	1929	1935	1,652	4,113	8,352		
113								
114	camp dead	1927	1930			900	Kosyk,62,79	[2,100 total dead, if proportionated over 1928-35]
115	camp dead	1930	1933			1,300	Kosyk,62,79	[3,033 total dead, if proportionated over 1928-35]
116	camp dead	1933	1936			1,900	Kosyk,62,79	[4,453 total dead, if proportionated over 1928-35]
117	unnatural deaths due to camps	1928	1939			2,600	Wiles,53,App.II,2	from census; women assumed to be 230,000 of the total
118	CONSOLIDATED CAMP DEAD	1929	1935	1,500	2,500	4,500	[based on proportionating lines 114-117 for 1929-35]	
119	SUM CAMP/TRANSIT DEAD	1929	1935	1,632	4,113	8,352	[from line 112]	
120	AVERAGE CAMP/TRANSIT DEAD	1929	1935	1,566	3,306	6,426	[average of lines 118-119]	
121								
122	FAMINE DEAD							
123	UKRAINIAN DEAD							
124	Ukraine	1932	1933	3,000		3,500	Wheatcroft,85,134	from census; even 3-35 million may be an overestimate.
125	Ukraine	1932	1933	6,000		7,000	Mace,85,136	
126	Ukraine	1932	1933	4,000	5,000	10,000	Conquest,86,303-4	diverse Soviet sources; Stalin given an approximation of 8-9 million out of a farm population of 20-25 million.
127	Ukraine	1932	1933			5,000	Conquest,86,249	
128	Ukraine	1932	1933			7,000	Ulam,85,vii	
129	Ukraine	1932	1933	5,000		9,000	Souvarine,39,670	diverse estimates, including from high Soviet officials.
130	Ukraine	1932	1933	4,000		7,000	wytwycky,80,53	
131	Ukraine	1932	1933	4,800		6,000	Manning,53,101	the low is Manning's preferred estimate
132	Ukraine	1932	1933	6,000		7,000	Kosyk,62,77	
133	Ukraine	1933			7,500		Mace,84,39	from census.
134	Ukraine	1933		5,000		7,000	Mace,86,11	
135	Ukraine	1933		5,000		7,000	Mace,84a,78	based on census; figure even may be higher than 7 million.

TABLE 4A (continued)

Line	Category	Year (from)	Year (to)	Low ('000)	High ('000)	Source	Notes
136	Ukraine/N Caucasus	1932			9,000	Tawdul,35,2	in Procyk,86,47.
137	Ukraine/N Caucasus	1933			8,000	Dalrymple,83,6	from M Skrypnyk as told to Tawdul
138	CONSOLIDATION	1932			8,000		
139			1935	3,000	5,000 10,000		
140	**OVERALL FAMINE DEAD**						
141	children	1932	1934	3,000		Medvedev,79,75	quoted from Soviet demographer M. Maksudov.
142	famine/attendant epidemics	1932	1934	10,000		Westwood,80,87	
143	peasants	?	1932		11,000	Weissberg,52,414	starved by 1932; due to Stalin's agrarian policies
144		1928			5,000	Elliot,72,40	
145		1930	1933	10,000		Zinsmeister,88,24	especially during the Winter of 1931–2
146		1931	1932	1,000		Sorlin,68,152	
147		1931	1932	2,500		Dujardin,78,50	
148		1931	1933			Prpic,67,51	
149		1931	1933		5,000	Dalrymple,64,250	general opinion of Moscow diplomats; from US Department of State
150		1931	1933	7,000		Dalrymple,65,472	
151		1931	1933		8,000	Mace,85,136	in Procyk,86,47.
152		1931	1933		9,000	Tawdul,35,2	from Alexander Ouralov, a high state security official,
153		1931	1933	3,300		Dziak,88,57	who says that the OGPU reported these figures to Stalin
154						Costa,88	Alexandra Costa is a former Soviet government official
155		1931	1933	5,000	10,000	Dziak,88,57	estimates of foreign journalists, from A. Ouralov,
156		1931	1935				a high state security official.
157					7,000	Lyons,67,330	communist sources: 3.5 million; noncommunist sources: 5–7 million
158							from diverse sources.
159		1931	1935	3,500	4,000	Steward-Smith,64,87	
160		1931	1933	3,000	7,000	Antonov-Ovseyenko,81,65	Ukraine = 5 million; North Caucasus = 1 million; Elsewhere = 1 million
161		1931	1933		6,000	Elliot,72,223–5	in Procyk,86,47; estimate given Stalin by Levin and Belinsky
162		1932	1933	5,000		Conquest,86,306	
163		1932	1935	7,000		Tawdul,35,2	in Dana Dalrymple's contribution to the seminar
164		1932	1933	10,000		Procyk,86,26	
165		1932	1933	6,000	8,000	Conquest,84,13	from Soviet authorities told privately to Dr. W Horsley Gantt;
166		1932	1934	7,000		Dalrymple,65,471	deaths include those from epidemics.
167		1932	?		15,000		
168		1932	?	6,000	6,000	Ramzer,86,20	from 20 different estimates of journalists, scholars, Soviet officials
169		1933	1935	1,000		Stewart-Smith,64,222	census derived.
170		1933			10,000	Dalrymple,64,259	from Soviet officials.
171		1933		8,000	8,000	Timasheff,46,290	figure circulated among Soviet elite.
172		1933			15,000	Mace,84a,78	
173		1933			10,000	Mace,86,11	
174	CONSOLIDATED OVERALL	1932	1933	3,000	7,000 15,000		
175	CONSOLIDATED UKRAINE	1932	1933	3,000	5,000 10,000		[from line 138]
176	*TOTAL CONSOLIDATED DEAD*	1932	1933	4,000	7,000 15,000		[from line 174; low raised by a million to account for areas outside of the Ukraine]
177							
178	*OVERALL DEAD*						
179	*DEMOCIDE ESTIMATES*						
180	children	?	1934	4,000		Conquest,86,297	in dekulakization and famine.
181	collect./dekula./fam./camps	1930	1937	14,500		Conquest,86,301,305–6	based on census; includes 3.5 million sent to camps who subsequently
182							died; excludes peasants arrested in general terror of 1937–38.
183	collect./dekulak./famine	1930	1932	22,000		Antonov-Ovseyenko,81,65,213	from "experienced" Soviet statisticians;
184							excludes camps and deportations

TABLE 4A (continued)

Line							Source	Notes
185	collectivization & camps	1930	1936	7,000			Conquest,68,533	those who died in collectivization and those
186								sent to camps who died in subsequent years
187	collectivization/dekulakization	1930	1937	11,000			Conquest,86,301,304-6	excludes 7 million famine dead and 3.5 million peasants dying in camps
188	dekulakization	1929	?		15,000		Solzhenitsyn,78,350	author calls this a "plague which starved
189								fifteen million of our peasants to death"
190	dekulakization	?	1933	5,000	15,000		Kuper,81,148	different estimates, excludes famine
191	dekulakization/famine	1929	?	16,000			Panin,76,93n	
192	exec./privation/dekula./fam./camp	1929	?	10,000			Elliot,72,40	includes 3 million dying in labor camps.
193	Kalmyks	1926	1939	20			Conquest,86,197	10% of population of Kalmykia.
194	Kazakhs	1930	1937	1,000			Conquest,86,190,305-6	dead from repression/famine of over 4 million population, from census
195	Kazakhs	1933c					d'Encausse,81,20	out of a population of 4 million
196	Kazakhstan unnatural deaths	1926	1932	3,000			Antonov-Ovseyenko,81,207	based on Turar Ryskulov's figures given to the Central Committee.
197	purges	1921	1939	1,000			Stewart-Smith,64,222	
198	purges	?	1941	10,000			Roeder,58,197	estimate generally accepted in the camps
199	shot/famine	?	1934	20,000			Antonov-Ovseyenko,81,104	credited to Stalin's account, omitting civil war and deported peasants.
200	Ukraine	1931	1932	4,200			Dujardin,78,50	1.2 million executed/liquidated, 3 million died from deportation
201	Ukraine unnatural deaths	1927	1938	2,320	4,400	5,900	Maksudov,86,37-40	high/low give range of possible over/under
202								estimation of population loss
203	unnatural deaths	1926	1930	3,000			Dyadkin,83,59	population deficit, were there no repression since 1926
204	unnatural deaths	1926	1937	30,400			Antonov-Ovseyenko,81,207	
205	unnatural deaths (Ukraine)	1926	1939	8,500	9,000		Dushnyk,83,36	from census; at least 90% of these died from hunger;
206								calculated by D Solovy, Ukrainian demographer.
207	unnatural deaths	1926	1939	5,522			Swianiewicz,65,100	from Frank Lorimer; excess deaths
208	unnatural deaths	1929	1936	9,500	15,000	16,000	Dyadkin,83,25,48	from census, deaths from privation, either in camps or rural areas
209	unnatural deaths	1926	1937	32,000			Souvarine,39,669	from census, assuming birthrate of 2.3% per annum (about 3 million)
210	unnatural deaths	1930	1935	11,000			Dyadkin,83,59	population deficit, were there no repression since 1926
211	unnatural deaths	1933c	1935c	16,700			d'Encausse,81,44	based on census of 1937
212	unnatural deaths	1929	1935	15,000			Legters,84,60	died as a consequence of forced collectivization
213	CONSOLIDATED DEAD	1929	1935	5,522	15,000	22,000		
214								
215	COMPONENTS OF DEMOCIDE							
216	TERRORISM	1929	1935	677	1,733	3,592		[collectivization and dekulakization line 50 minus line 49]
217	DEPORTATIONS	1929	1935	985	1,400	2,863		[from line 44]
218	CAMP/TRANSIT	1929	1935	1,566	3,306	6,426		[from line 120]
219	FAMINE	1932	1933	3,000	5,000	10,000		[Ukraine; from line 138]
220								
221	DEMOCIDE	1929	1935	6,227	11,440	22,880		[sum of lines 216 to 219]
222	DEMOCIDE (CIVILIANS)	1929	1935	6,227	11,440	22,880		[from line 222]
223	DEMOCIDE (FOREIGNERS)	1929	1935	?				[in Mongolia, no estimates available]
224								
225								
226	OTHER DEAD							
227	WAR	1929 & 1932	12 1933	1,000	0.20	2,000	Small & Singer,82,90	Sino-Soviet War
228	FAMINE	1932	1933		5,000			outside of the Ukraine [from line 174 minus line 175]
229	DEMOCIDE RATE							
230	population	1929		153,410			Dyadkin,83,24	
231	population	1930		154,000			Dyadkin,83,59	
232	population	1935		160,000			Dyadkin,83,59	
233	MID-PERICO POP	1932		157,000				
234	DEMOCIDE RATE	1929	1935	3.97%	7.29%	14.57%		[((line 223/line 233)×100)]
235	ANNUAL DEMOCIDE RATE	1929	1935	0.57%	1.04%	2.08%		[(line 234)/7]

Appendix 4.1

The many estimates of those killed during this period create a problem of organization, discrimination, and separation. A particular problem is that many estimates overlap, as in estimates of those killed in the process of collectivization, in the related, but separate, dekulakization of the countryside, in peasant/kulak deportations, and in the camps. Some estimates of the collectivization dead include kulaks killed; similarly, some estimates of the kulaks killed include deported dead. Moreover, to further complicate this, since a large number of the deported were sent to camps, estimates of deported dead may overlap with estimates of those killed in the camps.

To handle all this, estimates of the collectivization, dekulakization, and deportation are classified and consolidated separately in table 4A, respectively giving midestimates of 5,000,000, 3,000,000, and 1,400,000 dead. Then, these three totals are averaged to get a midestimate of 3,133,000 killed for overall collectivization/dekulakization (line 50), surely a very conservative approach. Low and high estimates were similarly determined.

Because of the overlap between the estimates of the deported and camp dead, the deportation total used in these calculations was derived in the following way. First, the number deported was determined from the estimates, which came to a midestimate of 10,000,000 (line 30). Then, half of these were assumed sent to camp (a reasonable assumption based on the references) and thus will be picked up by the camp population estimates. From the remaining half, and the deportation death rate derived in appendix 1.2 (26 percent for the midestimate), the number killed (in pickup, transit, and settlements) was calculated as 1,300,000 deportees (line 31).

But this is not all. As shown in the table (lines 34 to 39), there are also separate estimates of deported dead, for which a midestimate of 3,000,000 killed seems appropriate. Half of these are assumed to have died in the camps. There were then two estimates of deportees killed outside of the camps: one derived from the deathrate applied to the deported numbers (lines 31 and 43); the second determined from estimates of deported dead (line 41). These two are then averaged (line 44) to get a final deportation dead, midestimate of 1,400,000, which is the number used to get the overall collectivization/dekulakization total described above.

A separate problem is estimating camp/transit killed. First, the camp population was estimated for each year during the period, and then using the midcamp deathrate of 20 percent (from appendix 1.2), the annual midestimates of camp dead were calculated. From the camp population estimates, transit deaths for the whole period could also be determined (line 111). Summing annual camp deaths and transit dead gave a midestimate of 4,113,000 over the period (line 112). But there were also several overall estimates of the camp dead (lines 114 to 117), which give a consolidated midestimate of 2,500,000. Clearly there is a significant difference between the two ways of determining camp deaths, with no reason to favor one way over the other. Thus, they were averaged to get the final midestimate of 3,306,000 camp/transit dead (line 120). The similarly determined low was 1,566,000; the high 6,426,000.

Then there is the Soviet famine of 1932–33. The weight of evidence suggests that the attempt to collectivize the peasant, even the nomad, and liquidate the kulak as a class, massively disrupted the agricultural system and brought about the famine. A mild drought did occur but served more to exacerbate the famine than to cause it. As described in the text, the Ukraine was a special case. There the famine was less a by-product of a reckless policy than a policy itself. The Ukraine was purposely starved.

Now, although a strong argument could be made to include all famine deaths during this period as democide, to be conservative, only those in the Ukraine will be counted. Accordingly, two sets of estimates are listed in the table. The first are for the Ukraine, and yield a range of 3,000,000 to 10,000,000 starved to death, with a midestimate of 5,000,000 (line 138). The second set of estimates is for the toll of the famine overall, which initially gives a midestimate of 7,000,000 and a high of 15,000,000 (line 174). The low was 3,000,000, the same as for the Ukraine. Because the Ukrainian famine was only part of a general famine that also occurred in the North Caucasus and elsewhere, however, this overall low of 3,000,000 is raised by a million in the final total famine dead (line 176).

As for previous periods, the components of democide are listed in the table and when summed give a range of total democide figures, the midestimate of which is 11,440,000 (line 222). However, there is another source from which to estimate the total democide. In the table are listed (lines 180 to 212) estimates of overall democide given in the references, including those based on census data. Consolidating these gives a different range of estimates than those drived from the democide components. For comparison, these two ways of estimating the democide are, in thousands:

From components	6,227	11,440	22,880	(line 222)
From references	5,522	15,000	22,000	(line 213)

These two sets could be averaged, but this would yield a range of estimates no longer tied to the components. The lows and highs of each range are fairly close; it is only the midestimates that differ greatly, and the one from the components is lower. Therefore, to continue on the conservative side and lacking a significant reason to average or to adopt the estimates in the references, those based on the components are the final democide figures used in the text.

The census-based calculations of unnatural deaths given on lines 203 to 211 of the table provide a useful check on the final democide estimates. Those census figures that nearly cover the period are generally millions higher than the middemocide estimate. Dyadkin's, perhaps the best in the group, give a range of 9,500,000 to 16,000,000, with a midestimate of 15,000,000 unnatural deaths (line 208).[67] If we subtract from this the 2,000,000 midestimate of the dead in the famine outside of the Ukraine, we still get a midcensus-based estimate over a million higher than the final democide midestimate accepted here.

Estimates of two kinds of democide are omitted from the totals. I could find no estimates of those who died in the general terror and purges outside of the process of collectivization and dekulakization. It is clear that a great many "enemies of the people," "traitors," and "wreckers" were killed, aside from those sent to camps. Perhaps this number might be in six digits, but I am unwilling to add a pure guess to the democide total. It is clear, however, that were there available some reasonable estimates of those murdered in the general terror, the democide estimates would be significantly higher.

As far as the number of foreigners killed is concerned, the Soviets in effect controlled the Mongolian People's Republic during this period and doubtlessly played a role in the forced collectivization of the country in the early 1930s. "Widescale revolt raged"[68] and presumably the same agents of murder were applied as then were being used in the Soviet Union. The Soviets did send in tanks and aircraft to deal with a very serious rebellion in 1932.[69] Moreover, there was a high level purge in which, according to the official history of the country, "quite a few party and other responsible persons" perished.[70] How many died overall, and how many of these should be attributed to Soviet direct action, is unknown. Consequently, foreign democide is left with a question mark in the table.

Epigraph quoted in Kravchenco (1946, pp. 91–92).

Notes

1. Conquest (1986, p. 155).
2. Swianiewicz (1965, p. 88).
3. Ulam (1985, p. viii).
4. Dolot (1985, p. 92).
5. Prpic (1967, p. 50).
6. Grossman (1972, p. 142).
7. Ibid., p. 143.
8. Quoted in Conquest (1986, p. 20).
9. Ibid., p. 75.
10. Ibid., p. 118.
11. Churchill (1950, pp. 498–99).
12. Lewin (1968, p. 520n.4).
13. Ibid., p. 508.
14. Conquest (1986, p. 127).
15. See the opening quote in chap. 1.
16. Hingley (1974, p. 206); Weissberg (1952, p. 320)
17. Ambartsumov (1988).
18. Conquest (1986, p. 190).
19. Mace (1986, pp. 6–7).
20. Conquest (1986, p. 222).
21. Grossman (1972, p. 149).
22. Ibid., p. 150.
23. Kostiuk (1960, p. 38).
24. Dolot (1985, p. 167).
25. Grossman (1972, p. 150).
26. Mace (1986, pp. 7–8).
27. Quoted in Conquest (1986, p. 245).
28. Dolot (1985, p. 152).
29. Ibid., p. 153.
30. Kravchenko (1946, p. 113).
31. Ibid., p. 118.
32. Conquest (1986, pp. 235–36).
33. Swianiewicz (1965, p. 89).

34. Conquest (1986, p. 235).
35. Quoted in Kostiuk (1960, p. 44).
36. Conquest (1986, p. 262).
37. Ibid., p. 3.
38. Kravchenko (1946, p. 130).
39. Conquest (1986, p. 249).
40. Wheatcroft (1985, p. 134).
41. Conquest (1986, p. 304).
42. Ibid., p. 303.
43. Ibid., p. 306.
44. Dolot (1985, p. 175).
45. Mace (1986, p. 11).
46. Conquest (1986, p. 272). Conquest (p. 329) summarizes his evidence of the famine as an intentional policy to defeat Ukrainian nationalism into five major and five subsidiary items of evidence. Mace (1984, pp. 40–45) also provides evidence for the Ukrainian famine being intentional. Also, says Manning (1953, p. 104): "The famine was obviously intended not only to crush the population already impoverished by the collectivization but to administer a sound chastisement to all classes who were interested in the preservation and development of local and republic interests." And "it had been the policy of the government to allow the famine to run its course in the hope of breaking any possible opposition on the part of the collective farms and the individual peasants." (pp. 105–6) For opposing arguments, see Wheatcroft (1985, p. 134) and Tottle (1987), the latter an unabashed, book-length argumentum ad hominem.
47. Krawchenko (1986, p. 22).
48. See, for example, Tawdul (1935).
49. Quoted in Procyk (1986, pp. 53–54).
50. Conquest (1968, p. 87).
51. Ibid., p. 291.
52. Ibid., p. 242.
53. Ibid., p. 226.
54. Rosefielde (1981, p. 65).
55. Kosyk (1962, pp. 16–17); Chyz (1962, p. 95).
56. Solzhenitsyn (1975a, pp. 98, 102).
57. Petrov (1973, p. 163).
58. Tchernavin (1935, pp. 38–39).
59. Ibid., p. 40.
60. Swianiewicz (1965, p. 134).
61. Petrov (1973, p. 163).
62. Roeder (1958, p. 198).
63. Kosyk (1962, p. 79).
64. Wiles (1953, app. 2, p. 2).
65. Antonov-Ovseyenko (1981, p. 65).
66. Conquest (1986, pp. 301, 305–6). His estimate includes those subsequently dying in the camps.

67. Dyadkin (1983, pp. 25, 48).
68. Rupen (1979, p. 55).
69. Ibid., p. 60; Bawden (1968, pp. 315, 320).
70. Rupen (1979, p. 60).

5

4,345,000 Victims: The Great Terror Period, 1936–1938

> *What is so hard to convey about the feeling of Soviet citizens through 1936–38 is the similar long-drawn-out sweat of fear, night after night, that the moment of arrest might arrive before the next dawn. . . [J]ust as in the mud-holes of Verdun and Ypres, anyone at all could feel that he might be the next victim.*
>
> —Robert Conquest

By 1934, the Peasant War was over. But it left an aftertaste. Some activists and party officials in the field could not quite accept the horrors of the previous years with ideological equanimity. Shooting children as kulaks? Starving to death helpless old women? Is this what Marxism means? Moreover, many old Bolsheviks in the party who could contrast Bolshevik ideals with the present still had the old rebellious spirit. Then, there were the top contenders for Stalin's power, each with his own followers, each willing to criticize Stalin's policies and argue alternatives. Stalin ruled, but with an increasingly shaky party beneath him and the real possibility of a palace coup, he did not rule securely.

This was underlined at the January 1934 Party Congress of the Communist Party of the Soviet Union. Most delegates had decided to replace Stalin; some with Sergei Kirov, a popular member of the Politburo, a Russian, unlike Stalin, and head of the Leningrad Party.[1] Obviously, a major purge was needed, and Stalin was a man of action.

Surmounting this early challenge by directly confronting his opponents, Stalin launched a "'coup d'état' by inches."[2] First, he had Kirov assassinated; then under the guise of exposing the perpetrators of this abominable deed, he set up special staffs of NKVD in every district Executive Committee of Leningrad to uncover all those involved in the assassination (which turned out to be almost the whole Leningrad party, of course). They then shot the "conspirators" or sent them to labor camps, and one could not appeal. "It is . . . believed that a quarter of Leningrad was purged—*cleaned out*—in 1934–1935."[3]

This bloody purge was extended to other major cities and eventually to the whole country. It was to reach its zenith with Stalin's appointment of a supreme headhunter, Nikolai Yezhov, as chief of the NKVD in 1936. Immediately justifying Stalin's faith in him, Yezhov inaugurated his reign by having all the NKVD People's Commissars in the Union Republics, and usually their deputies, shot.[4] And no NKVD officer who had served under the former head, Yagoda, was safe either. In 1937 alone, 3,000 were shot.[5]

So effective, so fearsome, was Yezhov that the Great Terror is also called the *Yezhovshchina*. To this day, many who remember the terror hold him alone responsible for all the killing, and believe that Stalin really did not know what was going on. The party today knows who to blame, however, as they give amnesty posthumously to millions of "Stalin's victims."

As the murderous purge embraced one party bureau and then another, one government agency and then another, and one social institution and then another, its nature, extent, and scope began to defy reason and belief. The Red Terror, collectivization, Ukrainian famine, camps, and the like were horrible but explicable in the light of Marxism enforced under Soviet conditions and as interpreted by Lenin. Like Ghenghis Khan massacring all the inhabitants of a city that resisted him as a lesson to others, it was evil but rational. But the Great Terror seems wholly irrational.

Yet, one can impute a rationality to it. Stalin may have wanted to go beyond simply exterminating the opposition and to create a new party in abject fear of him that would work in lockstep to achieve his utopia. Now, consider these aspects of what came to be called the Great Terror, and see if this is not the only way in which they can be understood.

Throughout the vast country, top and middle echelons of the party

and government were executed or sent to camps to die. Their replacements, and sometimes even their replacements again, also were subsequently murdered or sent to labor camps. In 1938 in Tbilisi. . . the
Chairman of the City Executive Committee, his first deputy, department chiefs, their assistants, all the chief accountants, all the chief
economists were arrested. New ones were appointed in their places.
Two months passed, and the arrests began again: the chairman, the
deputy, all eleven department chiefs, all the chief accountants, all the
chief economists. The only people left at liberty were ordinary accountants, stenographers, charwomen, and messengers. . . .[6]

Many old Bolsheviks and other top communists were given show
trials during which they confessed to spying, counterrevolutionary
plotting, and other "crimes," and were sentenced to death. "'Zachto—
why?'—the last words of Yakov Livshits, Old Bolshevik and Deputy
People's Commissar, as he awaited execution on 30 January 1937, got
no answer."[7]

In August 1936, after a dramatic public trial, sixteen top party
leaders, such as Lev Kamemev, Ivan Smirnov, and Grigori Zinoviev,
were executed as Trotskyites. In January 1937, another public trial of
seventeen more top communists, including Karl Radek, was held and
all but four were later executed. In March of 1938, more top party
members, among them Nikolai Bukharin, Alexei Rykov, and Genrikh
Yagoda, were tried and executed. Many Westerners, including the
American ambassador, were completely duped by these trials. They
thought them legitimate, and these top party men guilty. They could
not believe that all the confessions of these high officials were false.
But they were. The party now admits that all was a sham, and has
rehabilitated many of those shot.

The chief of Soviet Military Intelligence was also shot. Military
intelligence agents serving abroad were brought home and shot. Major
Soviet officers and diplomats who had played a role in the Spanish
Civil War were shot.[8]

The top military echelons of the Red Army and navy were shot.
Marshall M. N. Tukhachevsky, the chief of staff, along with seven
high ranking generals, was shot for plotting against the country (the
marshall was posthumously exonerated in 1956).[9] Overall, about half
of the Red Army officer corps were shot or imprisoned—35,000 men.
These included three marshals out of five, thirteen out of fifteen com-

manders, eight out of the eight admirals, 220 out of 406 brigade commanders, seventy-five out of eighty sitting on the supreme military council, all military district commanders, and all eleven vice-commissars of war.[10] Heroes of the Soviet Union, many were, unto their death. There is no evidence that they plotted against Stalin, party, or country, or even tried to use their military forces to save themselves.

Not only were the officers, officials, or workers in the party or government executed or sent to labor camps, often with an impossible twenty-five-year sentence, but so were their wives, parents, and children, and often associates and friends.

It was assumed that all those arrested and interrogated had to be part of a plot or conspiracy. NKVD interrogators labored over each prisoner (interrogators themselves could and were arrested for "wrecking" if they seemed insufficiently dedicated) to "uncover" names and dates, often supplied by the interrogators themselves. But this was vicious. One was forced to confess to at least two coconspirators; these in turn were arrested and each confessed to at least two more; and in turn came more new names. It was a mathematical certainty that except for themselves and Stalin, the NKVD would eventually interrogate every adult in the Soviet Union.

The country-wide scope of these arrests, the sheer mass of those raked in, is unimaginable. Even race and ethnicity were bases for arrest. In 1937, Greeks were arrested "everywhere"; Chinese were arrested en bloc; and national minorities in Russian towns were "virtually eliminated."[11] All Koreans from the Far East were arrested; all those in Leningrad with Estonian family names were arrested; all Latvian Riflemen and Chekists were arrested.[12]

Indeed, the whole country came under an arrest *quota*: "Orders were . . . issued to arrest a certain percentage of the entire population."[13] How many were arrested? About 8,000,000 people just between the middle of 1936 and the end of 1938,[14] and possibly as many as 14,000,000 people were under NKVD detention,[15] or about 9 percent of the population. These were not all party members or officials; most were simple peasants and workers. They had nothing to do with the party, with Stalin's power over the party and thus the country. They had done nothing wrong. Yet they were arrested by the millions. Why?

Only one answer is plausible. As mentioned in the last chapter, there was a growing labor shortage. Needing more forced laborers for its enterprises, the NKVD had developed a quota system for arrests, and now it collected its slaves. "It is . . . difficult, without taking into consideration the bottleneck in [forced] labour, to explain the *scale* of arrests which affected a mass of ordinary people never connected with any political activity."[16] This becomes even more plausible when those whose camp terms were expiring—those who against the odds had managed to survive the deadly camp conditions—were given *second* terms. This, without interrogation or hearing, for nothing the prisoner had done, disclosed to the prisoners as they stood in brigades called up to the administration building for the purpose, and for which they were even made to sign their names.[17]

The millions and millions of arrests during 1937 and 1938 got out of hand. Interrogators were swamped, prison cells stuffed with new arrivals, and the system was at a breakdown by the end of 1938. In some places, for example, to find space for the daily crowd of newly arrested, holes were dug in the ground, a roof put over the top, and prisoners herded in. Small prisons teemed with thousands of arrivals. A prison in Kharkov built for around 800 held about 12,000 prisoners. Not at all unusual, Butyrka Prison in Moscow had 140 men squeezed into a cell for 24.[18]

The Great Terror had to end. His purpose accomplished, Stalin did this by purging the top purger, Yezhov himself, and replacing him with Lavrenti Beria. Yezhov was given a token position and soon disappeared.

Then, arguing that NKVD fascists had been responsible for the terror, and like Yezhov before him, Beria made an "almost clean sweep" through the NKVD, executing nearly all senior officers and sending most of the others to the camps[19] (many camp inmates briefly enjoyed seeing their former interrogators and torturers joining them). As told by a former official in the Secretariat of the Politburo, Beria had a way about him:

> He invited the Ministers of the Interior of all the republics and all the higher *Cheka* officials who had especially distinguished themselves during the purges to a conference in Moscow. Having been asked to leave their weapons in the cloakroom, they were received in the banqueting hall with lavish hospitality. Everybody was in excellent spirits when Beria appeared. Instead of the expected address he uttered just one sentence: "You are under arrest." They were led from the hall and shot in the cellar the same night.[20]

Executions during the Great Terror were not limited to those purged.

There still was an absolute requirement to liquidate "enemies of the people," party members with insufficient revolutionary conscious-ness, independent thinkers, and the like. Of those arrested, how many were executed cannot be known confidently, even within 500,000 lives. Elliot believes 1,000,000 people were executed in prison alone.[21] Medvedev considers this a low number just for the party members alone "struck down" from 1936 to 1939;[22] however, Ulum mentions "loose estimates" of only 500,000 executed.[23] Conquest gives esti-mates that vary from 500,000 to 2,000,000 executed.[24] A prudent estimate, I believe, is 1,000,000 individuals executed—murder in the first degree.

Why did local officials, "quite ordinary decent human beings, with a normal hatred of injustice and cruelty,"[25] carry out these merciless purges and executions? Simple, sweating, trembling, *fear*. Consider what Vladimir and Evdokia Petrov, in their book appropriately titled *Empire of Fear*, wrote about what a friend, who is called M——, said of his experience

> as an N.K.V.D. official in a country town in the Novo-Sibirsk region. The number of victims demanded by Moscow from this town was five hundred. M—— went through all the local dossiers, and found nothing but trivial offenses recorded. But Moscow's requirements were impla-cable; he was driven to desperate measures. He listed priests and their relatives; he put down anyone who was reported to have spoken criti-cally about conditions in the Soviet Union; he included all former members of Admiral Kolchak's White Army. Even though the Soviet Government had decreed that it was not an offense to have served in Kolchak's Army, since its personnel had been forcibly conscripted, it was more than M——'s life was worth not to fulfill his quota. He made up his list of five hundred enemies of the people, had them quickly charged and executed and reported to Moscow: "Task accomplished in accordance with your instructions."
>
> M—— . . . detested what he had to do. He was by nature a decent, honest, kindly man. He told me the story with savage resentment. Years afterwards its horror and injustice lay heavy on his conscience.
>
> But M—— did what he was ordered. Apart from a man's ordinary desire to remain alive, M—— had a mother, a father, a wife and two children.[26]

While the Great Terror focused on the party, it still fell hardest on peasants, workers, intellectuals, and the religious. One evidence of this terror was uncovered during the 1943 Nazi occupation of the

Ukraine. In Vinnitsa, a mass grave was discovered that contained over 9,000 bodies, more than 13 percent of Vinnitsa's prewar population. The Nazis invited an international commission of medical experts to examine the bodies. Almost all were found to have been shot in the back of the neck, all apparently in 1938. Note that a number of those murdered had been sentenced to forced labor "without the right of correspondence," an apparently normal way the party hid many executions.[27]

The result of the Great Terror was a whole new party. Of 139 members and candidates of the party's central committee, 98 were shot. Only 59 delegates of 1,966 to the Party Congress in 1934 were alive to attend the Congress in 1939.[28] In total, the purge eliminated 850,000 members from the party, or 36 percent.[29] Throughout the country extravagant adulation of Stalin became common, while the population learned silence and obedience, fear and submission. "A new political system had been established."[30]

It was a revolution, not in structure but in personnel. Virtually all the old guard and party faithful who lived through the Bolshevik Revolution were murdered. Stalin had liquidated the old party; the new party was totally terrorized into obeying his slightest whim or command. Stalin's power was absolute. He needed to obey no laws, no customs, no tradition. He feared no man under him. With no competing vision, he was free to achieve his own version of utopia, unhindered by any norms, traditions, ethics.

Although the Great Terror wound down in 1938, there were still nests of plotters to be uncovered and people who had been overlooked. NKVD interrogators and camp guards had no fear of unemployment, especially since waves of foreigners were soon to engulf them.

How many were killed overall during this terror? The probable 1,000,000 people executed does not cover camp and transit deaths. In 1936, the camp population was largely due to the collectivization campaign. Alexander Ouralov gives this population as 7,500,000 prisoners, which Kosyk considers too low;[31] Rosefielde as 7,300,000.[32] Others place it as low as 5,000,000 prisoners. By 1938, in spite of more than 2,000,000 inmates probably killed in the interval, the camp population increased to a probable high of 8,000,000. Given these estimated populations and growth from 1936 to 1938, the probable camp and transit death toll is from 1,508,000 to 8,678,000; most likely about 3,280,000, as given in table 5.1. Figure 5.2 compares this toll

TABLE 5.1
Great Terror Period Democide

FACTORS	DEAD ESTIMATES (000)		
	LOW	MID EST.	HIGH
DEMOCIDE	2,044	4,345	10,821
PERIOD RATE	1.26%	2.68%	6.72%
ANNUAL RATE	0.42%	0.89%	2.24%
FOREIGNERS		?	
DEMOCIDE COMPONENTS			
TERROR	500	1,000	2,000
DEPORTATIONS	36	65	143
CAMP/TRANSIT	1,508	3,280	8,678
FAMINE	0	0	0
OTHER KILLED		1.20	
WAR/REBELLION		1.20	
FAMINE/DISEASE		0	

*From appendix 5.1

to that, among others, for previous periods.

When these camp deaths are included, along with an estimated 65,000 dying from deportation, and with the number shot, the total probably murdered in the Great Terror years is 4,345,000. As shown in figure 5.1, the democide could be as high as about 10,821,000, or as low as 2,044,000.

Even this very conservative, absolute low is not to be taken lightly. If it alone were the only estimate for democide in the Soviet Union in this century, it would still be terribly significant. It is more than twice the number of Armenians probably murdered by the Turks during World War I. It likely exceeds the number of Cambodians killed by Khmer Rouge during their brief reign; it is over twice Japan's battle dead in all of World War II, almost twice the overall battle dead in the Vietnam War, and much greater than the total battle dead in the Korean War.[33] Yet, this low is probably too low by over 2,000,000 lives. And even the more likely estimate of 4,345,000, as shown in figure 5.3, is less than *one-third* the democide of the previous collectivization period!

However, from Stalin's perspective, the cost of his revolution from

FIGURE 5.1
Range of Great Terror Democide Estimates*

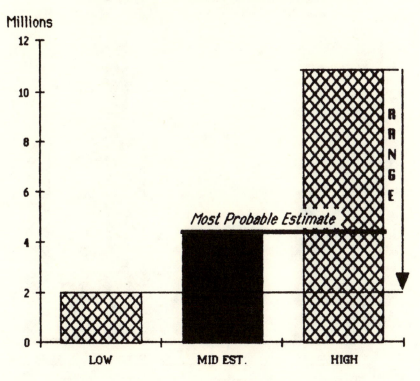

*From appendix 5.1

above was regrettable, but less important than achieving his "New World." Only a few million out of 162,000,000 were killed, or almost three out of every 100 men, women, children, aged, and infants. Wars also have killed millions, but for lesser causes than that of utopia.

Appendix 5.1

In covering this period, the references almost exclusively focus on the purge of the Communist party, and most available democide estimates are of those executed in the purge. These, as well as some estimates of others executed or killed in the continuing general terror, are given in table 5A (lines 77 to 92). Consolidated, these estimates

FIGURE 5.2
Democide Components for Four Periods*

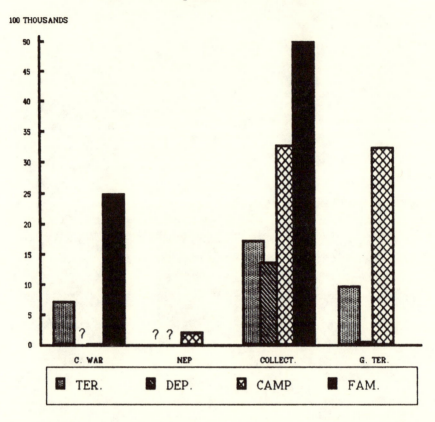

*From tables 2.1–5.1

give a range of 500,000 to 2,000,000 killed in the terror, with a midestimate of 1,000,000.

This midestimate of the terror is meant not only to cover executed party members, but also those peasants, workers, and professionals in the general population killed as "enemies of the people." It surely is very conservative, therefore, since many estimate the number of party members killed alone to be at least this number. The Soviet historian Medvedev, for example, estimates that of those who died at least 1,000,000 were communists.[34]

Deportations also continued into this period, but overall estimates

FIGURE 5.3
Soviet Democide and Annual Rate by Period*

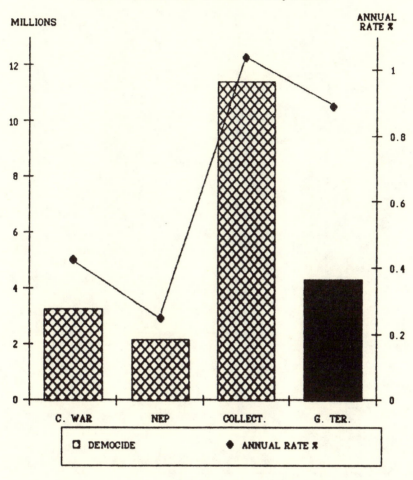

*From tables 2.1–5.1

are unavailable. There are some estimates, however, for the deportation of ethnic Germans, Poles, and Koreans, and these are given in the table (lines 3 to 6). Overall, a midestimate of 500,000 deportees is made (line 7), largely based on these deportations of these ethnics, but also taking into consideration the continuing deportations of other groups and peasants (as partly picked up by Dujardin's estimate on line

TABLE 5A
4,345,000 Victims during the Great Terror: Sources, Calculations, and Estimates*

LINE	EVENT/PROCESS/STRUCTURE	BEGIN YEAR M	END YEAR M	ESTIMATES (000) LOW	MID	HIGH	SOURCE	NOTES
1	*DEPORTED*							
2	Deported/arrested	1937 1	1938 12		7,000		Dujardin,78,50	after Robert Conquest.
3	German/Polish-Soviets	1936	1938	54			Fleischhauer & Pinkus,86,64	[R.J Rummel estimate based on context.]
4	German/Polish-Soviets	1936	1938			18	Fleischhauer & Pinkus,86,64	[R.J Rummel estimate based on context.]
5	Koreans	1937		250			Rupen,79,51	from Vladivostok area to Tashkent and other Central Asian localities
6	Koreans	1937			300		Andics,69,153	all Koreans in settlement areas deported to Uzbek and Kazakh Republics
7	CONSOLIDATED DEAD	1936	1938	400	500	665		[50% assumed deported to camps/forced labor; 50% to resettlement]
8	CALCULATED DEAD	1936	1938	36	65	143		[only for 50% assumed resettled; other 50% assumed picked up by camp/forced labor figures, below]
9								
10	*CAMP/FORCED LABOR POPULATION/DEAD*							
11	POPULATION/DEAD							
12	sent to camps	1936	1937		5,000		Elliot,72,43	added to camps in these years
13	camps	1935	1937	5,000		6,000	Dallin & Nicolaevsky,47,58	from M. Z. Nikonov-Smorodin
14	camps	1935	1937	5,000		6,000	Rosefielde,81,62	from calculations by a former land-surveyor, M. Z. Nikonov-Smorodin
15	forced labor	1936		6,500			Swianiewicz,65,37	from A. Avtorkhanov (pseud of A. Ouralov)
16	prisons	1936			6,500		Kosyk,62,16,79	from A. Ouralov, mid-estimate for camps
17	prisons	1936			7,500		Weissberg,52,320	from arrested former GPU men
18	prisons	1936			1,000		Rosefielde,81,65	
19	GULAG	1936			7,300		Dembin,72,216	in custody by 1937-8
20		1936			5,000		Dujardin,78,50	
21	CONSOLIDATED CAMP POPULATION	1936		5,000	6,500	7,300		
22	CALCULATED CAMP DEAD	1936		500	1,300	2,044		
23								
24	sent to camps	1935	1940		11,840		Antonov-Ovseyenko,81,212	destruction camps, from a 1956 report the Politburo requested of its Organs.
25	(arrested)	1936	1938		8,000		Weisberg,52,1	
26	prisons	1936	1938	7,000		14,000	Beck & Godin,51,67	under NKVD detention, estimated as 5-10% of population
27	arrests	1936	1938	6,000		9,000	Conquest,68,526-7	diverse estimates
28	arrests	1937	1938		7,000		Dembin,72,216	from the most "reliable experts", this gives a total of 12 million held
29	arrests	1937	1938		9,000		Weissberg,52,314-19	includes 2 mil. criminals, 7 mil politicals confirmed by former GULAG officials
30	prisons	1937	1936		1,000		Conquest,68,526	at any moment
31	camps	1937			2,000		Timasheff,48,150	based on election and population data
32	camps	1937 2				4,000	Wheatcroft,81,289	a revision of Timasheff's estimate
33	camp/jail	1937 1			5,000		Conquest,68,532	politicals/criminals.
34	camps/prisons/isolators	1937 1			2,000		Wiles,53,35	politicals/criminals
35	camps/prisons/isolators	1937 12			3,000		Wiles,53,35	deportees
36	forced labor camps	1937		5,000		6,000	Chyz,62,95	
37	GULAG	1937			9,000		Rosefielde,81,65	condemned.
38		1937			15,000		Souvarine,39,641	
39	(arrested)	?			8,000		Rassanovsky,77,559	by the political police
40	CONSOLIDATED CAMP POPULATION	1937		2,000	5,000	9,000		
41	CALCULATED CAMP DEAD	1937		200	1,000	2,520		
42								

TABLE 5A (continued)

Line	Item	Low	Mid	High	Dates	Source	Notes
43	sent to camps	3,000		12,000	1937, 1939	Ulam,76,130-1	low is "very conservative"
44	camps			10,000	1938	Conquest,68,531	from arrested GULAG officials
45	camps			8,000	1938 [12]	Conquest,68,532	
46	camps			7,000	1938	Souvarine,39,640	from communist communique
47	camps			8,000	1938	Weissberg,52,414	arctic camps, these prisoners "would never return"
48	camps/prisons			9,000	1938	Derabin,72,216	by climax of purge in 1938
49	camps/prisons			16,000	1938	Antonov-Ovseyenko,81,210	
50	camp/prisons				1938	Kosyk,62,16	from A. Ouralov.
51	forced labor		11,500		1938	Swianiewicz,55,37	from A. Avtorkhanov (pseud. of A. Ouralov).
52	camps			10,600	1938	Rosefielde,81,05	
53	GULAG			11,500	1938	Dujardin,78,50	
54	CONSOLIDATED CAMP POPULATION	7,000	8,000	10,600	1938		
55	CALCULATED CAMP DEAD	700	1,000	2,968	1938		
	ESTIMATES OF OVERALL CAMP DEAD						
58	camp famine	200		2,000	1936, 1937	Swianiewicz,65,95	after Robert Conquest.
59	camp/prison			2,000	1937, 1938	Dujardin,78,50	prison/camp executions, camp starvation, artificial epidemics
60	camp/prison			7,000	1934, 1941 [6]	Panin,76,93n	from V. Kosyk.
61	camps			2,800	1936, 1939	Conquest,68,365	
62	camps			2,800	1936, 1939	Kosyk,62,79	
63	camps			2,000	1937, 1938	Conquest,68,532	
64	camps	9,000			1937, 1938	Hingley,74,284-5	includes those who subsequently died in the camps
65	camps/prison/transit			2,000	1937, 1938	Derabin,72,216	based on figures Deriabin gives
66	camps/prison/transit			3,000	1936, 1938	Conquest,68,366	not counting those subsequently dying in camps
67	CONSOLIDATED DEAD	2,000	2,300	3,000	1936		
	OVERALL CAMP/FORCED LABOR DEAD						
70	MAXIMUM CAMP POPULATION	7,000	8,000	10,600	1936, 1938		[for Great Terror Period]
71	CALCULATED TRANSIT	108	361	1,146	1936, 1938		
72	SUM CAMP/TRANSIT	1,508	4,261	8,678	1936, 1938		[sum of lines 22, 41, 55, and 71]
73	CONSOLIDATED	2,000	2,300	3,000	1936, 1938		[from line 67]
74	OVERALL CAMP/TRANSIT DEAD	1,508	3,280	8,678	1936, 1938		low/high from line 72, mid-estimate an average of lines 72 and 73]
	EXECUTIONS (TERROR)						
77	executed (in prison)	7,000			1935, 1940	Antonov-Ovseyenko,81,212	shot; from a 1956 report the Politburo requested of its Organs.
78	executed (in prison)	1,000			1936, 1937	Elliot,72,43	
79	executed	2,000			1936, 1938	Petrov,56,72	shot.
80	Ukraine		300		1936, 1938	Maksudov,86,33	victims.
81	communists	200			1936, 1939	Medvedev,79,102	
82	executed	1,000			1936, 1940	Ramaer,86,20	
83	executed/suicides	500		2,000	1936, 1941 [6]	Lyons,67,335	includes CPSU purges"
84	executed	1,000		2,000	1937, 1938	Conquest,68,532	high is the estimate of Soviet defectors
85	executed	1,000			1937, 1938	Conquest,68,50	
86	executed	500		2,000	1937, 1938	Conquest,68,529	after Robert Conquest.
87	executed			2,000	1937, 1938	Hingley,74,284-5	diverse estimates.
88	executed	500			1937, 1939	Ulam,76,130	loose estimates
89	executed	500		1,700	1937, 1939 [1]	Solzhenitsyn,73,438-39	
90	executed (Baikal-Amour)	980		50	1937	Dujardin,78,50	shot; low includes 480,000 "habitual thieves", from former NKVD Yezhov men secretly shot in camps around the Baikal-Amour railroad

TABLE 5A (continued)

#	Category	Date1	Date2	Low	Mid	High	Source	Note
91	Trotskyists	1938		1,000		?	Medvedev,79,117	Indiscriminate massacre of all Trotskyists (actual and former) in the camps
92	communists	1930a		500		2,000	Medvedev,79,108	of those "who died"
93	CONSOLIDATED EXECUTIONS	1936		1,000		2,000		
94								
95	**WAR**							
96	Changkufeng (Manchurian) War	1938 7	1938 8	1,000		1.2	Small & Singer,82,90	
97		1938				2,000		
98	**OVERALL DEAD**							
99	**DIVERSE DEMOCIDE ESTIMATES**							
100		1935	1941	19,000			Antonov-Ovseyenko,81,213	population deficit, were there no repression since 1926
101		1936	1938	3,000			Lyons,67,335	
102		1937	1938	4,000			Legters,84,60	
103	CONSOLIDATED	1936	1938	3,000	6,000	8,143		mid-estimate is proportionated line 102; high is proportionated line 100
104								
105	**CENSUS BASED ESTIMATES**							
106	unnatural deaths	1935	1940	6,000			Dyadkin,83,59	from census
107	unnatural deaths	1937	1938	1,260	1,420	1,580	Dyadkin,83,41	from census
108	unnatural deaths	1937	1940	2,980		3,480	Dyadkin,83,41	from census
109	unnatural deaths	1937		660	790	920	Dyadkin,83,41	from census
110	unnatural deaths	1938		530	630	730	Dyadkin,83,41	from census
111	CONSOLIDATED	1936	1938	1,838	2,130	2,423		[average and proportionating of lines 107, and 109-110. (((109+110)/2) x 3)+((107/2) x 3))/2]
112	CONSOLIDATED TOTAL	1936	1938	1,838	4,065	6,143		[low/high from 111, mid-estimate is an average of lines 103 and 111]
113								
114	**COMPONENTS OF DEMOCIDE**							
115	TERRORISM	1936	1938	500	1,000	2,000	[from line 93]	
116	DEPORTATIONS	1936	1938	36	65	143	[from line 8]	
117	CAMP/TRANSIT	1936	1938	1,508	3,280	6,578	[from line 74]	
118	FAMINE	1936	1938	0	0	0		
119	DEMOCIDE	1936	1938	2,044	4,345	10,821	[sum of lines 115 to 118]	
120	DEMOCIDE (CIVILIANS)	1936	1938	2,044	4,345	10,821	[from line 119]	
121	DEMOCIDE (FOREIGNERS)	1936	1938			?		
122								
123	**OTHER DEAD**							
124	WAR	1936	1938		1.2		[from line 96]	
127								
128	**DEMOCIDE RATE**							
129	population	1937		163,772			Conquest,86,300	census, the most specific figure given in Soviet demographic studies
130	population	1937		163,770			Dyadkin,83,24	census
131	population	1937		156,000			Antonov-Ovseyenko,81,207	census
132	population	1937		164,000			d'Encausse,81,44	census, Second Five Year Plan forecast 180 7 million
133	population	1938		160,000			Antonov-Ovseyenko,81,211	
134	population	1938		166,900			Timasheff,48,150	
135	MID-PERIOD POP	1937		161,886			[average of 1937 estimates]	
136	DEMOCIDE RATE	1936	1938	1.26%	2.68%	6.68%	[((line 120/line 135) x 100)]	
137	ANNUAL DEMOCIDE RATE	1936	1938	0.42%	0.89%	2.23%	[line 136/3]	

*See notes to table 1A, appendix 1.1.

2). Half of these deportees are assumed resettled, and applying to this half the deportee deathrates determined in appendix 1.2 gives a range of deportation deaths of 36,000 to 143,000 (line 8). The other half are assumed to have been sent to the camps.

Estimates of the labor camp population for 1936, 1937, and 1938 are given in the table (lines 12 to 53). The camp dead for each year and the transit dead (line 71) are calculated from the death rates determined in appendix 1.2. These summed (line 72) give a range of 1,508,000 to 8,678,000 killed in the camps.

Aside from these death rate-based numbers, the references give for overlapping years a variety of estimates of the total camp dead, as listed in the table (lines 58 to 66). Consolidated, these yield a range of 2,000,000 to 3,000,000 dead, which is within the range of the calculated toll (see lines 72 to 73). Of the two sets of estimates for camp dead during the period, the lowest low and highest high are selected for the final figures, and the two midestimates are averaged (line 74).

To my knowledge, there was no famine during this period. There was a limited war fought in Asia in 1938 (line 96).

Turning to the overall democide, available estimates are organized into those of Dyadkin based on census reports (lines 106 to 110) and others (lines 100 to 102). These are consolidated into two sets of estimates, which are then combined into one by taking the lowest low and highest high and averaging both midestimates (line 112).

The resulting totals can now be compared to the sum of the democide components (lines 115 to 118). This sum (line 119) gives a democide range of 2,044,000 to 10,821,000 killed, with a conservative midestimate of 4,345,000. Both the low and midestimate are close to those from the other overall estimates (line 112), while the high is higher by more than 2,000,000 killed.

When Dyadkin's[35] census-based calculations are averaged and proportionated for this period (line 111), they give a low close to that here, but a *high* that is more than 2,000,000 *lower* than the midestimate given by the democide components. But it should be immediately noted that Dyadkin relied only on census reports available to the Soviet citizen, and at least regarding the 1937 census results, these were altered by the party to give a rosier view of Soviet population growth. The Second Five Year Plan had assessed the population of 1937 as 180,700,000, but the census came in with a figure of almost 164,000,000, or a deficit of nearly 16,700,000 between expected and actual.[36] As a result, the census results were annulled and high officials responsible for the census were arrested. The party subsequently revised the 1937 census results upward by about 14,300,000.[37]

Moreover, the 1926 census results for the population were under-reported, perhaps by 800,000.[38] Even without taking all this into account, the population deficit between the 1926 and 1937 census results was around 30,400,000.[39] Because of a too low estimate at one end and a too high estimate at the other, Dyadkin apparently under-estimated the number of unnatural deaths during this period, and could have been too low by several million deaths, even assuming that his birthrate assumptions were correct. All this makes the middemocide estimate of 4,345,000 more reasonable and conservative.

As for the NEP and collectivization periods, the Soviets were militarily involved in Mongolia. The Red Army entered Mongolia in force in 1937 and participated in the wide scale destruction of Buddhist monasteries.[40] In effect, the Soviets controlled the country. During this period, an intensive purge of the Buddhist church and nobles was carried out. According to an official history, "high lamas who had clearly demonstrated that they were irreconcilable . . . were defeated and liquidated by means of revolutionary violence."[41] A terror paralleling that in the Soviet Union was imposed on the Mongolian party. One indication of the extent of the purge and the violence throughout the country is that for the period of 1935 to 1938, the female population rose by 12,500, while males fell by 3,200 (total population in 1938 was 747,000).[42] Over the period 1935 to 1940, the population aged eight and over dropped by 9,300.[43]

Nonetheless, I could find no estimates of Mongolians killed by the Soviets, and thus in the table foreign democide is given a question mark.

Notes

1. Levytsky (1972, p. 79).
2. Conquest (1968, pp. 73–74).
3. Solzhenitsyn (1973, p. 58).
4. Levytsky (1972, p. 93).
5. Conquest (1968, p. 199).
6. Solzhenitsyn (1973, pp. 68–69).
7. Conquest (1968, p. 479).
8. Ibid., pp. 230–31.
9. Prpic (1967, p. 60).

10. Grey (1967, p. 294); Grey's figures for brigade commanders and commanders differ slightly from those given by Conquest (1968, p. 485).
11. Conquest (1968, p. 299).
12. Solzhenitsyn (1973, p. 72).
13. Riasanovsky (1977, p. 559).
14. Weissberg (1952, p. 1); Riasanovsky (1977, p. 559).
15. Beck and Godin (1951, p. 67).
16. Swianiewicz (1965, p. 164).
17. Solzhenitsyn (1975a, p. 376).
18. Conquest (1968, p. 290).
19. Grey (1967, p. 299); Conquest (1968, pp. 464–65).
20. Roeder (1958, pp. 205–6).
21. Elliot (1972, p. 43).
22. Medvedev (1979, p. 102).
23. Ulum (1976, p. 130).
24. Conquest (1968, pp. 527–29).
25. Petrov (1956, p. 75).
26. Ibid., pp. 75–76.
27. Conquest (1968, pp. 528–29).
28. Grey (1967, p. 251).
29. Prpic (1967, p. 57).
30. Conquest (1968, p. 481).
31. Kosyk (1962, p. 16).
32. Rosefielde (1981, p. 65).
33. See Small and Singer (1982, table 4.2). Estimates of those killed in the Armenian genocide (1914–18) vary from 300,000 to 1,500,000. A prudent estimate is that 1,000,000 Armenians were murdered.
34. Medvedev (1979, p. 108).
35. Dyadkin (1983).
36. d'Encausse (1981, p. 44).
37. Conquest (1986, p. 300).
38. Ibid., p. 299.
39. Antonov-Ovseyenko (1981, p. 207).
40. Rupen (1979, p. 60).
41. Quoted in ibid., pp. 50–51.
42. Ibid., p. 57.
43. Bawden (1968, p. 345).

6

5,104,000 Victims: Pre–World War II Period, 1939–June 1941

> *We did wrong in ever opposing Hitler. Po-*
> *land should never have fought. Nothing*
> *could have been worse than our plight here.*
> —A Polish Jew and deportee

> *I think with horror and shame of a Europe*
> *divided into two parts by the line of the*
> *Bug, on one side of which millions of so-*
> *viet slaves prayed for liberation by the*
> *armies of Hitler, and on the other millions*
> *of victims of German concentration camps*
> *awaited deliverance by the Red Army as*
> *their last hope.*
> —A Polish prisoner of the Soviets

Nineteen thirty-nine was a great year for Stalin. Now the most absolutist of rulers, he secured himself against a dangerous war, at least for a couple of years, by a nonaggression pact with Hitler; and by secret agreement he was given a free hand against the sovereign Baltic states and half of Poland. When World War II started with Hitler's invasion of Poland from the West on 1 September 1939, by the agreement Stalin was free to invade Poland from the East. This he did seventeen days later. Thus stabbed in the back while fighting the Nazis, the Poles put up little resistance. In fact, they first thought that the Red Army had crossed the Soviet-Polish border to help them against the Nazis. In short order, the Red Army occupied Poland up to the line agreed upon with the Nazis, taking over 13,000,000 people and 77,720 square miles. The Nazis conquered more Poles (22,000,000), but less land (72,806 square miles).[1]

The Soviets wasted no time with their half of Poland. In a little over a month, the Polish Western Ukraine and Western Byelorussia were made constituent parts of the Ukrainian and Byelorussian Soviet Republics.

Meanwhile, a Soviet attempt to pressure the Finns into ceding them bases failed. So Stalin abrogated their nonaggression pact, broke off diplomatic relations on 29 November, and within a day invaded Finland. Fiercely resisting, Finnish forces destroyed division after divison of Red Army troops and killed possibly as many as 1,000,000 (so believed Khrushchev).[2] But by sheer weight of numbers and resources, in a little over three months the Soviets won, forcing Finland to concede about 10 percent of her territory.

Perhaps for fear that the Soviet POWs held by Finland had probably been subjected to anti-Soviet, antirevolutionary propaganda, possibly believing that they had shown insufficient dedication to the revolution by allowing themselves to be captured, they were all given special treatment when released by Finland. They were welcomed back, triumphantly marched under a banner saying "The Homeland Greets Its Heroes" and down the length of the city, and then ordered into railroad cars with barred windows. When the train reached its destination, many POWs were shot, others were sent to labor camps, most of them probably to die.[3]

Next came the small Baltic states. In June 1940 (a month after the Nazi invasion of Belgium, Holland, and Luxembourg and with France close to defeat), the Soviets issued ultimatums to Lithuania, Latvia, and Estonia, demanding they set up pro-Soviet governments and allow the Red Army to establish military bases in their countries for their own protection. In no way could these nations militarily resist the Soviet giant. With one face-saving formula or another, they capitulated to Soviet demands, and were occupied, effectively taken over, and "voluntarily" absorbed into the Soviet Union after the war.

Moreover, in less than two weeks the Soviets also demanded that Rumania concede Bessarabia and Northern Bukovina to them. With appeals to Hitler for support getting nowhere, Rumania complied and the Red Army occupied this region within days.

By the end of the World War II, Soviet "annexations" included not only the three Baltic states, parts of Finland and half of Poland, but also northern Bessarabia and Bukovina, South Sakhalin, and four northern Japanese islands. All told, an area of at least 182,239 square miles with 24,379,000 people.[4] This is an area almost as large as Spain, with a population the size of, Belgium and the Netherlands together. The bulk of these "adjustments" in Soviet territory were done by ultimatums and conquest in this pre–World War II period.

Of the four great dictatorships—Nazi Germany, Fascist Italy, militarized Japan, and the communist Soviet Union—that invaded and conquered neighboring territory from 1 September 1939 to 21 June 1941, only the Soviet Union has kept what it took, and has even added to those booties as a result of becoming an ally of the democracies after the Nazi invasion in 1941. Moreover, in the spirit of decolonization after the war, the United States, United Kingdom, France, and other democracies freed at least forty colonies with a combined population of 850,000,000 people.[5] The Soviet Union has only now begun to free parts of its empire.

But all this is another story and is relevant here only because of the plight of the inhabitants. The party had developed and honed through the collectivization and Great Terror periods precise instructions and rules for processing actual or potentially hostile populations. These only needed some refinement in application to foreign nationals, such as in the correct handling of foreign military officers or police officials: shoot them.

In each newly acquired territory, the Red Army was immediately followed by the NKVD, with well-prepared lists. Many former high officials, top military, and police officials were arrested, most shot. Also, leading clergy, bourgeoisie, teachers, and other professionals were arrested and usually shot. Now, this is not path-breaking behavior for the Soviets. In fact, it is quite in keeping with Lenin's treatment of the Poles conquered during the short Soviet-Polish War of 1919–20. For example, in a note to Efraim Sklyansky (deputy chairman of the Revolutionary Military Council of the Republic) at a meeting, Lenin wrote:

> A superb plan. Complete it *together* with Dzerzhinsky. Under the guise of "Greens" (and we will pin it on them later) we shall move forward 10–20 versts and hang the *kulaks*, priests and landowners. Bounty: 100,000 rubles for each man hanged.[6]

By 1939, the party needed to offer no bounty. Soviet officers and NKVD had learned their duty during the collectivization and Great Terror years.

Besides those shot in the newly occupied territories, others—middle echelon officials, intellectuals, professionals, and lowly common folk—were deported en masse to Soviet labor camps. Waves of arrests, shootings, and deportations followed as the NKVD hunted deeper into the foreign population to liquidate any possible source of anti-Soviet behavior or thoughts. The directive was simple. Kill actual or possible leaders. Of others who might have opposing ideas or thoughts, get some work out of them before they die; the remainder will be terrorized into obeying every command.

These murders took place in four phases. First, as the Red Army moved in, looting, beating, robbery, rape, and indiscriminate murder by soldiers were not rare. This was most true in Poland, less true in the Baltic states during this period (but true in every foreign mile the Red Army conquered or reconquered during World War II). Second, upon entering villages Red Army officers and party representatives encouraged workers and peasants to "take what belonged to them," to get even with their former "exploiters," with the capitalist or rich land owner or police official, and to beat and even kill them. If they could not do this on their own, the Red Army promised to help.

Throughout occupied Poland, for example, the Red Army decreed a period of lawlessness. Local communists were given carte blanche to square accounts with enemies.[7] "A brutal, nightmarish bloodbath ensued."[8] It was hopeless to appeal to Soviet authorities. At best such pleas were met with "indifference or rebuke."[9] Moreover, the Soviets gave some local authority to village committees they set up, with instructions to shoot anyone who disobeyed or ignored their orders.[10]

Third came massive arrests. Former officials, officers, social categories like the clergy that were natural "enemies of the people," and most people of importance, were arrested. But there were also individual arrests and roundups on the street.[11] In Soviet occupied Poland, about 500,000 were arrested and imprisoned at one time or another—about one in ten of all adult males.[12]

Arrest, however, was just the beginning. The NKVD then systematically shot former leaders, officials, and officers. In Bessarabia and Northern Bukovina, for example, there were massive arrests and deportations and countless summary executions, particularly along the Rumanian border.[13]

Poland was treated with special care. In one well investigated case, the NKVD executed possibly 14,471 mainly Polish officers (with some civilian professionals included) in three camps.[14] Some 4,254 of these were uncovered in mass graves in Katyn Forest by the Nazis in 1941, who then invited an international group of neutral representatives and doctors to study the corpses and confirm Soviet guilt.[15] In cold calculation, the Soviets transported these Poles to their place of execution and shot each in the back of the head.

Fourth came the deportations, and here there were three stages of death: during roundup, when people might be shot for falling or straying out of line, disobeying an order, and such; during transit to resettlement or camps in the Soviet Union; and in the deadly resettlement area or camps themselves. People were deported often because of who they were (landowner, businessman, clergy, writer, etc.) or because of being denounced "by a wide network of secret freelance collaborators."[16] Their roundup for deportation involved standard operating procedures. These are detailed in a captured NKVD order regarding deportations from the Baltic states:

> In view of the fact that a large number of the deportees must be arrested and placed in special camps and their families settled at special points in distant regions, it is necessary to execute the operation of deporting both the members of his family as well as the deportee simultaneously, without informing them of the separation confronting them. . . . The moving of the entire family to the station . . . should be done in one vehicle, and only at the station should the head of the family be placed separately from his family in a railway car especially intended for heads of families. . . . While gathering together the family in the home of the deportee, the head of the family should be warned that personal male articles are to be packed into a separate suitcase, as a sanitary inspection will be made of the deported men separately from the women and children.[17]

Now those deported to settlements rather than camps or into exile could not consider themselves lucky. Special settlements "may be described briefly as concentration camps without barbed wire fences, and with a somewhat less rigorous discipline."[18] The death rate in special settlements was about 10 to 15 percent annually.[19] In two ways the life of the exile was worse than for camp inmates. The camps at least had a place to sleep under a roof—usually. And no matter how little the food or how deficient in vital nutrients it was, at least there was a daily ration; exiles ate only what they could scrounge. Since they were generally unfit for work, they did not get bread cards nor were they entitled to food allotments.[20]

For Poland, the deportations took place in four waves. With the temperature at minus forty degrees Fahrenheit on a February day in 1940, the first wave of 220,000 Poles were forcibly distributed among 110 trains, and then slowly carted northeast to the Soviet Arckhangeilsk region by the White Sea.[21] These were mainly the staffs of Polish public services and those to be resettled along with their families, around 10 percent—22,000—of whom perished during the deportation alone.[22] A few months later there was a second deportation, this time consisting of 320,000 villagers along the Soviet border, land owners, families of the former Polish military and police, and so on. These Poles ended up in the southern part of Asiatic Russia. Then, during the summer, there was a third deportation of around 240,000 Poles, mainly refugees who thought they had escaped the Nazi hell. The final deportation wave of about 200,000 Poles comprised more refugees, the families of those arrested, and intellectuals, craftsmen, and the like.[23] Poles were also deported in many minor waves. Overall, for Poland *alone*, an estimated 1,200,000 were deported,[24] with possibly 270,000 of them being murdered by thirst, starvation, disease, cold, and overwork within a few years.[25]

Then there were the Soviet deportations of the Baltic peoples. On 13–14 June 1941, one Latvian study estimates that 662 boxcars left Latvia for Soviet camps and forced settlements carrying 15,081 deportees (3,332 children under sixteen), or eight out of every 1,000 Latvians; from Estonia, it is estimated that 490 boxcars carted 10,205 people (3,018 under sixteen) eastward, nine out of every 1,000 Latvians; and some days later, 34,260 Lithuanians were similarly deported, or eleven of every 1,000 Lithuanians. Men generally went to camps; women and children into exile.[26] Overall, about 127,000 Balts were deported before the war, among whom 17,000 probably died.[27]

The story of one Latvian girl, Ruta Upite, deported twice to Siberia, exemplifies the appalling lot of these deportees. She

cried out her sufferings in her diary "Dear God, I wanted to live!" On Bilina Island, Ob River, in the winter of 1943, she saw one-fourth of all Latvians in the group of 200 deportees die of cold and starvation in a period of four months. Her health was destroyed by the slave labor conditions in Siberia, and she died while still young.[28]

And then there was Bessarabia, from which, as with a broom, the

Soviets swept up and deported to the gulag 200,000 to 300,000 intelligentsia and politically articulate sectors of Bessarabia's population of about 2,000,000.[29]

When all the deportations from conquered territories are added up, most likely about 280,000 foreigners perished during transit, in the settlements, or during exile. Of those sent to camps, probably another 250,000 died.[30] I can find no estimates on the number of Soviet citizens deported or who perished from deportation during this period.

Aside from the deportations, of course, general terror was applied to all conquered territories. For example, a list of seventy-eight names of those executed by the Soviets was found in Latvia after the Soviets were driven out by the Nazis:

> On the list the charges preferred against them were stated, a selection of which read: "she was caught singing Latvian folk-songs," "his ancestors were bourgeois," "he exploited the labour of others," "he was caught hiding in the woods," "he was a member of a students' organization," "he was a police officer," "he fought in the Latvian army against bolshevism," "he had anti-bolshevist convictions," "he ignored soldiers of the Red Army," "he insulted the Communist Party." Across this list, Shustin, who was chief of the M.V.D. in Latvia, scrawled in red-ink these words, "Considering the social danger they represent, all must be shot."[31]

In one year, 1940 to 1941, the Soviets murdered 1,950 Estonians, 1,488 Latvians, and 1,114 Lithuanians.[32]

Everyone now knows how abominable, fearsome, and deadly was the Nazi occupation of Eastern Europe. Yet, from his study of the Soviet occupation of Poland, Jan Gross concludes that in terms of loss of life, forced resettlement, deportations, confiscations, and fiscal measures, the Soviet occupation was worse than that of the Nazis.[33]

Now, we need an overall estimate for this period that takes executed, deported, and camps into account for both these foreigners and Soviet citizens. For although attention is naturally drawn to the drama in the conquered territories, life at home was only less terroristic than in 1936 to 1938. The massive murdering of citizens for one reason or another, or for no reason whatsoever, still was carried out mercilessly. For example, in Kuropaty Wood near Minsk, the capital of Byelorussia, mass graves were found holding perhaps as many as 30,000 to 200,000 bodies.[34] Exhuming the corpses and the questioning of local villagers revealed that these dead had been murdered from 1937 to 1941 by the NKVD. According to one current Soviet report based on a news article by Zenon Poznyak in the *Moscow News:*

> Examination of the clothes of the victims shows that most of them were ordinary country folk, many of them women, along with intellectuals and town dwellers.
>
> Household goods and purses buried with them suggest that they were taken straight from home or work and shot without trial, [Poznyak] surmises.
>
> A villager described how his village of 120 homesteads, containing about 800 people, had been reduced to 30 by the time Hitler invaded in 1941.
>
> The population was terrorized by a few people—the collective farm chairman, the head of the village council, a foreman and a couple of hangers-on.
>
> The trouble was, for every "enemy of the people" exposed, the denouncer-informer received about 15 rubles a head.[35]

A Soviet archaeologist who dug up some of the graves reported that similar mass murders had taken place "near other big Byelorussian towns."[36]

Avoiding this fast death of the bullet only meant for many the slow death of the labor camp. Although in smaller waves than during the Great Terror, enemies of the people continued to wash into the camps and prisons. "'Normal' arrests by the thousands, executions without trial, arbitrary exile of 'undesirable elements' whose labor was desirable in forsaken regions, tortures and inquisitions continued."[37]

Moreover, there was a whole new basis for arresting and shipping people off to camps. Beginning in 1938, all workers had to have a workbook filled in by their bosses, and those who were late for work, quit early for lunch, or left before closing time were punished. Then in 1939, those who were more than twenty minutes late for work three times in a month had their poor work attitude dealt with in a corrective-labor camp (which was milder than the forced labor camp); and then beginning in 1940, leaving a job without permission was made a crime punishable by internment in a forced labor camp.[38]

The deathrate in the camps during this period was near its highest. Conditions had become so ruinous to life that "about a third of the new intake—already physically exhausted, and quite unprepared for heavy manual labour on a minimal ration—died in the first year."[39] The population of the camps still increased in spite of this toll, partially due to the influx of foreigners. For 1941, Conquest gives estimates of the camp prisoner population varying from 6,000,000 to over 15,000,000, and an estimate of 12,000,000 to 14,000,000 prisoners was given by a colonel connected to the inspectorate of camp guards.[40] Swianiewicz notes that estimates of Western experts range from a low of 3,000,000 to 13,000,000 prisoners,[41] and the estimates of many prisoners and NKVD officials range from 12,000,000 to 20,000,000.[42] And Kosyk gives what he believes to be an underestimate of 13,500,000 for 1941.[43] Taking these and other estimates into account, the most reasonable estimate for 1941 is of 10,000,000 camp inmates.

Moreover, there was a correlative increase in numbers of prisoners sent off to the death camps in Kolyma. Their inmate population grew from 150,000 in 1937 to possibly 300,000 to 400,000 in 1940, reaching its largest number of 500,000 after the war.[44] Such numbers are very misleading, however, since there was a constant need to replace those who died. In these mining camps prisoners doing general labor in the arctic cold and dangerous mines hardly lasted a year, and as they died, new inmates replaced them.

In the late 1930s, gold production in the Kolyma mines seems to have reached 300 tons a year; after the war it possibly went up to 400-500 tons a year (perhaps a third of world production). One estimate is that every ton cost 1,000 lives. Moreover, at least during 1940 to 1941 there were lead mines where the lack of safety measures was such that all prisoner-miners eventually died of lead poisoning. The 3,000 Poles sent into these mines in August 1940 were all dead by the following year when Poles were amnestied.[45]

Actually, out of a total of 10,000 to 12,000 Poles sent to Kolyma, only 583 survived to be amnestied a year or so later, or a 75- to 80-percent deathrate per annum. But it is difficult to calculate an overall deathrate in these camps, since in some all prisoners died, leaving no one to tell the tale.[46] For those camps with survivors, however, Conquest calculates in his book *Kolyma* the average death rate for miners to be 30 to 35 percent and 25 percent per year for Kolyma overall.[47] Against these death rates, one should weigh the ten-, fifteen-, and twenty-five-year sentences of prisoners sent there.

And one must not forget the toll from transit to or from these camps, all by ship over dangerous waters. For example, carrying 2,500 freed prisoners—those who had miraculously survived their term—in its hold on a trip from Magadan to Vladivostok, the transit ship *Indigirka*

FIGURE 6.1
Range in Pre-World War II Democide Estimates*

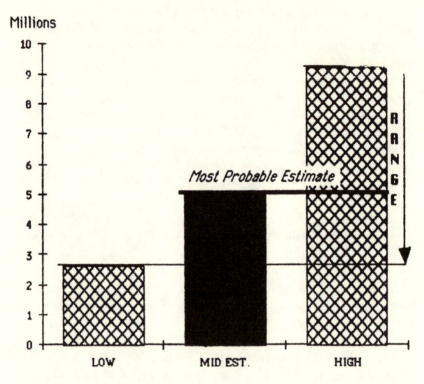

Millions

Most Probable Estimate

LOW   MID EST.   HIGH

R R N G E

---

*From appendix 6.1

struck a rock. As the hold full of former prisoners began to fill with freezing water, officials refused to unlock the holds to let them out, while themselves escaping on lifeboats. Only about thirty former prisoners survived.[48]

Taking all this into account (deportations, settlements, camps, and terror), surely no less than 2,646,000 and possibly even 9,192,000 Soviet citizens and foreigners were murdered during this period. My prudent estimate is a democide of 5,104,000 people, of which 666,000 were most likely foreigners. Figure 6.1 shows the range in possible democide during this period, and the most probable estimate. Table 6.1 gives the actual numbers.

TABLE 6.1
Pre-World War II Period Democide

FACTORS	DEAD ESTIMATES (000)		
	LOW	MID EST.	HIGH
DEMOCIDE	2,646	5,104	9,192
PERIOD RATE	1.33%	2.55%	4.45%
ANNUAL RATE	0.53%	1.02%	1.78%
FOREIGNERS	340	666	1,445
DEMOCIDE COMPONENTS			
TERROR	1,049	1,932	2,232
DEPORTATIONS	180	283	685
CAMP/TRANSIT	1,418	2,889	6,275
FAMINE	0	0	0
OTHER KILLED	54	256	1,006
WAR/REBELLION	54	256	1,006
FAMINE/DISEASE		0	

*From appendix 6.1

Figure 6.2 compares the components of democide during this period against those of the previous ones. Note that this period's increase in camp population was the largest of any so far and resulted in camp deaths also being the greatest.

As can also be seen from figure 6.2, terror in the occupied teritories and at home apparently reaped more victims in this period than during the Great Terror. However, this is probably an artifact of the available estimates of terror during this previous period focusing on the execution of party members and government officials rather than on the general terror against common folk.

A comparison of the most probable overall democide of this period with that of the previous ones is illustrated in figure 6.3. Note that the prewar years were, judging from the annual deathrate, almost as deadly as during collectivization, even considering the famine then. This results largely from the camps' more than doubling in size by this period and the continuing terror and purges.

By normal standards, the democide toll of 5,104,000 for this period is a catastrophe in human lives. For most nations it would be the

FIGURE 6.2
Democide Components for Five Periods*

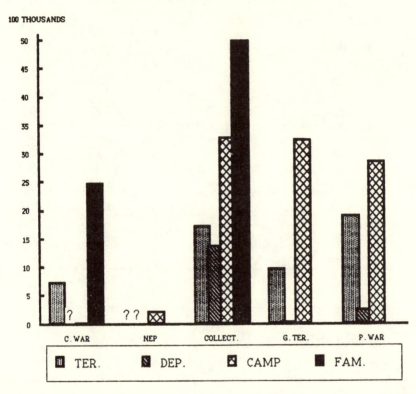

100 THOUSANDS

C. WAR   NEP   COLLECT.   G. TER.   P. WAR

▨ TER.   ▨ DEP.   ▨ CAMP   ■ FAM.

---

*From tables 2.1-6.1

fixation of endless books and speeches, the dead remembered and mourned for centuries. It is more than equivalent to wiping out all human life in Finland or Denmark. But in the history of the Soviet Union, by now so inured to mass murder as a tool of a utopian dream, this period seems hardly remarkable—a "breather" between the collectivization and Great Terror of the 1930s and the blood bath of World War II.

Appendix 6.1

In this period not only is the citizen subject to terror and the labor camps, but so are millions of foreigners in territory newly occupied by

FIGURE 6.3
Soviet Democide and Annual Rate by Period*

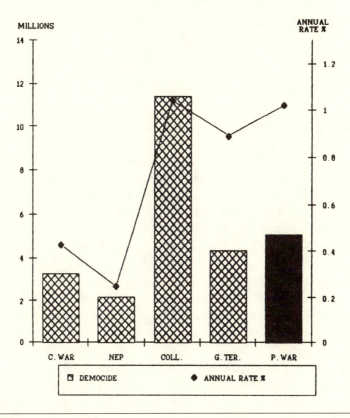

*From tables 2.1-6.1

Soviet forces. In table 6A, I try to untangle the various agents of death for these foreigners in the same fashion applied to citizens and to organize relevant estimates by national groups.

For example, estimates of the number of Estonians deported by the Soviets after their occupation of Estonia are shown (lines 4 to 13), yielding a range of 57,000 to 67,000 deportees. Half of these are assumed to have been sent to camps, and thus will be picked up in the camp estimates to be considered subsequently. The other half is assumed to have been sent to settlements, and for these the number of dead is calculated (line 15) using the deportation death rates determined in appendix 1.2. This gives a range of 5,000 to 14,000 dead.

Then, estimates of the number that died in the Soviet terror in Estonia are listed (lines 18 to 23) and consolidated (line 24), giving an estimated range of 2,000 to 63,000 killed (excluding deportations). The deported and terror-dead are then summed to give the overall range of Estonian dead as 7,000 to 77,000, with a midestimate of 18,000.

As estimates in the references allow, the same procedure is also applied to Latvians, Lithuanians, Bessarabians and Bukovians, Poles, Rumanian-Bessarabians, and together for West Byelorussians, Moldavians, and West Ukrainians. For Poland, there are a number of estimates of those who died in the deportations (lines 106 to 111), and a consolidation of these (line 112) are compared to the number calculated (line 113) from the numbers of deported. Both the consolidated and calculated sets are close and are averaged to get a range of 113,000 to 349,000 Polish deportees killed in the settlements.

Summing all the foreign deportation (settlements) and terror killed gives a total of 229,000 to 965,000 people, with a midestimate of 415,000 (line 153). This is exclusive of those foreigners who died in the labor camps.

Concerning these, I could not find any overall estimates of their number for this period, and thus applied the following procedure. Since half of the deportees were assumed to have been sent to camps, and deportation totals for each nation already have been determined, the total deportees in the camps can be calculated (line 209). I assume that the resulting estimates approximate the total number of foreigners in the camps. Since there is no reason to believe that the death rates for foreigners were higher or lower than for Soviet citizens, foreign camp-dead can be calculated as a ratio of the Soviet camp population to number of camp inmates that died. Since the (maximum) camp population (line 204) must include foreigners, in calculating this ratio the foreign camp population (line 209) first has to be subtracted from the camp population. Using the maximum population is a conservative approach, since the higher the assumed camp population for a given number of dead and foreign camp population, the lower the number of foreign-dead that will be calculated from the ratio.

The result is a foreign-, camp- and transit-dead range of 111,000 to 480,000, with a midestimate of 251,000 (line 210). This is a reasonably conservative conclusion, since estimates among experts of just those Polish deportees that died in the settlements and camps is 270,000 to 300,000 (lines 108 to 111).

Adding these foreign camp deaths to those who died from terror in the occupied territories and in the Soviet deportation settlements gives a most probable foreign democide of 666,000 people over two-and-a-half years (line 243). This is a democide rate of 3.31 percent (line 268)—about one out of every thirty foreigners in the Soviet occupied territories.

Turning to the components of democide among Soviet citizens, I could not find estimates of deportations and I suspect that that those carried out were relatively small in number and size.

On terror, only one estimate of those citizens killed for the period was given in the references, and that was for both purges and the Soviet-Finnish War from 1939 to 1940.[49] Subtracting the war-dead estimates gives a range of 1,000,000 to 1,952,000 killed in terror (line 215), and, conservatively, I will assume this applies to the whole period up to June 1941.

Estimates of the camp population abound, and these are organized by year in the table. As for previous periods, these are consolidated into one range of population estimates for each year; and to these, assumed camp and transit death rates are applied to calculate a range of camp/transit-dead. The sum of dead for the period is 2,243,000 to 14,835,000 (line 206). Now, Kosyk gives an estimate of 1,800,000 camp-dead for 1939 and 1940.[50] If we proportionate this over the period and assume conservatively a lower estimate two-thirds that of Kosyk's and a high one-third higher, we get a range of 1,005,000 to 1,995,000 camp-dead (line 201). This gives a set of estimates significantly lower, particularly at the high end (a difference of about 13,000,000) than that derived from the deathrates (both sets are shown together on lines 206-7).

Kosyk's estimate is only one, while those calculated from the camp population and death rate figures are based on many dozens of independent estimtaes. But the latter give a midestimate almost 3,000,000 dead higher, and a high about 12,000,000 higher, than census-based estimates of unnatural deaths during this period (line 231).

Now, calculation of unnatural deaths is very sensitive to birthrate and total population assumptions and, as pointed out in appendix 5.1, the party has manipulated census results for political purposes. Even a reasonable change in Dyadkin's assumptions could mean an annual change in millions of unnatural deaths. Referring to his table including deaths from privation and repressions for 1937–40, among other years,

Dyadkin points this out: "If we ever discover that in those years the average birth rate was at least at the 1937 level, the number of persons who perished would increase by 2 million annually. . . ."[51] This would amount to an increase of 5,000,000 unnatural deaths for the period, or a total of almost 7.5 million unnatural deaths at the high end. And this is without even taking into consideration the politically altered population totals used in the calculations.

Nonetheless, to bring the camp/transit death figures into greater consistency with the possible range of demographic calculations, the figures based on Kosyk's estimates and those derived from the camp population are averaged, with Kosyk's much lower estimates weighted double that of the latter (line 208). This gives a range of camp and transit deaths of 1,418,000 to 6,275,000.

Summing now the democide components for Soviet citizens, the democide during this period amounted to probably 4,438,000 people, with a possible low of 2,307,000 and high of 7,747,000 (line 237). The midestimate is nearly twice as high as unnatural deaths for this period given by demographic calculations (line 231). While this suggests caution in accepting these results as final, it does not invalidate them (for the reasons given above). Indeed, the midestimate may still be too low. Antonov-Ovseyenko, for example, estimates that from 1935 to 1941, 19,000,000 Soviet citizens were killed in the terror.[52] Prorated, this yields almost 6,786,000 dead during this period—more than 2,000,000 higher than the midestimate accepted here.

The democide period and annual democide rates are calculated in the table (lines 266 and 267). One out of every thirty-nine citizens was killed by the party during this period.

Finally, now adding foreigners to the democide total gives an overall midtotal of 5,104,000 people killed (line 249).

Aside from democide, 54,000 to possibly over 1,000,000 Soviet citizens were killed in war during this pre-World War II period. There was a small war against Japan in 1939, the very short war against Poland in September 1939 (resulting in splitting Poland between the Soviets and Nazis), and the major war against Finland in 1940. These are listed in the table (lines 218 to 223), along with the estimated battle-dead.

Epigraphs quoted in Dallin and Nicolaevsky (1947, p. 47) and Conquest (1968, p. 491).

TABLE 6A

5,104,000 Victims during the Pre-World War II Period: Sources, Calculations, and Estimates*

LINE	EVENT/PROCESS/STRUCTURE/EPISODE	BEGIN YEAR	M	END YEAR	M	LOW	MID	EST.	HIGH	SOURCE	NOTES
1	*OCCUPIED STATES/TERRITORIES DEAD*										
2	ESTONIANS										
3	DEPORTED NUMBER										
4	Estonians	1940		1941					60	Mass Deportations,81,17	murdered, arrested, or deported
5	Estonians	1940		1941					67	Swianiewicz,65,42	from Estonian National Council/Red Cross
6	Estonians	1940		1941					57	Herling,51,217	
7	Estonians	1941	3	1941	6				60	Herling,51,72	"disappeared"; from former Estonian Minister of Foreign Affairs Kaarel R. Pusta, Sr
8											
9	Estonians	1941			6				12	Vizulis,85,103	
10	Estonians	1941							12	Tolstoy,81,219	
11	Estonians	1941			6				10	Shtromas,86,186	
12	Estonians	1941			6				10	Misiunas & Taagepera,83,41	
13	Estonians	1941			6				10	Swettenham,52,139	
14	CONSOLIDATED DEPORTED	1940		1941	6	57	60		67		to GULAG
15	CALCULATED DEPORTED DEAD	1940		1941	6	5	8		14		[only for 50% assumed resettled; other 50% assumed picked up by camp/forced labor figures, below]
16											
17	TERROR DEAD										
18	Estonians	1940		1941					63	Swettenham,52,141-2	bodies found in mass graves after Soviet occupation
19	Estonians	1940		1941					2	Herling,51,217	from Estonian National Council/Red Cross
20	Estonians	1940		1941					2	Mass Deportations,81,28	
21	Estonians	1940		1941					2	Vizulis,85,103	
22	Estonians	1941			6	10				Taagepera,80,381	
23	Estonians	1940		1943					27	Misiunas & Taagepera,83,276	executions 1940-41 and deportee (1940-3) and evacuee (1941-3) dead
24	CONSOLIDATED TERROR DEAD	1940		1941	6	2	10		63	[excludes deported dead]	
25	CALCULATED DEPORTED DEAD	1940		1941	6	5	8		14	[from line 15]	
26	SUM ESTONIAN DEAD	1940		1941	6	7	18		77	[sum of lines 24-25,excludes camp/forced labor dead]	
27											
28	LATVIANS										
29	DEPORTED NUMBER										
30	Latvians	1940		1941					30	Vairogs,n.d,33	murdered, arrested, or deported
31	Latvians	1940		1941					34	Mass Deportations,81,17	
32	Latvians	1941							21	Vizulis,85,102	
33	Latvians	1941							15	Tolstoy,81,219	
34	Latvians	1941			6				15	Shtromas,86,186	
35	Latvians	1941			6				15	Misiunas & Taagepera,83,41-2	
36	Latvians	1941			6				15	Herling,51,72	from former Estonian Minister of foreign Affairs Kaarel R. Pusta,Sr
37	CONSOLIDATED DEPORTED	1940		1941	6	15	21		30		to GULAG
38	CALCULATED DEPORTED DEAD	1940		1941	6	1	3		6		[only for 50% assumed resettled; other 50% assumed picked up by camp/forced labor figures, below]
39											
40	TERROR DEAD										
41	Latvians	1941							1	Vizulis,85,102	bodies found in mass graves after Soviet occupation
42	Latvians	1940		1941					64	Swettenham,52,141-2	1.8% of Latvia's population
43	Latvians	1940		1941					35	These Names,82,XXX	

Table 6A (continued)

#	Category	Period	Figures	Source / Notes
44	Latvians	1940–1941, 6	1	Mass Deportations,81,28
45	Latvians	1940–1943	32	Misiunas & Taagepera,83,276 [executions 1940–41, and deportee (1940–3) and evacuee (1941–3) dead]
46	Latvians	1940–?	1	Vairogs,n.d.,35 — killed in Latvia
47	CONSOLIDATED TERROR DEAD	1940–1941, 6	35 / 64	[excludes deported dead]
48	CALCULATED DEPORTED DEAD	1940–1941, 6	3 / 6	[from line 38]
49	SUM LATVIAN DEAD	1940–1941, 6	2 / 38 / 70	[sum of lines 47–48, excludes camp/forced labor dead]
50				
51	**LITHUANIANS**			
52	DEPORTED NUMBER			
53	Lithuanians	1940	65 / 65	Swettenham,52,139 — exiled/evacuated; includes Vilna region.
54	Lithuanians	1940	75	Mass Deportations,81,17 — murdered, arrested, or deported
55	Lithuanians	1940	75	Vizulis,85,104 — deported/killed
56	Lithuanians	1941, 6	34 / 46	Misiunas & Taagepera,83,418 — high from Leonardas Kerelis.
57	Lithuanians	1941	34	Tolstoy,81,219 — to GULAG.
58	Lithuanians	1941, 6	34	Shtromas,86,186
59	Lithuanians	1941, 6	30	Swettenham,52,139
60	CONSOLIDATED DEPORTED	1940–1941, 6	30 / 46 / 65	[only for 50% assumed resettled; other 50% assumed picked up by camp/forced labor figures, below]
61	CALCULATED DEPORTED DEAD	1940–1941, 6	3 / 6 / 14	
62				
63	TERROR DEAD			
64	Lithuanians	1940–1941	65 / 65	Swettenham,52,141–2 — bodies found in mass graves after Soviet occupation
65	Lithuanians	1940–1941	1	Mass Deportations,81,28
66	Lithuanians	1940–1943	26 / 26	Misiunas & Taagepera,83,276 [executions 1940–3) and deportee (1940–10, and deportee (1940–3) and evacuee (1941–3) dead]
67	CONSOLIDATED TERROR DEAD	1940–1941, 6	1 / 20 / 65	[excludes deported dead]
68	CALCULATED DEPORTED DEAD	1940–1941, 6	3 / 6 / 14	[from line 61]
69	SUM LITHUANIAN DEAD	1940–1941, 6	4 / 26 / 79	[sum of lines 67–68, excludes camp/forced labor dead]
70				
71	**BESSARABIANS/BUKOVIANS**			
72				
73	Bessarabians/Bukovians	1940, 7–1941, 6	150 / 150	Dima,82,44 — for just before outbreak of war; from former deporte; other deportations previously carried out.
74				
75	Bessarabians	1941	200 / 300	Hingley,70,185
76	CONSOLIDATED DEPORTED	1940–1941, 6	150 / 200 / 300	[only for 50% assumed resettled; other 50% assumed picked up by camp/forced labor figures, below]
77	CALCULATED DEPORTED DEAD	1940–1941, 6	14 / 26 / 65	
78				
79	TERROR DEAD			
80	Bessarabians/Bukovians	1940, 7–1941, 6	2 / 2	Dima,82,44–5 — "massive arrests and deportations. countless summary executions". [R. J Rummel estimate]
81				
82	CALCULATED DEPORTED DEAD	1940–1941, 6	14 / 26 / 65	[from line 77]
83	SUM BESS./BUKOVIAN DEAD	1940–1941, 6	15 / 27 / 67	[sum of lines 80 and 82; excludes camp/forced labor dead]
84				
85	**POLES**			
86	DEPORTED NUMBER			
87	Poles	1939–1940	1,000 / 1,060 / 1,500	Swianiewicz,65,41 — to forced labor/settlements, from Polish Embassy in Kuibyshev; includes POWs, half to forced labor.
88				
89	Poles	1939–1941	1,200	Tolstoy,81,102 — includes POWs
90	Poles	1939–1941	1,000	Bouscaren,63,48
91	Poles	1939–1941	1,000	Kusnierz,49,86 — excluding those sent to forced labor camps
92	Poles	1939–1941	1,250	Gross,88,146 — includes POWs

Table 6A (continued)

#	Category	Subject	Year(s)	N1	N2	N3	Source	Notes
93		Poles	1939		1,200		Zawodny,62,5	not including 250 thousand POWs
94		Poles	1939		1,500		Kusnierz,49,80	of which 250,000 were those arrested; Polish estimates
95		Poles	1939		1,250		Gross,88,194	deported or moved east, about 450 thousand
96								went to camp; from the Polish Foreign Ministry
97		Poles	1939 1941		1,200		Grudzinska-Gross,81,xxii	resettled, estimates of Polish authorities;
98								includes 180 thousand POWs, 440 thousand to labor camps.
99		Poles	1939		980		Kusnierz,49,69	in four waves
100		Poles	1939 1942		1,060		Conquest,68,532	to camps/forced settlement
101		Polish POWs	1939		1,000		Elliot,72,84	to labor camps
102	CONSOLIDATED DEPORTED		1939	1,000	1,200	1,500		
103	CALCULATED DEPORTED DEAD		1939	90	156	323		[only for 50% assumed picked up by camp/forced labor figures, below]
104								
105	DEPORTED DEAD							
106		Poles	1941		709		Kusnierz,49,86	of deported, excludes forced labor camp dead, from Vyshinsky,
107		Poles	1939			750	Gross,88,229	if accept from Norman Davies a deportation total of 1.5 million
108		Poles	1939		300		Gross,88,229	of deportees and concentration camp inmates by end of 1941.
109		Poles	1939 1942		270		Conquest,68,532	of those sent to labor camps and forced resettlement during these years.
110		Poles	1939 1943		270		Tolstoy,81,102	of deported and POWs
111		Poles	1940 1943		270		Swianiewicz,85,42	of deported, from Polish Embassy in Kuibyshev.
112	CONSOLIDATED DEPORTED DEAD		1939	135	135	375	[only for 50% assumed resettled, other 50% assumed picked up by camp/forced labor figures, below]
113	CALCULATED DEPORTED DEAD		1939	90	156	323	[from line 103]
114	AVERAGE DEPORTED DEAD		1939	113	146	349	[average of lines 112-113]
115								
116	TERROR DEAD							
117		Poles	1939		15		Zawodny,62,5	POWs
118		Poles	1940		4		Conquest,68,483	Katyn Forest massacre
119		Poles	1940		14		FitzGibbon,75,446	executed POWs; includes those killed at Katyn
120		Poles	1940		4		Zawodny,62,24	Polish POWs murdered in Katyn Forest.
121		Poles	1939		50		[R.J.Rummel estimate of general terror]	
122	CONSOLIDATED TERROR		1939	44	65	86		
123								
124	TOTAL DEAD							
125	AVERAGE DEPORTED DEAD		1939	113	146	349	[from line 114]
126	CONSOLIDATED TERROR		1939	44	65	86	[from line 122]
127	SUM:POLISH DEAD		1939	156	211	435	[sum of lines 125-126, excludes camp/forced labor dead]
128								
129	RUHANIAN-BESSARABIANS DEPORTED NUMBER							
130		Rumanian-Bessarabians	1940	200		300	Tolstoy,81,200	possibly also includes occupied Bukovina
131		Rumanian-Bessarabians/N.Bukovinians	1940			300	Herling,51,113	from former Prime Minister Radescu
132	CONSOLIDATED DEPORTED		1940	200	233	300		
133	CALCULATED DEPORTED DEAD		1940	18	30	65	[only for 50% assumed resettled; other 50% assumed picked up by camp/forced labor figures, below]
134								
135								
136	MISCELLANEOUS DEPORTED NUMBER							
137		Byelorussians (West)	1939 9 1941 6		300		Lubachko,72,145	up to invasion of Germans, deported to eastern and northern USSR.
138		Finns (Soviet Karelia)	1939		?		Tolstoy,81,283	deported "en masse"
139		Leningrad Finns/Estonians	1940		?		Solzhenitsyn,78,387	to Karelia
140		Lith./Byelo./Russians	1941 1 1941 3		21		Schechtman,46,465	by treaty from Memel region and Suwalki region

Table 6A (continued)

Line	Category	Years	Pop (low)	Pop (mid)	Pop (high)	Source	Notes
142	Moldavians	1941 4c.		300		Dima,82,44	evacuated, but "better said deported," mainly Rumanians
143	Poles/Belts/Bess./Bukov.	1940 1941		1,500		Swianiewicz,65,31	at least half to forced labor camps
144	Poles/Belts/Rumanians	1939 1941	2,000			Hingley,74,303	total, including POWs
145	Poles/Jews/Ukrainians/Byelo	1939 1941	1,500			Swianiewicz,65,25-6	to camps and forced settlements
146	Ukrainians/Byelorussians/Russians	1940 2		35		Schechtman,46,485	by treaty from German dominated Polish provinces
147	CONSOLIDATED DEPORTED	1939 1941 6	300	300			[for West Belorussians, Moldavians, and West Ukrainians]
148	CALCULATED DEPORTED DEAD	1939 1941 6	27	65			[only for 50% assumed resettled; other 50% assumed picked up by camp/forced labor figures, below]
149							
150	TOTAL OCCUPIED STATES/TERRITORIES DEAD						
151	*OVERALL DEPORTED DEAD*	1939 1941 6	180	283			[from lines 15, 38, 61, 77, 114, 134, and 148]
152	*TERROR DEAD*	1939 1941 6	49	132			[from lines 24, 47, 67, 80, and 122]
153	*SUB DEAD*	1939 1941 6	229	415			[sum of lines 151-152]
154							
155	*CAMP/FORCED LABOR POPULATION/DEAD*						
156	POPULATION/DEAD						
157	camps	1939	8,000	8,000	17,000	Heller & Nekrich,86,318,784	concentration camps, variation in estimates; author's consider their estimate "probably too low"
158							
159	camps/prisons/isolators	1939 1		8,000		Wiles,53,35	politicals/criminals
160	GULAG	1939		10,400		Rosefielde,81,65	
161	prisoners	1939	10,000	12,500		Kosyk,62,16,79	low from S Schwarz, mid-estimate for camps
162	CONSOLIDATED CAMP POPULATION	1939	8,000		17,000		
163	CALCULATED CAMP DEAD	1939	800	1,600	4,760		
164							
165	forced labor	1940		13,000		Forced Labor,52,4	from Harry Schwartz.
166	GULAG	1940	11,200			Rosefielde,81,65	
167	GULAG	1940 1941		16,000		These Names,82,VI	estimates in the camps and by many arrested NKVD officials
168	camps	1938 1941	15,000			Conquest,68,531	from former "checkists" and prisoners in position to know or count.
169	camps	1939 1941		20,000		Panin,76,92n	
170	repatriated Soviet POWs	1940		?		Antonov-Ovseyenko,81,280	from war with Finland, many shot
171	CONSOLIDATED CAMP POPULATION	1940	11,200	13,000	20,000		
172	CALCULATED CAMP DEAD	1940	1,120	2,600	5,600		
173							
174	camps/prisons	1940 1942	15,000			Dallin & Nicolaevsky,47,62	inmates, a conservative estimate based on former prisoner reports
175	camps	1940 1942	10,000			Dallin & Nicolaevsky,47,59	prisoners; from Ernst Tallgren
176	camps	1940 1942	15,000			Rosefielde,81,63	from Polish Officers who systematically debriefed former Polish prisoners
177	camps	1941	6,000	14,000		Conquest,68,531	low is from an official, high is from a colonel connected with the inspectorate of camp guards.
178							
179	camps	1941 5		10,000		Floyd,58,xiii	decline from 8 million of 1939 due to high death rate, from "most cautious and conservative estimates made by Western researchers."
180	camps	1941 6		6,500		Heller & Nekrich,86,319	
181							
182	camps/prisons/isolators	1941 6		9,000		Wiles,53,36	politicals/criminals
183	forced labor	1941		3,500		Jasny,51,416	from camps, from calculations based on 1941 Plan.
184	forced labor	1941		7,000		Swianiewicz,65,161	estimates by Western experts
185	forced labor	1941	3,000	13,000		Swianiewicz,65,29	a correction of N Jasny's estimate, which was based on the 1941 Plan.
186	forced labor	1941		6,900		Swianiewicz,65,31	from A. Avtorkhanov (pseud of A. Ouralov). unpublished estimate of Nazi government
187	forced labor	1941		13,500		Swianiewicz,65,37	
188	forced labor	1941 1		9,600		Dallin & Nicolaevsky,47,86	estimate includes foreign forced laborers
189	forced labor	1941 6	6,500	10,000		Swianiewicz,65,37-8	estimate of many prisoners and NKVD officials
190	forced labor camps	1941 6	7,000	12,000	20,000	Swianiewicz,65,26-29	

Table 6A (continued)

#	Item	Year			Low	Mid	High	Source / Notes
191	GULAG prisoners	1941			13,500		10,600	Rosefielde,81,65
192	prisoners	1941						Kosyk,62,16,79
193		1941			13,500			Dujardin,78,50
194	CONSOLIDATED CAMP POPULATION	1941			3,000	10,000	20,000	
195	CALCULATED CAMP DEAD	1941			300	2,000	5,600	
196	HALF-YEAR CAMP DEAD	1941	6		150	1,000	2,800	[for first 6 months of 1941]
197								
198	**OVERALL CAMP/FORCED LABOR DEAD**							
199	**ESTIMATED DEAD**							
200	camp dead	1939	1941			1,800		Kosyk,62,79
201	CALCULATED DEAD	1939	1941	6	1,005	1,500	1,995	[line 200 proportionately reduced to 1939–June, 1941, where low is assumed 2/3rds of mid-estimate and high is assumed 1/3rd higher]
202	CALCULATED DEAD							
203	**TOTAL DEAD**							
204	MAXIMUM POPULATION	1939	1941		11,200	13,000	20,000	[for Pre–War Period]
205	CALCULATED TRANSIT DEAD	1939	1941		173	468	1,675	
206	SUM CAMP/TRANSIT DEAD	1939	1941	6	2,243	5,668	14,835	[from lines 163, 172, 196, and 206]
207	CALCULATED DEAD	1939	1941	6	1,005	1,500	1,995	[from line 201]
208	CONSOLIDATED CAMP/TRAN DEAD	1939	1941	6	1,418	2,889	6,275	[the weighted average of lines 206–207: ((2 × line 207)+line 206)/3]
209	FOREIGN CAMP POPULATION	1939	1941		876	1,130	1,531	[assumed half of those deported, lines 14, 37, 60, 76, 102, 133, and 147]
210	FOREIGN CAMP DEAD	1939	1941	6	111	251	480	[assumed proportionately the same as for Soviet citizens]
211								
212	**TERROR/PURGE DEAD**							
213	purges and Finnish War	1939	1940			2,000	2,000	Legters,84,60
214	dead	1937	1941		30	200	200	Church,89,71 Killed by NKVD, found in graves outside Minsk.
215								low estimate of the Soviet-Finnish War Soviet dead is 48,000, high
216	TOTAL	1939		6	1,000	1,800	1,952	is a million, mid-est is 200,000; see lines 219 to 222]
217	**WARS 1929–1940**							
218	Finnish/Manchurian Wars	1939				500	500	Stewart-Smith,64,222 [a small number of Soviets were killed in battle]
219	Soviet-Polish War	1939	9 1939	9		?	?	Tolstoy,81,283 high estimated by Khrushchev.
220	Soviet-Finnish War	1939	1940		250	250	1,000	Smell & Singer,82,90
221	Soviet-Finnish War	1939	1940	3		50	50	Jacobson,61,273n47
222	Soviet-Finnish War	1939	1940		48		200	Smell & Singer,82,90
223	Nomohan War	1939	5 1939	9			5	low is Soviet figure, high is from Finnish intelligence estimates battle deaths, USSR and Mongolia versus Japan.
224	CONSOLIDATED	1939	1940		54	256	1,006	
225								
226	**OVERALL DEAD**							
227	**CENSUS ESTIMATES (CITIZENS)**							
228	unnatural deaths	1939			1,630	1,810	1,990	Dyadkin,83,41 from census
229	unnatural deaths	1939			640	780	920	Dyadkin,83,41 from census
230	unnatural deaths	1940			910	1,030	1,150	Dyadkin,83,41 from census
231	CONSOLIDATED (CITIZENS)	1939		6	2,038	2,263	2,488	[line 228 extrapolated to and including June, 1941]
232								
233	**COMPONENTS OF DEMOCIDE (CITIZENS)**							
234	TERROR/PURGE	1939			1,000	1,800	1,952	[from line 215]
235	DEPORTATIONS	1939			?	?	?	[no estimates or sufficient data for an estimate available]
236	CAMP/TRANS	1939			1,307	2,638	5,795	[line 208 minus line 210]
237	DEMOCIDE (CITIZENS)	1939		6	2,307	4,438	7,747	[the sum of from lines 234–236]
238								from Alexander Durolov

Table 6A (continued)

239	COMPONENTS OF DEMOCIDE (FOREIGNERS)						
240	*TERROR(SY)*	1939	6	49	132	280	[from line 152]
241	*DEPORTATIONS*	1939	6	180	283	685	[from line 151]
242	*CAMPS/TRANSIT*	1939	6	111	251	480	[from line 210]
243	*DEMOCIDE (FOREIGNERS)*	1939	6	340	666	1,445	[sum of lines 240-242]
244							
245	OVERALL COMPONENTS OF DEMOCIDE						
246	*TERROR(SY)*	1939	6	1,049	1,932	2,232	[sum of lines 234 and 240]
247	*DEPORTATIONS*	1939	6	180	283	685	[sum of lines 235 and 241]
248	*CAMPS/TRANSIT*	1939	6	1,418	2,889	6,275	[sum of lines 236 and 242]
249	*OVERALL DEMOCIDE*	1939	6	2,646	5,104	9,192	[sum lines 246 to 248]
250							
251	TOTAL KILLED						
252	*OVERALL DEMOCIDE*	1939	6	2,646	5,104	9,192	[from line 249]
253	*WAR*	1939	6	54	256	1,006	[from line 224]
254	*OVERALL KILLED*	1939	6	2,701	5,361	10,198	[sum of lines 252 and 253]
255							
256	DEMOCIDE RATE						
257	population	1939		170,557			Dyadkin,83,16
258	population	1939		170,600			Heller & Nekrich,86,316.
259	population	1939		170,467			Conquest,68,531
260	population	1940		194,100			Dyadkin,83,24
261	population	1940		174,000			Dyadkin,83,59
262	population	1940		194,000			Eason,59,600
263							
264	annexed territories	1940		20,100			Dujardin,78,150 [excluding annexed territories]
265	MID-PERIOD POP	1940		174,000			
266	*DEMOCIDE RATE (CITIZENS)*	1939	6	1.33%	2.55%	4.45%	[(line 243/line 271) X 100]
267	*ANNUAL DEMOCIDE RATE (CIT.)*	1939	6	0.53%	1.02%	1.78%	[line 266/25]
268	*DEMOCIDE RATE (FOREIGNERS)*	1939	6	1.69%	3.31%	7.19%	[(line 243/line 264) X 100]

excludes 20 million in newly conquered territories on territory comparable to post-war Russia, excluding emigration since post-war Russia increase in population from conquered territories]

*See notes to table 1A, appendix 1.1

Notes

1. *Dark Side* (1946, p. 45).
2. Tolstoy (1981, p. 283).
3. Antonov-Ovseyenko (1981, p. 280).
4. Vizulis (1985, p. 127); Schmid (1985, p. 2).
5. Vizulis (1985, p. 127).
6. Quoted in McCauley (1975, p. 165).
7. Gross, (1988, p. 36).
8. Ibid., p. 37.
9. Ibid., p. 39.
10. Ibid., p. 67.
11. Ibid., p. 147.
12. Ibid., p. 155.
13. Dima (1982, p. 44).
14. FitzGibbon (1975, p. 446).
15. Zawodny (1962, p. 24). He gives a total of approximately 4,443 bodies found in Katyn Forest.
16. Gross (1988, p. 146).
17. Herling (1951, p. 211).
18. Kuznierz (1949, p. 83).
19. Ibid., p. 84.
20. Ibid., p. 85.
21. Ibid., p. 69.
22. Ibid., p. 74.
23. Ibid., p. 69.
24. See appendix 6.1.
25. See, for example, Swianiewicz (1965, p. 42).
26. Misiunas and Taagepera (1983, pp. 40-42, 41n.50).
27. See, for example, Herling (1951, p. 217); Misiunas and Taagepera (1983, pp. 41, 276).
28. *These Names* (1982, p. VII).
29. Tolstoy (1981, p. 200); Herling (1951, p. 113).
30. See appendix 6.1.
31. Swettenham (1952, p. 137).
32. *Mass Deportations* (1981, p. 28).
33. Gross (1988, p. 226).
34. Church (1989, p. 71).
35. "Soviet Union: 102,000 in a Single Stalin Grave," (1988).
36. Ibid.
37. Kravchenko (1946, p. 302).
38. Swianiewicz (1965, pp. 154-55).
39. Conquest (1978, p. 218).
40. Conquest (1968, p. 531).
41. Swianiewicz (1965, p. 29).
42. Ibid., pp. 28-29.

43. Kosyk (1962, p. 16).
44. Conquest (1978, pp. 215-16).
45. Ibid., p. 110.
46. Ibid., p. 219.
47. Ibid., p. 220.
48. Petrov (1949, pp. 403-6).
49. Legters (1984, p. 60).
50. (1962, p. 79). There is an ambiguity in Kosyk's presentation of this number. He lists it for 1939–41, but the estimate for the previous period is given as for 1938–39, and the subsequent period as for 1941–45. Accordingly, I assume that 1939–41 means up to, but not including, 1941.
51. Dyadkin (1983, p. 48).
52. (1981, p. 213).

7

13,053,000 Victims: World War II Period June 1941–1945

> *It isn't only in comparison with your life*
> *as a convict, but compared to everything*
> *in the thirties, even to my favorable con-*
> *ditions at the university, in the midst of*
> *books and money and comfort; even to me*
> *there, the war came as a breath of fresh*
> *air, an omen of deliverance, a purifying*
> *storm. . . . And when the war broke out,*
> *its real horrors, its real dangers, its men-*
> *ace of real death, were a blessing com-*
> *pared with the inhuman power of the*
> *life. . . .*
>
> —Boris Pasternak

Hitler invaded the Soviet Union on 22 June 1941. Khrushchev claimed that in the next four years, 20,000,000 Soviet citizens died in battle and occupation.[1] Stalin had set this number at 7,000,000 in a March 1946 statement:

> As a result of the German invasion, the Soviet Union has irrevocably lost in battles with the Germans, and also during the German occupation and through the deportation of Soviet citizens to German slave labor camps, about 7,000,000 people. In other words, the Soviet Union has lost in men several times as many as Britain and the United States together.[2]

Stalin's estimate notwithstanding, Khrushchev's 20,000,000 figure, undocumented and unanalyzed, has been widely accepted in the West. But then, based upon census results, Timasheff claimed that 37,500,000 were lost between 1941 and 1945;[3] Tolstoy believes 30,000,000 died;[4] Dyadkin estimates 30,200,000;[5] Eason gives war-dead as 25,000,000 of those born before 1940.[6] No one that I could find believes 20,000,000 dead to be compatible with postwar census figures.

There is, as one might suspect by now, a simple reason for this discrepancy. Possibly 20,000,000 were killed in the war against the Nazis and from Nazi occupation, but many more millions were killed in Stalin's simultaneous war on his own people.

In gauging the Soviet toll during this period, there are a number of sources of death to consider. First are the military battle-killed, probably almost 7,000,000.[7] Second are the civilians who died from bombing or as armies clashed across their land and cities, possibly 500,000.[8] Third are those the Nazis executed or massacred, or who otherwise died from Nazi repression, possibly 7,000,000 overall.[9] This includes at least 750,000[10] and possibly 2,500,000[11] Jews murdered. Then there were those starved to death by the Nazis during their occupation of Soviet territory, possibly 1,000,000 in the Ukraine.[12] And we cannot ignore those Soviet citizens who died from deportation to Germany and forced labor there, possibly up to 500,000.[13] Nor should we forget the 2,000,000 to 3,000,000 Soviet POWs killed in the Nazi concentration camps.[14] All these civilian and military deaths due directly or indirectly to war battles, and those otherwise killed by the Nazis, total a probable 19,625,000, surprisingly close to Khrushchev's figure (see appendix 7.1).

But this still leaves many millions of corpses to explain. Now, the Soviet people were under attack from two directions: the Nazi military machine and the Soviet Communist Party. The imprisonment and killing of enemies of the people by the party not only continued during the war, but was intensified. A large number of the Soviet World War II dead were killed by Stalin, not Hitler—probably 10,000,000 more. Had Ripley written a "Believe It or Not" of incredible tales of murder and death, the two-front war suffered by Soviet citizens and foreigners subject to Soviet occupation surely would provide prominent entries.

As the Red Army retreated before Nazi invasion forces, the NKVD often tried to deport prisoners east before the Nazis arrived. In some cases prisoners were beaten and shot in death marches along the roads or, if evacuation were impossible or too difficult, prisoners were shot en masse in the prisons,[15] whether pickpockets. crooks, black marketeers, or political prisoners. For example, they were shot as prisons were evacuated in Tallin, Smolensk, Kiev, Kharkov, Zaporozhye, Dnepropetrovsk, and Orel; in Tartu at least 192 prisoners were killed.[16] Upon the approach of German forces, all in Minsk's prison were killed. It held about 10,000 inmates, although constructed for 1,000.[17] All prisoners doing forced labor at a mining complex near Nalchik were machine gunned to death. At the Olginskaya camp, more than 2,000 of those sentenced for over four years were shot.[18] And in the Ukraine:

> In the majority of prisons NKVD troops shot all inmates who had been sentenced to more than three years. In some towns the NKVD burned prisons with all their inmates. According to Ukrainian sources, 10,000 prisoners were shot in Lvov, Zolochevo, Rovno, Dubno, Lutsk, and other cities.[19]

In all, perhaps 80,000 Ukrainians were massacred during the Red Army retreat.[20]

Now, one's mind can soon become dulled by all the figures being given here; one can read about 80,000 Ukrainians murdered but not absorb this magnitude. But consider: more Ukrainians were apparently murdered in this retreat than all the Englishmen killed (70,000) by *all* the Nazi bombs dropped on England during the war;[21] it is more than *all* the American Marine and Navy battle-dead in all theaters of action in World War II (56,683);[22] it is virtually equal to *all* the American battle dead in the Korean and Vietnam wars together (80,950).[23]

To continue, the party's understandable paranoia about loyalty to Marxist ideals (which during the war was cleverly transliterated by Stalin to mean "Russia" or the "Motherland") was sharpened by the enthusiastic welcome initially given Nazi soldiers by Soviet citizens. Moreover, in a number of places open rebellions were launched against Soviet forces then in disarray and retreat. Lithuania revolted on the first day of the war: a provisional government was proclaimed, units of the former Lithuanian army mutinied against its Soviet command, and local uprisings harassed the retreating Red Army. This was not a small operation. About 100,000 to 125,000 insurgents may have been active, suffering perhaps as many as 12,000 casualties, with 4,000 killed in action.[24] Similar insurgences broke out in Latvia and Estonia.[25] In the latter, there were 5,000 active guerrillas in the north,[26] and they lost 541 dead and missing, with comparable losses for the Red Army in two months of fighting.[27]

Whether rising up against the Soviets or welcoming the Nazis, all soon realized that one horror, one death machine, was being replaced by another—that the SS and NKVD were brothers in blood. Only then did they turn on the Nazis. In the early months of the war Stalin feared his own people more than the Nazis, a fear that drove the NKVD to an especially refined search for and definition of "enemy of the people." Arrests, interrogations, executions, deportations, and sentences to twenty-five years at forced labor continued throughout the war.

As the Nazi occupation of Soviet territory settled in behind the front lines, partisans attacked Nazi logistics and installations. But as the Nazis made clear that for every soldier killed, scores of innocent people would be rounded up and shot, the party organized "partisan attacks" in order to provoke Nazi reprisals, and thus turn the population even more against the Nazis (and conversely, to make the Red Army's return more welcome). In the Baltic states, for example, it became clear from experience and explicit warnings that any attack on the Nazi occupation authorities or soldiers would be met with mass reprisals. Still, Soviet partisans launched various assaults on the Nazis, one resulting in the Nazis' executing all 235 inhabitants of Audrini village in Latvia; another in the Nazis' burning to death 119 peasants in the village of Pirciupis in Lithuania.[28]

While many partisans fought Nazis behind the front lines, similar anticommunist, partisan units of Soviet citizens or those conquered by the Soviet Union before the Nazi invasion fought the Red Army. In the Ukraine, Byelorussia, Baltic states, and Poland—as the Red Army forced Nazis back toward Germany—organized, anticommunist guerrilla units sprang up. Indeed, protracted guerrilla wars continued in these regions into the 1950s, virtually unaided and apparently invisible to the West (they are still ignored in political scientists' compilations of guerrilla or civil wars).

One would think that in the early, dark days of the war when it looked like Moscow would fall, when every able-bodied person was needed for the defense and war effort, millions of prisoners would have been released from the camps. Some in fact were released, many to be put in expendable penal battalions. Such battalions, untrained and often unarmed, sometimes without camouflaged uniforms so as to draw fire, were hurled in waves against Nazi positions, while NKVD troops would be behind them with machine guns ready to fire on those who hesitated or retreated. These former prisoners were also forced to clear mine fields by walking through them. When the head of the Soviet Military Mission in Britain, General Ratov, was offered British mine detectors, he declined, explaining that "in the Soviet Union we use people."[29]

The population of the camps may have decreased in the early days of the war, from an estimated 10,000,000 prisoners in 1941 to 9,000,000 in 1942 (see appendix 7.1). But that would be only because the inflow to the camps, which continued in a broad stream, was insufficient to cover those prisoners who were killed—probably 2,000,000 in 1941 and 3,400,000 in 1942. In 1943, when the war effort was not as bleak, but the outcome still could have gone either way, the camp population actually appears to have increased to a likely 11,200,000.[30] And during the whole war, the number of these unfortunates who were usually guilty of nothing, who were dying a slow, miserable, death in the camps, may have reached 15,000,000.[31] Even this figure may be too conservative. Says Kravchenko about 1942 alone:

> In official circles twenty millions became the accepted estimate of this labor reservoir [of prisoners]. The estimate did not include the boys and girls from 14 to 16 forcibly torn away from their parents and assigned to regions and industries in which manpower shortages were sharpest.[32]

As before the war, these camp prisoners were used as slave labor. They were auctioned and sold, their bodies contracted for as though so much machinery. Kravchenko also gives us a feel for this:

> I recall vividly an interview which I arranged . . . with one of the top administrators of GULAG. He was to supply a certain commissariat some hundreds of prisoners for a rush assignment. We were under terrific pressure . . . and I had summoned the GULAG official for a showdown on this manpower.
>
> "But Comrade Kravchenko, be reasonable," he interrupted my speech. "After all, your Sovnarkom is not the only one howling for workers. The State Defense Committee needs them, Comrade Mikoyan makes life miserable for us, Malenkov and Vosnessensky need workers, Voroshilov is calling for road builders. Naturally everyone thinks his own job is the most important. What are we to do? The fact is *we haven't as yet fulfilled our plans for imprisonments*. Demand is greater than supply."[33]

During the war, the camp regime was especially severe, increasing markedly the camp death rate. For example, out of 50,000 prisoners at the railroad camp of Pechorlag in the fall of 1941, there were 10,000 left alive the following spring; out of 50 people in the central sector barracks of Burepolom Camp in February 1943, at least four died a night, and one night twelve died (in the morning the dead would be replaced).[34] Moreover, special categories of enemies were massacred periodically throughout the camps, such as the shooting in every camp of all former and actual Trotskyites in 1942.[35] Moreover, camp administrators and guards were constantly on watch for ways to justify their exemption from duty at the front—"plots" and "conspiracies" among prisoners were regularly "discovered," usually resulting in batches of prisoners being shot.

And in the 1941–42 period, the usual sources of death just intensified. Inmates fought for their lives against a starvation diet, and with food rations cut even below prewar levels, numerous camp complexes suffered from famine. Even then, already starvation-level rations were cut when wholly unrealistic production quotas were not achieved. Add that in most camps there was no issue of cold weather clothing—wear what you came in—that in the northern camps there was often a twice a day trek of three to over six miles, frequently in deep snow, between the work area and barracks for these hungry, ill-clothed prisoners. And in 1941 to 1942, there was a dreadful winter, when in many camps the termperature was never above minus thirty-one degrees Fahrenheit, but men worked anyway. Moreover, there was no day of rest, there were hordes of bedbugs and lice, and the barracks were unheated and freezing.[36]

As if this were not enough, beginning in April 1943, prisoners could be sentenced to Katorga (hard labor). This meant surviving under especially severe conditions, often working on twelve-hour shifts with no days off and even less gruel and rotten potatoes than before. And the twelve work hours did not include the slow trek to and from the work site, nor the time spent being counted before and after the trek. Moreover, the prisoners may have been packed into nothing more than tents. The Vorkuta mines, one camp system to which Katorgans were sent, "were, undisguisedly, murder camps: but in the Gulag tradition murder was protracted, so that the doomed would suffer longer and put a little work in before they died."[37] Not one of the first group of 28,000 prisoners sent to this camp survived for a year.[38]

In thinking about these abhorrent camp conditions during the war, whether Katorga or otherwise, also note that as the war progressed, fewer and fewer prisoners were released, even after miraculously surviving their sentence. They were just automatically resentenced. For the greater majority of prisoners this meant a sentence to camp was a sentence to death by hunger, malnutrition, hard labor, cold, disease, or at the hand of the criminals or camp guards, or by the teeth of guard dogs.

How many died under these wartime conditions in the camps? Tolstoy says that one "former prisoner, who with his comrades conducted a rough-and-ready estimate, reckoned that seven million gulag inmates were slaughtered in the first year of the war."[39] Although Tolstoy believes that this need not be an exaggeration, a more prudent estimate of the total murdered in transit to or in the camps during the whole war period is 8,518,000 Soviet citizens (see appendix 7.1).

What irony, indeed. The democracies fought alongside the Soviet Union to eradicate the horror of fascism from the world. And afterwards, the democracies shook their collective head over the documented mass, inhuman murder of Jews and heaved a sigh of relief and thankfulness that this abominable Nazi system was utterly defeated. Yet, the democracies' major ally and a victor sitting in judgment with them at the Nuremberg trials was, during that very war, murdering more innocent people just in their labor camps than the Nazis were machine gunning in the gullies and gassing in their concentration camps.

Then there were the Soviet deportations. Whole cultural, ethnic, and linguistically homogeneous nations of suspect loyalty were deported. Naturally, all German-Soviets were not trusted, no matter if they had lived in the Soviet Union for generations or had been heroes in the Red Army. In August 1941, the loyalty of the Volga Germans was tested by parachuting men in Nazi uniforms from planes with Nazi markings among villages. They asked to be hidden until the Nazi Army came. If the villagers complied, the village was immediately liquidated.[40] But even when villagers reported the parachutists, their reprieve was short anyway. They were all eventually deported, whether their sons were at the front fighting or they were loyal party members. In total about 412,000 Volga Germans,[41] with perhaps another 400,000 or more ethnic Germans from other parts of the European Soviet Union,[42] were whisked away.

Their deportation was less harsh than that of many other nations, such as the Crimean Tatars. The Germans often had several days' warning, and sometimes they were seen off at the stations by friends of other nationalities. Still, the Volga Germans were packed forty to sixty to a cattle car for many days and sometimes weeks; among those who had to cross the Central Asian deserts, many died from lack of water. Most deportees were transported to Siberia and Northern Kazakstan.[43]

Also, those nations that had presumably "cooperated" or "collaborated" (by party definition) with the occupying Nazi forces, or that might do so, had to go. Even minorities living in sensitive areas were deported, although, as Khrushchev later admitted, at the time there was no military necessity to do so, since the Nazis were already being forced to retreat.[44] Thus, the party deported to the inhospitable far reaches of the country not only all German-Soviets, but also Greek-Soviets, Chechens, Ingushi, Karachai, Balkars, Kalmyks, Crimean Tatars, and Meskhetians—nine entire nations. No one was excepted, not even deputies to the Supreme Soviet.[45] As to how some of these deportations were carried out, we have the following account regarding the Chechens:

> NKVD units, dressed as ordinary troops, entered the republic in early February 1944, as if for manoeuvers. The population was assembled in the villages on the evening of 22 February 1944, to celebrate Red Army Day. They were surrounded by troops and the deportation decree was read to them by security officers. Stormy scenes ensued, in which many of the weaponless Chechens and Ingushi were shot down. The rest were rounded up and allowed to collect 50 kilograms of baggage per family. . . . They were then driven away in trucks—mainly lease-lend Studebakers, we are told by Lt.-Col. Burlitsky, who took part in the deportation of the Chechen village of Novoselskoye.[46]

Of just 1,600,000 deported among eight nations, about 530,000 probably died.[47]

Much other nonbattle-related killing took place during the war years, not all directly attributed to Stalin, but for which he bears a major responsibility. For example, I have excluded the Soviet POWs killed by the Nazis from Stalin's side of the ledger. But Stalin was certainly partially to blame for their deaths. Consider:

> Stalin went out of his way to invite Nazi ill-treatment and later extermination of Russian prisoners-of-war. He absolutely refused to permit the provisions of the Geneva Convention to apply to them, ignored International Red Cross efforts to intervene on their behalf, and even declined to allow the British to send them comforts. He was fully aware of the appalling mortality that resulted from this policy and referred to

it repeatedly in his speeches as evidence of Nazi cruelty. It is quite clear, therefore, that the deaths of over three million Russians in German custody was a piece of deliberate Soviet policy, the aim of which was to cause the liquidation of men regarded automatically as potential traitors, whilst arousing the anger of the Soviet people against the perpetrators of the crime.[48]

Evidence for this analysis is amply provided by the treatment accorded those POWs that survived and were repatriated to the Soviet Union. They were usually shot, sent off to labor camps, or exiled. More on this will be discussed subsequently.

As predictable from Soviet behavior in the territories it occupied before the war, foreigners were also ill-treated. As the Red Army forced the Nazis to retreat back across the Baltic states and into Eastern Europe, the ghastly prewar story of indiscriminate Red Army killing, of NKVD roundups, executions, and deportations, was replayed. As the Soviets reconquered Lithuania, for example, 400 to 700 people were executed in Kaunas, Zarasai, and Siauliai.[49] About 20 percent of the German-Balts disappeared.[50] And in the first wave of deportations in 1944, 30,000 Estonians, 38,000 Latvians, and probably a larger number of Lithuanians were freighted into the Soviet Union, mainly for "labor service."[51]

All Eastern European states suffered the ravages, the looting, rapes, and murder by Red Army soldiers. But German civilians in the former German territories and East Germany suffered the most. Already vengeful over what the Nazis had done in occupied territory, the soldiers were spurred on to kill Germans, and kill again. For example, Ilya Ehrenburg's 1943 book *Voina* (The war) contains a passage:

> We shall not speak any more. We shall not get excited. We shall kill. If you have not killed at least one German a day, you have wasted that day . . . . If you kill one German, kill another—there is nothing funnier for us than a pile of German corpses. Do not count days, do not count versts. Count only the number of Germans killed by you. . . . Do not miss. Do not let through. Kill.[52]

This was included in leaflets as guides to Soviet troops entering East Prussia.[53]

Given a free reign for weeks in the newly "liberated" regions, soldiers raped, tortured, and murdered helpless masses of German civilians. I have avoided atrocity and torture stories in this book, but the following is necessary to fully understand the plight of these German civilians in the path of the Red Army.

In October 1944, the Red Army broke into East Prussia and captured the districts of Goldap and Gumbinnen, but was driven out by a Nazi counterattack in November. In the region that had been occupied few civilian survivors remained. One formerly occupied village, Nemmersdorf, became a symbol to Germans of Soviet barbarism and, like the Katyn Forest murders, is one of the best documented atrocities of the war. In the village, civilians were systematically killed, some rolled over by tanks on the roads, some nailed to barn doors, some raped and shot, some tortured before death. One German who later entered the village reported that in one farm yard "stood a cart, to which four naked women were nailed through their hands in a cruciform position."[54] In another place

> stood a barn and to each of its two doors a naked woman was nailed through the hands, in a crucified posture. In the dwellings we found a total of seventy-two women, including children, and one old man, 74, all dead . . . all murdered in a bestial manner, except only for a few who had bullet holes in their necks. Some babies had their heads bashed in. In one room we found a woman, 84 years old, sitting on a sofa . . . half of whose head had been sheared off with an axe or a spade . . . all the women, as well as the girls from eight to twelve years and even the woman of 84 years had been raped.[55]

As word of such atrocities spread to German civilians facing the oncoming Red Army, many fled west in panic; many died trying to escape by sea as ports were bombed or ships crowded with refugees were torpedoed or sunk. For example, the liner *Wilhelm Gustloff* was sunk, drowning about 7,700 people (this made the *Guinness Book of World Records*[56] as the greatest marine disaster, but in fact that honor should go to the Soviet ship *Dzhurma*, which got locked in the ice near Wrangel Island for the winter in 1933, with perhaps as many as 12,000 prisoners aboard dying),[57] and the *Goya* was sunk with only 183 surviving out of 6,000 to 7,000 refugees.[58] Fleeing civilians were also killed as they tried to escape across bays or inlets covered with ice that collapsed from their weight or shelling, or on roads packed with refugees as they were bombed and strafed. Many just committed suicide: 500 out of around 9,700 in the village of Trzcianka, 1,000 out of possibly 50,000 in Slupsk, 600 out of about 20,000 in Lebork.[59]

Now, armies that had fed on violence for years, that are inured to killing, and that of necessity have even developed a professional pride in killing, have always been difficult to control when occupying enemy territory. And doubtlessly, atrocity stories can be told about all armies. Consider the American Army in Vietnam and the My Lai atrocity.[60] But the Red Army was different. It was not only a matter of scale and enthusiasm, but of high politics:

> It was clear that the destruction of civilized life in occupied Germany was a matter of high policy. When reports were brought to Stalin of Soviet tanks regularly shelling civilian refugees, women and children, Stalin replied in high good humour: "We lecture our soldiers too much; let them have some initiative."[61]

In post-war conversation with Milovan Djilas, a member of the Yugoslavian Politburo, Stalin made his views even clearer. He ignored accusations of murder, rape, and looting. After sympathizing with a soldier who "has fun with a woman or takes some trifle,"[62] he said

> that he himself had once intervened to pardon a Red Army major sentenced to death for shooting a fellow-officer who was in the act of protecting a woman from violation. For good measure Stalin also told Djilas how much he approved the Red Army's alleged practice of wantonly massacring German civilian refugees, including women and children.[63]

Only when the looting, killing and rape began to endanger military efficiency did Marshall Konief put a stop to it. The number of defenseless German civilians murdered can only be roughly estimated, and may number hundreds of thousands.[64]

Not only Germans, but all those touched by the Red Army suffered. On driving the Nazi armies back into Poland the Soviets played a clever game. They knew that the underground Polish Home Army that had fought the Nazi occupation was a great threat to future Soviet control over Poland. When the Red Army fought to within a few miles of Warsaw, therefore, the Soviets encouraged the Home Army in Warsaw to rise up against the Nazis, promising aid and implying that Soviet troops would then move into Warsaw. But when the Home Army attacked the Nazis, the Red Army not only refused to move to their defense, but also refused to parachute aid to the Poles or to allow the United States or United Kingdom to do so—at least until the aid was too late.[65] The Home Army was destroyed, and around 150,000 to 250,000 Poles were killed.

Surely, the Soviets deserve some credit for this toll (although since the Nazis did the killing, I am not counting this into Soviet democide). As Hingley points out: "By a feat of masterly inactivity Stalin had allowed Hitler to perform the task of liquidating over 150,000 independent-minded Poles whom he might otherwise have had to liquidate himself."[66] Arthur Bliss Lane, the former American Ambassador to Poland, wrote about this Soviet trick that

> . . . in two essential respects the cold-blooded, premeditated crime against Poland, conceived by the Soviet government with the aid of its puppets, had succeeded: (1) The Polish government in London had been discredited; (2) The Polish Home Army had been broken, so that no leadership remained there to dispute the authority of the Lublin gang.

> The incredible betrayal was complete.[67]

The Soviets also took a personal hand in exterminating remnants of the underground, Polish Home Army, that had fought the Nazi occupiers. As Soviet forces took over all of Poland, Home Army leaders and officers were shot; lower echelon members were imprisoned or deported to camps; even underground civil administrators were arrested, later to be shot or deported.[68]

At the same time, among the Poles the usual "enemies of the people," the bourgeoisie, the intellectuals, and such, were either shot, depending on their status, or deported. In the district of Lida, the Soviets murdered around 9,800 Poles; in Szczuczyn, about 8,000; in Oszmiana, some 6,000.[69] As to the deportations, approximately 35,000 Poles alone were deported from Wilno. Generally, from "the few larger towns in North-eastern Poland an average of 2,000 to 2,500 people were deported to Central Russia every month in 1945."[70]

Rumania was given similar treatment after Soviet forces occupied it in 1944. Wrote former Rumanian Premier Nicolae Radescu: "During the extremely trying three months of my Premiership, Soviet troops were looting and killing at random. Every morning I received reports of the robberies and assassinations perpetrated during the preceding 24 hours."[71] And there were the predictable deportations. Some 130,000 Rumanians were deported east, in addition to 40,000 Rumanian civilians "kidnapped" from Moldavia and Transylvania. Then, there was the deportation of 72,000 German-Rumanians ("They were arrested at schools, seized in the streets, dragged from their homes, taken in the fields.")[72] and 20,000 Rumanian POWs whom the Nazis captured and subsequently turned over to the Soviets.[73]

The story varies by numbers for Bulgaria, Hungary, Czechoslovakia, and parts of Yugoslavia. In all, mass shootings and deportations were common. About 600,000 Hungarians alone were deported to the Soviet Union;[74] males were rounded up indiscriminately off the street in Budapest for deportation, with an exception given to those with a Communist party membership card.[75] Few Jews who were in labor battalions under the Germans escaped deportation, nor did many prisoners just liberated from Nazi death camps, such as Auschwitz, Buchenwald, and Ravenbrück.[76] Almost the entire Hungarian population of Ruthenia (which was annexed by the Soviet Union) was deported.[77] Then in 1945, the USSR requisitioned available food supplies and even seed grain, and drove columns of livestock into the Soviet Union. Left without food and reserves, Hungarians faced "rampant" starvation and "tens of thousands of infants and young mothers in the cities . . . perished from malnutrition."[78]

And so on and on throughout Soviet-occupied Europe. The killing, the terror, the deportations, and the atrocities all become so depressingly similar that one simply begs for some kind of totals and conclusion. But before skipping over other sorry numbers for Eastern European countries,[79] one more aspect of the Soviet occupation should be mentioned. Wherever ethnic Germans were found, no matter how many generations they had lived in some East European city or village, they were subject to special treatment. About 140,000 ethnic Germans remaining in Rumania, Hungary, and Yugoslavia were deported by the Soviets to Ukrainian labor camps.[80] The German Red Cross estimates that 218,000 ethnic Germans were deported to the Soviet Union from the former German Eastern Provinces, Gdansk, and Western Poland; another estimate is of 250,000 deported from the German Eastern Provinces alone.[81] Across all of Soviet-occupied Europe, from 1944 on, possibly as many as 700,000 Germans were deported to the Soviet Union.[82] For every 100 people deported, twenty-six generally suffered wretched deaths.[83]

Not counting those who subsequently died in camps, the deportations into the Soviet Union of the inhabitants of the newly occupied, or reoccupied, countries probably killed about 285,000 of them. Adding those also killed in the labor camps would probably raise the total to over 600,000 human beings.[84] For comparison, the total number of

American deaths in battle during World War II was 292,131; the number of Americans who were killed in all American wars, including the Revolutionary and Civil wars, totals 578,210.[85] That is, just in these deportations of foreigners, the Soviets killed more people than all the Americans who died in all American wars.

As the Allied and Soviet armies forced the Nazis back into Germany and with the German surrender, millions of Russian exiles, Soviet citizens deported by the Nazis, Soviet defectors, or Soviet citizens who voluntarily fought on the side of the Nazis (about 1,000,000) fell into Allied and Soviet hands. Many of these were simple, poor folk whom the Nazis had deported from occupied Soviet territory to Germany to do forced labor. Many others were refugees who had fled to Europe after the Bolshevik coup in 1917, established families, homes, and occupations in Europe. Those the Soviets captured were usually shot or deported to camps or into internal exile.

The Allies—France and especially Great Britain and the United States—also had on their hands millions of such people who had surrendered to them naively ("Americans would never turn us over to the Bolsheviks") or in good faith ("the British would never lie to us"). Nonetheless, Great Britain and the United States decided to repatriate them to the Soviet Union, regardless of their fate, over their protests, demonstrations, and physical resistance, and using deception, lies, bayonets, and bullets. Ostensibly this was justified by the Yalta Treaty signed by Stalin, Churchill, and Roosevelt, which committed the Allies to return all Soviet citizens, but *not* Russian exiles (for example, those who had emigrated during the revolution or civil war and carried international passports). Since the treaty was silent about those who did not want to return, those resisting repatriation could have been allowed to remain in Europe. But the British preferred to interpret the treaty to mean that all Soviet citizens or Russian exiles must be returned, even those who had fled during the civil war, and prevailed upon reluctant American authorities to go along, at least for awhile.[86] Wrote the British Foreign Office's legal adviser, Sir Patrick Dean, in June 1944: "In due course all those with whom the Soviet authorities desire to deal must be handed over to them, and *we are not concerned with the fact that they may be shot* or otherwise more harshly dealt with than they might be under English law."[87]

In fact, it was not just a matter of the Yalta Treaty, but of several treaties and domestic laws. Both the United States and Britain pre-

ferred to follow their interpretation of the Yalta Treaty, even in violation of their own laws and other treaties (such as the Geneva Treaty on
prisoners of war). Stalin was an ally, and both democracies believed
that a show of concern for Soviet interests would enhance postwar,
Anglo-Soviet cooperation.

Many repatriates resisted and fought Allied troops; some committed
suicide, sometimes whole families; some were shot by Allied soldiers,
or by NKVD agents allowed behind Allied lines to search for repatriates. Some allied soldiers and units refused to obey orders and either
did not participate in this forced repatriation or allowed repatriates
under their control to escape.

Returned Soviet POWs fared no better than repatriated civilians and
probably worse. Stalin considered them all traitors. As he told a foreign reporter, "In Hitler's camps there are no Russian prisoners of war,
only Russian traitors, and we shall do away with them when the war is
over."[88]

In total about 5,500,000 were repatriated to the Soviet Union;
2,272,000 by Great Britain and the United States.[89] Of the total, about
1,100,000 were consigned to labor camps for twenty-five years, clearly
a sentence to a slow death, or were executed outright,[90] some 300,000
of them.[91] Possibly over 1,100,000 were inducted or reinducted into
the Red Army,[92] but many may have ended in penal battalions that
were no better than forced labor camps.[93] Another 825,000 to 1,100,000
got sentences of five to ten years in camp.[94] Swianiewicz roughly
estimates that around 2,500,000 repatriates probably were sentenced to
forced labor.[95] With an estimated death rate varying from 10 to 28
percent per year in the camps,[96] the odds were against one surviving
even a five-year sentence. Overall, from execution, the penal battalions, or camps, well over half these repatriates must have been killed.

Now, Stalin and the party won the war against Hitler, and they won
the war on the home front. This latter victory was so complete and
achieved with such secrecy and repression that British and American
history books, even histories of World War II, generally seem ignorant
of it. Until recently in the Soviet Union, it was dangerous to even
mention any part of Stalin's war against his people.

In this war on the home front, a total of 10,000,000 citizens were
probably murdered, even as they fought the Nazis. Even if this estimate is in great error, I do not believe any correction can go below
5,071,000 or above 19,503,000. The prudent estimate of 10,000,000

FIGURE 7.1
Range in World War II Democide Estimates*

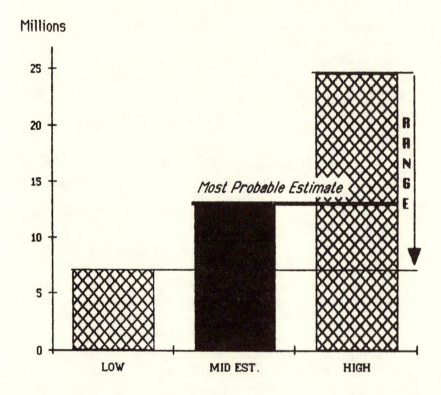

*From appendix 7.1

is at the lower end of this range. It is well below the estimate of the Soviet demographer, Maksudov, who believes that in addition to those soldiers and civilians killed as part of the Nazi war, 15,000,000 were killed "through Soviet action."[97] Regardless, it is incredible enough that possibly 10,000,000 citizens were murdered by their own government *while fighting a foreign war to preserve it*—about 1 out of every 20 citizens!

Of course, these 10,000,000 corpses must be added to the nearly 20,000,000 Soviet citizens that the Nazis likely killed, as calculated in appendix 7.1. But an estimate of 29,625,000 citizens killed overall still does not close the account for this most bloody period. To be

TABLE 7.1
War II Period Democide

FACTORS	DEAD ESTIMATES (000)		
	LOW	MID EST.	HIGH
DEMOCIDE	7,014	13,053	24,503
PERIOD RATE	2.76%	5.46%	10.77%
ANNUAL RATE	0.61%	1.21%	2.39%
FOREIGNERS	1,943	3,053	5,000
DEMOCIDE COMPONENTS			
TERROR	397	1,257	4,719
DEPORTATIONS	478	1,036	1,910
CAMP/TRANSIT	6,139	10,761	17,875
FAMINE	0	0	0
OTHER KILLED	16,625	26,125	34,360
WAR/REBELLION [1]	11,625	19,625	26,860
FAMINE/DISEASE [2]	5,000	6,500	7,500

* From Appendix 6.1.
1. Includes Nazi caused famine/disease.
2. Excludes Nazi famine/disease.

added are about 3,053,000 foreign civilians or POWs murdered by the Red Army or in NKVD executions, terror, deportations, and labor camps. Thus the Soviet wartime democide probably totals 13,053,000 people overall, with a range from 7,084,000 to 24,733,000. This is shown in figure 7.1. Table 7.1 gives the numbers.

Figure 7.2 compares the components of this slaughter with that of previous periods. As can be seen, the camps were by far the major murder weapon during World War II, accounting for more than twice the victims of any previous period. Even though thus eclipsed, the pile of corpses due to terror also reached a new height.

A comparison of the World War II democide totals and annual death rate to previous periods is shown in figure 7.3. Clearly, this period was the deadliest, not only in Nazi-Soviet war-dead, but in the history of the Communist party's murder of those under its control.

How can one conceivably understand, appreciate, or assimilate, the incredible number of largely innocent people killed by the Soviets during the war? Perhaps this might help. The total number of *battle-dead* for all nations involved in World War II, including Germany,

FIGURE 7.2
Democide Components for Six Periods

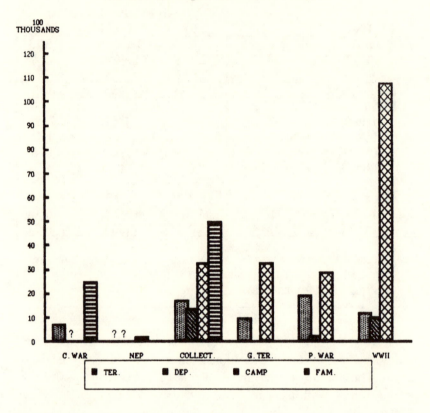

*From appendix 7.1

Japan, France, Great Britain, the United States, and the Soviet Union itself, was 15,000,000.[98] This number of corpses, produced in mankind's most intense, most universal, most lethal war, is only 15 percent greater than the 13,053,000 noncombatant civilians and foreigners the Communist Party of the Soviet Union probably murdered in its own war, not against governments, but on subject people.

Appendix 7.1

During World War II, Soviet citizens died not only from battle against the Nazis and in the Nazi occupation and repression, but also from a war that Stalin waged on his own people. Whole nations and

FIGURE 7.3
Soviet Democide and Annual Rate by Period*

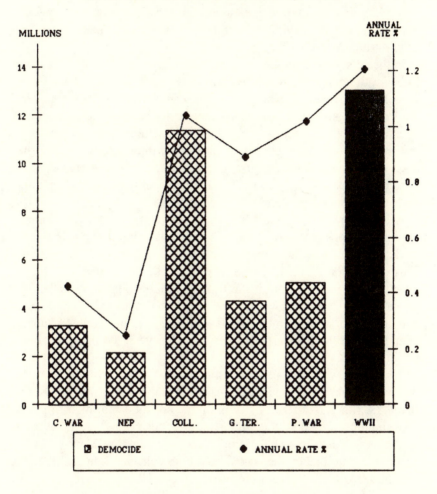

*From tables 2.1–7.1

ethnic groups were deported, NKVD prisoners were shot en masse, alleged Nazi collaborators were killed, repatriated Russians and Soviet citizens were executed, and prisoners and other "undesirables" were used as cannon fodder or to clear mine fields with their bodies. The Germans were purposely provoked into massacring Soviet civilians, millions were sent to labor camps and the camp regime made even more lethal, and everyday terror was magnified. Besides this democide, there were the terror and deportations that followed the Red Army into Eastern Europe and the Far East. All this requires carefully untangling and classifying the numerous, relevant estimates of Soviet dead during World War II.

Before discussing these, however, I must note that while it is easy to begin the period with the German invasion of the Soviet Union in June 1941, the period cannot be easily ended with the Japanese surrender in August 1945. At that time Soviet terror in the occupied territories and deportations into the Soviet Union were continuing, repatriations of Soviet citizens proceeded without a break, and the mass expulsion and killing of ethnic and Reich Germans throughout Eastern Europe was well underway. Estimates of this democide cannot be cleanly divided pre- and post-August 1945.

Accordingly, for democide beginning during the war and continuing into the near postwar period, such as the repatriation of Soviet citizens or deportation of Rumanians, it is treated as part of the war period. This causes some overlap between this and the subsequent period in events and some inflation of the former period's democide at the expense of the latter. However, and importantly, there is no double counting: democide counted in the war period is not counted subsequently, even though part of it may overlap years defining the next period.

Turning now to the specific estimates, in table 7A I first try to delimit the number of Soviet citizens killed in the war against the Nazis (table 7A, lines 2 to 59). Focusing on the consolidated midestimates, this amounts to 7,000,000 military battle-dead (line 9); 2,250,000 civilians (including Jews) killed from Nazi repression (line 24); 3,000,000 Soviet POWs killed by the Nazis, mainly in concentration camps (line 32); 500,000 civilians who died from forced labor in Germany (line 35); and 6,500,000 dying from Nazi-created famine and disease (line 41). This adds up to 19,250,000 Soviet citizens (line 57).

Aside from the specific estimates of war-dead, there are estimates of the overall war toll (lines 48 to 51). These provide a check on the above total. Consolidated, they give a range of 7,000,000 (Stalin's figure—lines 48 and 49) to 27,500,000 war-dead (line 51). The two sets of Soviet war-dead estimates are shown together in the table (lines 57 and 58). They are very close together at the middle and high end, and because there is no reason to claim one or the other better, they are

TABLE 7A
13,053,000 Victims during World War II:
Sources, Calculations, and Estimates*

LN	EVENT/PROCESS/STRUCTURE/EPISODE/	BEGIN YEAR	M	END YEAR	M	LOW	MID EST.	HIGH	SOURCE	NOTES
2	*WWII BATTLE/NAZI OCCUPATION KILLED*									
	MILITARY (BATTLE)									
3	military	1941	6	1945	7			7,000	Elliot,72,226	battle deaths, includes 2 million dying of wounds
4	military	1941	6	1945	7			7,000	Conquest,at el,84,36	sources with demographer M. Maksudov
5	military	1941	6	1945	7			7,500	Small & Singer,82,91	battle deaths.
6	military	1941	6	1945	7			7,000	Tirnasheff,48,155	
7	military	1941	6	1945	7			7,500	Medvedev,79,140	military battle deaths, from Soviet demographer M. Maksudov
8	Red Army	1941	6	1945	7			3,000	Kulischer,48,276-77	
9	CONSOLIDATED	1941	6	1945	7	7,000	7,000	7,500		
10	**KILLED BY NAZIS (NONBATTLE)**									
	REPRESSION									
13	civilians	1941	6	1945	5	500	500		Elliot,72,54-8	war actions
14	executed	1941	6	1945	5			1,000	Elliot,72,54-8	
15	partisans-related	1941	6	1945	5		250		Tolstoy,81,282	Nazi killings
16	repression	1941	6	1945	5			7,500	Medvedev,79,140	civilians killed by Germans in the fighting or repression; from Soviet demographer M. Maksudov
18	reprisals	1941	6	1945	5	500		1,000	Elliot,72,54-8	against peasants
19	Jews	1941	6	1945	5		1,000		Elliot,72,54-8	
20	Jews	1941	6	1945	5		750		Tolstoy,81,282	
21	Jews	1941	6	1945	5		1,252		Pearson,83,200	
22	Jews	1941	6	1945	5		1,000		Elliot,72,54-8	
23	Jews	1941	6	1945	5		2,500		Kulischer,48,276-77	
24	CONSOLIDATED REPRESSION	1941	6	1945	5	1,750	2,250	7,500		
26	**SOVIET POWS**									
27	Soviet POWs	1941	6	1945	5	3,000			Elliot,72,48-9	of 5 million POWs
28	Soviet POWs	1941	6	1945	5	2,000			Elliott,82,7-9	of 5.75 million captured Soviet soldiers
29	Soviet POWs	1941	6	1945	5	3,220		3,000	Heller & Nekrich,86,390	of at least 5,754,000 captured Soviet soldiers
30	Soviet POWs	1941	6	1945	5	3,000			Werth,64,708	of 5,754,000 war prisoners; from Alexander Dallin
31	Soviet POWs	1941	6	1945	5	3,000			Tolstoy,81,261-2	author says Stalin responsible for the death of Nazi held POWs.
32	CONSOLIDATED SOVIET POW	1941	6	1945	5	2,000	3,000	3,220		
34	**FORCED LABOR**									
35	forced labor	1941	6	1945	5		500		Tolstoy,81,282	in Germany.
37	**FAMINE**									
38	famine (Ukraine)	1941		1945			1,000		Tolstoy,81,282	Nazi caused
39	famine/disease	1941		1945			5,000		Medvedev,79,140	from Soviet demographer M. Maksudov
40	famine,disease/exposure	1941		1945				7,500	Elliot,72,54-8	privation
42	CONSOLIDATED FAMINE/DISEASE	1941		1945		5,000	6,500	7,500	Elliot,72,54-8	

TABLE 7A (continued)

Line	Item	Dates	Figures (000s)	Source	Notes
43	**TOTAL NONBATTLE KILLED**				
44	SUM NONBATTLE DEAD	1941 – 1945, 5	9,250 / 12,250 / 18,720		[sum of lines 24, 32, 35 (for low and high, 500,000 assumed the toll of forced labor in Germany), and 41]
45					
46					
47	**TOTAL WAR DEAD (BY NAZIS)**				
	OVERALL ESTIMATES				
48	battle/occupation killed	1941, 6 1945, 7	7,000	Kulischer,48,276	battle and German occupation/deportation dead, from Stalin
49	battle/occupation killed	1941, 6 1945, 7	7,000	Mihajlov,87	Stalin's figure; includes dead from German occupation
50	battle casualties	1941, 6 1945, 7	20,000	Dyadkin,83, 55	from census
51	citizen battle deaths	1941, 6 1945, 7	27,500	Antonov-Ovseyenko,81,279	according to demographers, died in battle against German troops
52	CONSOLIDATED	1941, 6 1945, 7	7,000 / 20,000 / 27,500		
53					
54	**OVERALL TOTAL**				
55	MILITARY DEAD	1941, 6 1945, 7	7,000 / 7,000 / 7,500		[from line 9]
56	SUM NONBATTLE DEAD	1941, 6 1945, 5	9,250 / 12,250 / 18,720		[from line 44]
57	SUM TOTAL	1941, 6 1945, 7	16,250 / 19,250 / 26,220		[sum of lines 55–56]
58	CONSOLIDATED ESTIMATES	1941, 6 1945, 7	7,000 / 20,000 / 27,500		[from line 52]
59	*BATTLE/OCCUPATION DEAD*	1941, 6 1945, 7	11,625 / 19,625 / 26,850		[average of lines 57–58]
60					
61	*CITIZENS KILLED BY STALIN AND PARTY: NATIONS/ETHNICS DEPORTED/DEAD*				
62	**CRIMEAN TATARS**				
63	*DEPORTED NUMBER*				
64	Crimean Tatars	1944, 5	194	Nekrich,78,112	
65	Crimean Tatars	1944, 5	232 / 242	Conquest,70b,64-5	
66	Crimean Tatars	1944, 5	200	Heller & Neckrich,86,535	
67	Crimean Tatars	1944, 5	200 / 250	Sheehy and Nahaylo,80,8	
68	CONSOLIDATED DEPORTED	1944, 5	194 / 232 / 250		
69					
70	*DEPORTED DEAD*				
71	Crimean Tatars	1944 1946	27 / 111	Conquest,70a,162	low is Soviet official estimate (omits transit dead); high from Tatar census
72	Crimean Tatars	1944 1946	44 / 115	Sheehy and Nahaylo,80,8	low is Soviet official estimate (omits transit dead); high from Tatar census
73	Crimean Tatars	1944 ?	24 / 89	Nekrich,78,112-4	low is from official documents and for those who died in Uzbekistan;
74					high from an official "Appeal of the Crimean Tatar People"
75	Crimean Tatars	1944 1946	35 / 92	Heller & Neckrich,36,535	
76	CONSOLIDATED DEAD	1944 1946	24 / 67 / 115		[mid-estimate is average between low and high]
77					
78	**GEORGIAN MESKHETIANS**				
79	*DEPORTED DEAD*				
80	Georgian Meskhetians/others	1944 11	200	Sheehy and Nahaylo,80, 24	includes Turkmans, Turkic Karapapakh Azerbaydzhanis,
81					Turkicized Kurds, and Khemshili Armenians.
82	Georgian Meskhetians	1944 ?	30 / 50	Sheehy and Nahaylo,80, 24	died from hunger and cold in Uzbekistan, to which deported
83	Georgian Meskhetians	1940s	50	Conquest,70b,109	excludes transit deaths and therefore a low figure
84	CONSOLIDATED DEAD	1944	30 / 40 / 50		
85					
86	**GREEK-SOVIETS**				
87	Greeks (Black Sea) deported	1944	?	Nekrich,78,104	out of population of 285 thousand in 1940
88	Greeks (Crimea) deported	1944	10	Conquest,70b,111	
89	CONSOLIDATED DEPORTED	1944 ?	10 / 10		
90	CALCULATED DEAD	1944 ?	1 / 2		[only for 50% assumed picked up by camp/forced labor figures, below. Calculations based on the mid-estimate of line 89]
91					

TABLE 7A (continued)

Line	Item	Year 1	Year 2	Est. 1	Est. 2	Est. 3	Source	Notes
92	**GERMAN-SOVIETS**							
93	**DEPORTED NUMBER**							
94	German-Soviets deported	1941		650		750	Fleischhauer & Pinkus,86,87	from European USSR; number is "probably" between 650,000 and 700,000.
95	German-Soviets deported	1941	12				Pearson,83,194	the entire German population of the European USSR.
96	German-Soviets deported	1941		412		1,400	Conquest,70a,64-5	Volga Germans
97	German-Soviets deported	1941	1942		800	800	Sheehy and Nahaylo,80, 19	Including 400 thousand from the Volga German Republic.
98	German-Soviets deported	1941	?	400			Conquest,70a,65-6	non-Volga Germans in Ukraine (200,000) and elsewhere in European USSR.
99	CONSOLIDATED DEPORTED	1941		412	650	800		[1,400 figure of line 95 ignored, since it implies zero deportations in 1944, below—it is treated as a total for 1941-1945]
100	German-Soviets deported	1941	1945		1,000	1,000	Tolstoy,81,283	excludes Volga Germans.
101	German-Soviets deported	1944	1945	20			Fleischhauer & Pinkus,86,86	from Leningrad, after the blockade was lifted.
102	German-Soviets deported	1944	1945	200			Fleischhauer & Pinkus,86,101	of 200,000 Soviet-Germans evacuated with German army and
103								overtaken by Red Army and deported; 15-30% died during transit
104								
105	German-Soviets deported	1944	?		300	300	de Zayas,79,203n31	those fleeing with retreating Nazi Army and
106								later repatriated, deported to labor camps.
107	Germans (Black Sea) deported	1944			120	120	Philipps,83,145	of those resettled in Warthegau, Poland,
108								by Nazis during their WWII occupation of the Black Sea region.
109	CONSOLIDATED DEPORTED	1944		300	450	600		
110	CONSOLIDATED DEPORTED	1941		412	650	800	[from line 99]	
111	SUM DEPORTED	1941		712	1,100	1,400	[sum of lines 109-110]	
112	CALCULATED DEAD	1941		64	143	301	[of line 111, only for 50% assumed resettled, other 50% assumed picked up by camp/forced labor figures, below]	
113								
114	NON-VOLGA GERMANS DEPORTED	1941		300	688	988	[line 111 minus 412,000 Volga Germans (line 96)]	
115	CALCULATED DEAD (NON-VOLGA)	1941		27	89	212	[of line 114, only for 50% assumed resettled, other 50% assumed picked up by camp/forced labor figures, below]	
116								
117	**DEPORTED DEAD**							
118	German-Soviet dead	1941	1955	64		300	Fleischhauer & Pinkus,86,144	
119	CALCULATED DEAD	1941	1945	64	143	301	[from line 112]	
120	TOTAL CONSOLIDATED DEAD	1941	1945	64	222	301	[mid-estimate an average of those for lines 118-119]	
121								
122	**UKRAINIANS**							
123	**DEPORTED NUMBER**							
124	Ukrainians deported	1941	1945	90		1,000	Tolstoy,81,283	
125	CALCULATED DEAD	1941	1945	130		215	[only for 50% assumed resettled, other 50% assumed picked up by camp/forced labor figures, below. Calculations based on the mid-estimate of line 124]	
126								
127	**SOVIET NATIONS GENERALLY**							
128	**DEPORTED NUMBER**							
129	nations deported overall	1941	1944		1,850	1,850	Conquest,70a,65-6	8 nations; includes 400,000 Germans from outside the Volga Republic; excludes Greeks
130								
131	nations deported overall	1943	1944	1,000			Nekrich,78,115-6	number deported, excludes Greeks
132	CONSOLIDATED DEPORTED	1941	1944	1,000	1,850	2,000	[of line 132, only for 50% assumed resettled, other 50% assumed picked up by camp/forced labor figures, below]	
133	CALCULATED DEAD	1941	1944	90	241	430		
134								
135	**DEPORTED DEAD**							
136	nations deported dead	1941	1944		530	530	Conquest,70a,162	of 8 nations, including Meskhetians, excludes non-Volga Germans, supported by census data
137								
138	nations deported dead	1959	1959	219			Nekrich,78,138	between census estimates of net losses, allowance made for wartime losses; for Balkars, Chechens, Ingush, Kalmyks, and Karachai.
139								

TABLE 7A (continued)

Line	Category	Date	Date	Est.	Est.	Est.	Source / Notes
140	CONSOLIDATED NATIONS DEAD	1941	1944	219	530	705	high is assumed a third higher than mid-estimate]
141	CALCULATED DEAD	1941	1944	90	241	430	from line 133]
142	SUM NATIONS DEAD	1941	1945	91	239	254	just for Tatars, Meskhetians, and Volga Germans,
143							sum of lines 76 and 84, and line 120 minus line 115]
144	**TOTAL DEPORTED DEAD**						
145	CONSOLIDATED NATIONS DEAD	1941	1944	219	530	705	from line 140]
146	GREEK-SOVIET DEAD	1941	?	1	1	2	from line 90]
147	NON-VOLGA GERMANS DEAD	1941	1945	27	89	212	from line 115]
148	UKRAINIAN DEAD	1941	1945	90	130	215	from line 125]
149	*SUM NATIONS ETHNICS DEAD*	1941 6	1945 8	337	751	1,134	sum of lines 145-148]
150	*FOREIGNERS KILLED BY STALIN AND PARTY. DEPORTED/DEAD*						
151							
152	**GERMANS**						
153	REICH GERMANS DEPORTED						
154	Germans	1944	1945	218	250	250	Schmitzek,66,316&n203 — low is for German Eastern Provinces, Gdansk, and Western Poland; high includes German Eastern Provinces
155							
156	Germans	1944		200	200		Tolstoy, 81,269 — to forced labor
157	CONSOLIDATED DEPORTED	1944	1945	200	218	250	
158							
159	GERMAN-RUMANIANS DEPORTED						
160	German-Rumanian	1944			72		Markham,49,410
161	German-Rumanian	1944			70		Bouscaren,63, 61
162	German-Rumanian	1945 ?			107		Werling,51,106
163	German-Rumanian	1945 ?			70		Bouscaren,63, 52-3
164	German-Rumanian	1945 1?			60		Markham,49,517
165	German-Rumanian	1944c			69		Schechtman,46,236
166	CONSOLIDATED DEPORTED	1944	1945	130	155	179	
167							
168	GERMAN-YUGOSLAVES DEPORTED						
169	German-Yugoslaves	1944	1945 3	100	100		Schechtman,46,242 — from diplomatic information reaching Washington, includes German POWs
170	German-Yugoslaves	1945 2c		100			Bouscaren,63, 61
171	CONSOLIDATED DEPORTED	1944	1945	100	100	133	
172							
173	ETHNIC GERMANS DEPORTED						
174	Germans (Rum./Hun./Yugo.)	1945 2c			140		Schoenberg,70,18
175	CONSOLIDATED GERMAN-RUM	1944	1945	130	155	179	from line 166]
176	CONSOLIDATED GERMAN-YUGO	1944	1945	100	100	133	from line 171]
177	CONSOLIDATED DEPORTED	1944	1945	230	255	312	
178							
179	REICH/ETHNIC GERMANS DEPORTED						
180	Germans (Reich/Ethnic)	1945c			700		Swianiewicz,65,42 — from Germany and Danubian countries; from German Federal government in 1952.
181							
182	Germans (Reich/Ethnic)	1944	?		700		de Zayas,79, 203n31 — includes Romanian, Hungarian, and Yugoslavian Germans, excludes
183							300,000 German-Soviets later repatriated and sent to labor camps
184	Germans (Reich/Ethnic)	1945		200			Schoenberg,70,19 — Germans fleeing Soviet advance and overtaken by Red Army.
185	CONSOLIDATED DEPORTED	1944	1945	469	700	931	
186	REICH GERMANS DEPORTED	1944	1945	200	218	250	from line 157]
187	ETHNIC GERMANS DEPORTED	1944	1945	230	255	312	from line 177]
188	TOTAL (CONSOLIDATED DEPORTED	1944	1945	430	473	700	(consolidation of lines 185-187]

TABLE 7A (continued)

Line	Category	Y1	M1	Y2	M2	n1	n2	n3	Source / Notes
189	**HUNGARIANS**								
190	DEPORTED NUMBER								
191	Hungarians deported	1944		1945			600		Tolstoy,81,267 — includes POWs; from Bela Varga, president of Hungarian National Council
192	Hungarians deported	1944		19457			600		Herling,51,143
193	Hungarians deported					200	295		Nagy,48,80
194	Hungarians deported	1945					600		Swianiewicz,65,42
195				1945c					
196	CONSOLIDATED DEPORTED	1944				400	798		
197									
198	**JAPANESE**								
199	DEPORTED NUMBER								
200	Japanese deported	1945					1,000		Tolstoy,81,431n64 — deported to forced labor
201	Japanese dep (Kurile)	1945					?		Bouscaren,63,56
202	Japanese dep (S. Sakhalin)	1945					400		Bouscaren,63,56
203	CONSOLIDATED DEPORTED	1945				650	1,000	1,300	
204									
205	**POLES**								
206	DEPORTED NUMBER								
207	Poles	1944		1945			50		Glückstein,52,148 — of Polish "partisans" who fought the Germans.
208	Poles	1945				59	50		Kusnierz,49,191 — [R. J. Rummel calculation from data and text, absolute minimum]
209	Poles	1944				73	109		Kusnierz,49,211 — Home Army soldiers executed or deported to labor/concentration camps
210	CONSOLIDATED DEPORTED	1944						145	
211									
212	**OTHER FOREIGNERS**								
213	DEPORTED NUMBER								
214	Rumanians	1944					390		Markham,49,410-1 — includes POWs and excludes 72,000 deported Germans-Romanians, 100,000 repatriated by end of 1946
215									
216	Romanians/Germans-Romanian	1944					250		Tolstoy,81,266 — to GULAG, "Few are likely to have survived…"
217	West Ukrainian/Byelorussians	1941	6				150		Gross,88,179 — Western Byelorussians/Ukrainian prisoners;
218									
219	Belorussians (West)	1941	6?				50		Lubachko,72,145 — killed or moved east on Nazi invasion
220	CONSOLIDATED DEPORTED	1944		1945		395	590	662	after invasion of Nazis
221									
222	**TOTAL FOREIGNERS DEPORTED/DEAD**								
223	foreign nationals deported	1941	6	1945	8	1,500			Swianiewicz,65,42 — deported to USSR during the war; excludes Poles
224	ADJUSTED FOR DEPORTED	1941	6	1945	8	1,573	1,609	1,645	[mid-estimate of line 223 added to line 210 to include the deportations of Poles]
225	SUM FOREIGNERS DEPORTED	1941	6	1945	8	1,948	2,772	3,605	[sum of lines 188, 196, 203, 210, and 220]
226	CONSOLIDATED FOR DEP	1941	6	1945	8	1,573	2,191	3,605	[mid-estimate is the average of lines 224 and 225]
227	*CALCULATED FOREIGN DEAD*	1941	6	1945	8	142	285	775	[of line 226, only for 50% assumed resettled, other 50% assumed picked up by camp/forced labor figures, below]
228									
229	**TOTAL DEPORTED/DEAD**								
230	NATIONS/ETHNICS DEAD	1941		1945		337	751	1,134	[from line 149]
231	FOREIGNERS DEPORTED DEAD	1941		1945		142	285	775	[from line 227]
232	*SUB DEPORTED DEAD*	1941	6	1945	8	478	1,036	1,910	[sum of lines 230 and 231]
233									
234	*KILLED BY STALIN AND PARTY: CAMP/FORCED LABOR POPULATION/DEAD*								
235	**1941 DEAD**								
236	1941 HALF-YEAR CAMP DEAD	1941	7	1941	12	150	1,000	2,800	[from line 196, Appendix 6.1]
237									

TABLE 7A (continued)

Line	Category				Date		Source	Notes
238	1942 POPULATION							
239	camps				1942		Panin,76,92n	from former "checklists" and prisoners in position to know or count.
240	camps/prisons		14,000		1942	?	Dallin & Nicolaevsky,47,277	inmates; different sources
241	forced labor camps	8,000		12,000	1942c.		Rosefielde,81,60	from data compiled by US Moscow Embassy, according to Ambassador Averell Harriman.
242								politicals/criminals
243	camps/prisons/isolators	6,500			1942c		Wiles,53,35	
244	GULAG		11,200		1942		Rosefielde,81,65	
245	prisoners			20,000	1942		Kravchenko,46,404	accepted estimate in official circles of labor reservoir of prisoners.
246								excludes forced labor of 14-15 year olds
247	CONSOLIDATED CAMP POP	6,500	9,000	16,000	1942			
248	CALCULATED CAMP DEAD	650	1,800	4,480	1942			
250	1942 DEAD							
251	zeks	7,500			1941	6 1942	Panin,76,93n	death through hunger and overwork.
252	PROPORTIONATED DEAD		5,000		1942			[line 251 proportionated for twelve months]
253	CALCULATED CAMP DEAD	650	1,800	4,480	1942			[from line 248]
254	AVERAGE DEAD	2,825	3,400	4,740	1942			[average of mid-estimate on line 252 with estimates on line 253]
256	1943 POPULATION/DEAD							
257	GULAG		11,200		1943		Rosefielde,81,65	
258	GULAG	10,000		15,000	1941		Solzhenitsyn,75a,205	at a time; from encyclopedia Rossiya-SSR; agrees with prisoner estimates
259	GULAG			15,000	1945		Solzhenitsyn,75a,205	the number reached during WWII, excludes
260	prisoners/deportees			30,000	1945		Chyz,62,28-9	forced child labor involving several million.
262	CONSOLIDATED CAMP POP	10,000	11,200	15,000	1943			
263	CALCULATED CAMP DEAD	1,000	2,240	4,200	1943			
265	1944 POPULATION/DEAD							
266	repatriated Russians/Soviets	2,500			1944	?	Elliott,82,202	sent to prisons or forced labor camps
267	GULAG		12,300		1944		Rosefielde,81,65	
268	camps/forced settlement	5,000		7,000	1941	1946?	Swianiewicz,65,13	influx of POWs and civilian deportees from conquered countries
269	CONSOLIDATED CAMP POP	10,000	12,300	15,000	1944			low and high assumed same as 1943
270	CALCULATED CAMP DEAD	1,000	2,460	4,200	1944			
272	1945 POPULATION/DEAD							
273	camps	15,000		17,000	1945	?	Conquest,68,531	from the commandant of a "repatriation camp" feeding the labor camps.
274	camps	8,000		15,000	1945	?	Heller & Nekrich,86,493	post-World War II; low from Robert Conquest; high from R. Roeder.
275	camps	18,000			1945		Kosyk,62,79	
276	GULAG		13,400		1945		Rosefielde,81,65	
277	forced labor camps/prisons	8,000		20,000	1940s		Herling,51,11	
278	forced labor camps		12,000		1945		Chyz,62,95	deportees, "exiled."
279	repatriated Russians/Soviets	1,250			1944	?	Elliott,82,207	of 25 million sent to prisons/camps
280	repatriated Russians/Soviets	2,250			1944	?	Tolstoy,81,283-4	of 5.5 million repatriated; 2.272 million by the US and UK.
281	repatriated Russians/Soviets	2,400			1945	1947	Swianiewicz,65,44	of 5.5 million repatriated, 2.4 million probably sent to forced labor
282	repat. Rus/Soviets/POWs	1,100			1943		Tolstoy,77,515	of 5.5 million repatriated, 20% executed or got 25 years in camp (an
283								extended death sentence), from a former officer of the NKVD
284	repat. Rus/Soviets/POWs	825		1,100	1945	1947	Tolstoy,77,515-6	out of 5.5 million repatriated, 15-20% received a sentence of 5 to 10 years
285	CONSOLIDATED CAMP POP	8,000	11,200	20,000	1945			mid-number assumed same as for previous year
286	CALCULATED CAMP DEAD	800	2,240	5,600	1945			

TABLE 7A (continued)

Line	Item	Year(s)	Low	Mid	High	Source	Notes
287	**OVERALL CAMP/FORCED LABOR DEAD (INCLUDES FOREIGNERS)**						
288	TRANSIT DEAD						
290	MAXIMUM POPULATION	1942	10,000	12,300	20,000		[for World War II Period]
291	CALCULATED TRANSIT DEAD	1942	1	91	455		
292							
293	CAMP DEAD						
294	forced labor camp dead	1941	10,000			Legters,84,60-1	based on "demographic indicators"
295	camp dead	1941	6,500			Kosyk,62,79	
296	camp dead	1943	5,000			Panin,76,93n	
297	CONSOLIDATED CAMP DEAD	1941 6 1945	6,500	10,000	13,300		[sum of lines 236, 254, 263, 270, and 286]
298	SUMMED CAMP DEAD	1941 6 1945	5,775	11,340	21,540		[average of lines 297 and 298]
299	AVERAGE CAMP DEAD	1941 6 1945	6,138	10,670	17,420		[sum of lines 291 and 299]
300	*SUM CAMP/TRANSIT DEAD*	1942 6 1945	6,139	10,761	17,875		[sum of lines 291 and 299]
301							
302	**FOREIGN CAMP/FORCED LABOR POPULATION/DEAD COMPONENT**						
303	POW POPULATION						
304	German POWs	1945	3,740			Swianiewicz,65,42	from Soviet war communiqués
305	Hungarian POWs	1945	325			Swianiewicz,65,43	
306	Japanese POWs	1945	594			Swianiewicz,65,43	POWs transferred from Manchuria to Siberia
307	Japanese POWS	1945	900			Dallin & Nicolaevsky,47,277	[low is sum of lines 304 to 306, mid-estimate is sum of lines 304, 305 and line 307]
308	SUM FOREIGN POWs	1945	4,659	4,965		Swianiewicz,65,43	
309	Foreign POWs	1945	5,000	5,330	6,000		
310	CONSOLIDATED POWs	1945	4659	5,330	6,000		[mid-estimate an average of low and high estimates]
311	CALCULATED POW CAMP DEAD	1945	466	1,066	1,680		
312							
313	POW DEAD						
314	POWs (German) dead	1941 ?	1,500		2,000	Elliott,82,233	sent to Soviet camps and who did not return; presumed dead
315	POWs (German) dead	1941 ?				Johnson,83,585	"vanished" into the USSR.
316	POWs (German) dead	1941 ?	1,000	1,150	1,500	Elliot,72,84	sent to Soviet labor camps and presumed dead
317	POWs (German) dead	? 1947	1,105		2,105	Dallin & Nicolaevsky,47,277	of an estimated 3–4 million POWs, Molotov claimed in 1947 that 1,003,974 were repatriated and 890,532 were still in the USSR
318							
319	POWs (Italian) dead	? 1947	200	47	300	Dallin & Nicolaevsky,47,277	12,513 POWs returned out of 60,000; from Italian government in 1947
320	POWs (Japanese) dead	1945 ?				Elliott,82,233	never released and presumed dead
321	CONSOLIDATED POW CAMP DEAD	1941 ?	1,247	1,747	2,247		[from line 311]
322	CALCULATED POW CAMP DEAD	1945 ?	466	1,066	1,680		
323	OVERALL POW CAMP DEAD	1941 ?	1,247	1,747	2,247		
324							
325	FOREIGN CIVILIAN POPULATION						
326	foreign civilians	1945	500	1,000		Swianiewicz,65,42	
327	FOR DEPORT CAMP POPULATION	1941 1945	787	1,095	1,832		[assumed half of those deported; from line 226]
328							
329	FOREIGN CIVILIAN DEAD						
330	TRANSIT DEAD	1941 1945	0	58	178		[calculated from line 327, low set to zero]
331	CALCULATED FOR CAMP DEAD	1941 1945	157	438	1,009		[calculated from line 327, since period is over four years, the death rate is conservatively doubled]
332	FOR CIV CAMP/TRANSIT DEAD	1941 1945	157	496	1,188		[sum of lines 330 and 331]
333							

TABLE 7A (continued)

								Source	Notes
334	OVERALL FOREIGN CAMP DEAD COMPONENT								
335	OVERALL POW CAMP DEAD	1941	?	1,247	1,747	2,247			[from line 323]
336	FOR CIV (CAMP/TRANSIT DEAD	1941	1941	157	496	1,188			[from line 332]
337	*SUB FOR CAMP/TRANSIT DEAD*	1941	?	1,404	2,243	3,435			[sum of lines 335–336]
338									
339	**KILLED BY STALIN AND PARTY: TERROR/REPRESSION**								
340	CITIZENS								
341	repatriated Russians/Soviets	1944	?	300				Elliot,82, 202	these are executed, out of 5.2 million repatriates, 2.5 million were
342									sent to prison or forced labor; 1.1 million inducted or reinducted
343	Soviet caused	1941	1945		15,000	15,000		Conquest, et al,84,36	from Maksudov; in addition to soldiers and civilians killed as part of WWII.
344	Soviet caused	1941	1945	10,000				Tolstoy,81,283	due to Stalin; includes Finnish War; epidemics from forced
345									evacuation purges, GULAG deaths, and killed among the repatriated
346	Ukrainians	1941			80			Dujardin,78,51	during Red Army retreat.
347	Ukrainians	1944			20			Mikolejczyk,48,99-100	executed German "collaborators" captured by the Red Army, from Stalin.
348	repressive actions	1941	1953		9,000			Antonov-Ovseyenko,81,307	German collaborators; includes repatriated,
349	collaborators	1944	?		3,000			Swianiewicz,85,44	from the Institute of the History and Culture of the USSR (Munich)
350									
351	CONSOLIDATED GENERAL DEAD	1941	1945	9,000	10,000	15,000			[one cause of death possibly included in the above; from line 149]
352	NATIONS/ETHNICS DEAD	1941	6 1945	8	337	751	1,134		[one cause of death possibly included in the above; line 300 minus line 337]
353	CAMP/TRANSIT DEAD (CITIZENS)	1941	6 1945	4,735	8,518	14,440			[low is high of lines 352 and 353 (set to 0, since
354	*GENERAL REPRESSION/TERROR*	1941	1945	0	731	3,929			[low is high of line 351 minus lows of lines 352 and 353;
355									result is negative), high is low of line 351 minus highs of lines 352 and 353,
356									mid-estimate of that of line 351 minus lines 352 and 353]
357	**OCCUPIED STATES/TERRITORIES DEAD**								
358	BALTS								
359	Baltic Germans	1944	?		?			Schoenberg,70,32	after reoccupation by Red Army, 20% disappeared
360	Balts	1941	1944		?			Misiunas & Tagepera,83,67	Soviet partisan provocations causing Nazi mass reprisals.
361	Balts	1944		3				Misiunas & Tagepera,83,68	[R. J Rummel estimate of summary executions upon Red Army
362									reoccupation; 400–700 alone executed in 3 cities of Lithuania]
363	CONSOLIDATED	1942	1945	3	4	6			
364	**REICH/ETHNIC GERMANS**								
365	Germans	1944		200	200			Tolstoy, 81,269	text unclear; possibly only for East Prussia;
366									excludes expelled from the former German territories
367	CONSOLIDATED	1944		200	266	400			
368									
369	**POLES**								
370	Poles	1941	6 ?	12	12			Gross,88,181	prisoners shot by NKVD in Brygidki prison in Lwów
371	Poles	1941	6 ?	50				Gross,88,185	[R. J Rummel estimate] hundreds of thousands were killed, deported,
372									or marched East by the NKVD in front of Nazi invasion forces.
373	Poles	1941	6 ?	24	2			Grudzinska-Gross,81,254n63	prisoners killed by the NKVD in the districts of Berdyczów and Glebokie
374	Poles	1944		74	96	144		Kusnierz,49,190	a low, since in 3 districts only.
375	CONSOLIDATED	1941	6 1944						
376									
377	**OTHER NATIONALS**								
378	Bulgarians	1944	1945						
379	Byelorussia/Ukraine	1941	6 1941 ?		100			Gross,88,229	Western Byelorussians/Ukrainians;
380									during evacuation of prisons after German invasion.
382	Czechs	1945		?	?				

TABLE 7A (continued)

Line	Item	Years	Low	Mid	High	Source / Note
383	Hungarians	1945		28		urban famine, Soviets wholly responsible
384	Koreans	1945		?		
385	Japanese	1945		?		
386	Yugoslavs	1944 6 1945		?	240	
387	CONSOLIDATED	1941 6 1945	120	160	240	Italy,48,104
388						
389	**OVERALL OCCUPATION DEAD**					
390	SUM FOREIGN DEAD	1941 6 1945	397	526	790	[sum of lines 363, 368, 376, and 387]
391						
392	**TOTAL TERROR/REPRESSION**					
393	*SUM TERROR/REPRESSION*	1941	397	1,257	4,719	[sum of lines 354 and 390]
394						
395	*OVERALL DEAD*					
396	**COMPONENTS OF DEMOCIDE (CITIZENS)**					
397	*TERRORISM*	1941 6 1945	0	731	3,929	[from line 354]
398	*DEPORTATIONS*	1941 6 1945	337	751	1,134	[from line 149]
399	*CAMP/TRANSIT*	1941 6 1945	4,735	8,518	14,440	[line 300 minus line 337]
400	*DEMOCIDE (CITIZENS)*	1941 6 1945	5,071	10,000	19,503	
401						
402	**COMPONENTS OF DEMOCIDE (FOREIGNERS)**					
403	*TERRORISM*	1941 6 1945	397	526	790	[from line 390]
404	*DEPORTATIONS*	1941 6 1945	142	285	775	[from line 227]
405	*CAMP/TRANSIT*	1941 6 1945	1,404	2,243	3,435	[from line 337]
406	*DEMOCIDE (FOREIGNERS)*	1941 6 1945	1,943	3,053	5,000	
407						
408	**OVERALL COMPONENTS OF DEMOCIDE**					
409	*TERRORISM*	1941 6 1945	397	1,257	4,719	[sum of lines 397 and 403]
410	*DEPORTATIONS*	1941 6 1945	478	1,036	1,910	[sum of lines 398 and 404]
411	*CAMP/TRANSIT*	1941 6 1945	6,139	10,761	17,875	[sum of lines 399 and 405]
412	*OVERALL DEMOCIDE*	1941 6 1945	7,014	13,053	24,503	[sum of lines 409 to 411]
413						
414	**OVERALL WORLD WAR II DEAD**					
415	**ESTIMATES SOVIET DEAD**					
416	Ukrainians					Krawchenko,86,23
417	total loss	1941	6,800			Timasheff,48,155 — census based
418	military/civilians	1941	37,500			Tolstoy,81,280
419		1941	30,000			from census; assumes at least a quarter of expected births took place, includes Soviet POWs.
420	civilians	1941	18,300			Timasheff,48,155
421	population deficit	1940	50,000			Dyadkin,83,59 — population deficit (including unborn) due to repressive policies and World War II.
422		1945				
423	unnatural deaths	1941	30,200			Dyadkin,83,49 — "an estimate of war losses"; from census.
424	unnatural deaths (draft age)	1941	25,600	26,000	27,800	Dyadkin,83,55 — from census, includes 18.8 million males.
425	deaths	1941 1949	44,000			Dyadkin,83,55
426						if assume 20 million war dead, 1941–45, then from the census, 24 million more adults had to die 1941–49, high includes
427	war loses	1940 1950	25,000	35,000	45,000	Eason,59,600-1 — those born before 1940, low is of those born after 1940, high includes
428						those not born or who died in infancy, mid is the average
429	CONSOLIDATION ESTIMATES	1941 6 1945	25,000	30,100	40,000	[mid-estimate is an average of lines 418 and 423]
430						of lines 418 and 423]

TABLE 7A (continued)

431	TOTALS SOVIET DEAD									
432	BATTLE/OCCUPATION DEAD	1941	6	1945	7	11,625	19,625	26,860		[from line 59]
433	SOVIET DEMOCIDE (CITIZENS)	1941	6	1945	6	5,071	10,000	19,503		[from line 400]
434	*OVERALL WWII CITIZEN DEAD*	1941		1945		16,696	29,625	46,363		[sum of lines 432 and 433]
435	Cf CONSOLIDATED ESTIMATES	1941		1945		25,000	30,100	40,000		[from line 429, Cf means "compare to"]
436										
437	DEMOCIDE RATE									
438	population	1941					200,500		Timasheff,48,155	
439	population	1941	1				196,700		Dyadkin,83, 49	
440	population	1941	7				200,000		Eason,59,600	
441	population	1941	5				174,000		Swianiewicz,65,39	
442										
443	population	1945					165,000		Dyadkin,83, 59	
444	population	1945					170,000		Eason,59,600	
445	MID-PERIOD POPULATION	1943					183,283		[includes annexed territories]	
446	*DEMOCIDE RATE (CITIZENS)*	1941		1945		2.77%	5.46%	10.64%		[line 298/line 452) X 100]
447	*ANNUAL DEMOCIDE RATE*	1941	6	1945		0.61%	1.21%	2.36%		[line 452/45]

the working age (15-60) population was about 84 million, [apparently excludes annexed territories]

*See notes, table 1A, appendix 1.1.

averaged to get overall totals (line 59): 11,625,000 to 26,860,000 dead, with a midestimate of 19,625,000. This final result is surprisingly close to the official Soviet figure of 20,000,000 war-dead.

Now putting this total aside, we can try to estimate the number of those who were killed in Stalin's war on his own people. The table first consolidates deportation numbers and death estimates (lines 62 to 142), organized by Soviet nation or ethnic group: Crimean Tatars, Georgian Meskhetians, Greek-Soviets, German-Soviets, Ukrainians, and others.

To the deportation totals, where necessary, the deportation death-rates from appendix 1.2 are applied to get the number of dead (outside of the camps). For example, the estimates of the number of Crimean Tatars deported in 1944 are shown (lines 64 to 67), and consolidated (line 68). Possibly 194,000 to 250,000 Crimean Tatars were deported. Estimates of those who died are shown next (lines 71 to 75), which when consolidated gives a range of 24,000 to 115,000 dead.

The consolidated deportation total for the Greek-Soviets (line 89) provides an example of where the dead had to be calculated (line 90) from the deportation death rates determined in appendix 1.2, since no deportation death estimates were available in the references. As for previous periods, this calculation was done only for half of the deportees, assuming the other half were sent to camps and their deaths would be picked up in the overall camp totals. Since the references seem to imply that most, if not virtually all, these nations were resettled rather than sent to camps, this procedure is surely conservative.[99]

The deportation of 712,000 to 1,400,000 German-Soviets (line 111) is a special problem, since a useful estimate of the overall dead from the deportations of Soviet nations excludes non–Volga Germans (line 136). Consequently, the number of Volga Germans deported is first estimated (line 96) as 412,000, then this is subtracted from the number of Germans deported during the war (line 111). This gives a range of 300,000 to 988,000 non–Volga Germans deported (line 114). Calculating for half of these the number who died (from the deportation death rate) gives 27,000 to 212,000 dead (line 115).

Two estimates of the number of nationals deported (lines 129 to 131) and the resulting dead (lines 136 to 139) are given. Using the deportation death rates, the number of dead from the deportation estimates was calculated as a test, and compared to the consolidated death estimates (lines 140 to 141). Since the calculated dead is applied to half of the number deported and also the midestimate and high is close to half of the estimated dead, the two sets of figures tend to confirm each other. Note that this also shows how conservative these calculated deaths are, since presumably the estimated deportation dead is exclusive of any sent to the camps.

The above consolidated dead (line 140) are for, among others, the Tatars, Meskhetians, and Volga Germans. Accordingly, as another test the calculated dead for these nations given elsewhere in the table (lines 76 and 84, and line 120 minus 115) is summed and shown (line 142) for comparison to the estimated dead. The result is also much less than half of the estimated amount, providing some further (although marginal) support to the death rates used and to the estimates.

Finally, to calculate the overall number of those who died from deportation, the consolidated estimates of the dead (line 145) are added to the calculated dead for those nations not included in these estimates (lines 146 to 148): Greek-Soviet, non–Volga German-Soviets, and Ukrainians. In sum (line 149), 337,000 to 1,134,000 Soviet citizens lost their lives in the deportation roundups, transit, and settlements, with a midestimate of 751,000.

No other deportation figures are available in the references, although it seems very likely that on ethnic, national, religious, or political grounds, many more, although possibly much smaller, groups were deported. Perhaps if included, they might add tens of thousands more dead to the total.

Next to consider is camp deaths. Numerous estimates of the camp population and dead during the war are available in the references, and these are organized by year in the table (lines 235 to 284). For each year (except 1941, for which the half-year calculated dead is taken from appendix 6.1), the dead is calculated from the consolidated population estimates, using the camp death rates. For 1944, estimates of the dead are also available, so the estimated dead is compared to the calculated and the two are averaged (lines 251 to 254). Note that 1945 camp population also includes estimates of repatriated Russians and Soviet citizens and also POWs. This average, along with the calculated dead for the other years, is summed to give a total of 5,775,000 to 21,540,000 camp dead during the war (line 298). This incredible high is due to the huge but common estimate of 20,000,000 camp prisoners during the war and the high but also not uncommon assumed annual death rate of 28 percent.

There are also overall estimates of the camp deaths during the war (lines 294 to 296), which when consolidated give a range of 6,500,000 to 13,300,000 dead. In the table, these are shown above the calculated toll (lines 297 to 298). As can be seen, the low and midestimates are very close, while the high for the consolidated one is much lower. This is due, in part, to the high for the consolidated being made, by assumption (since no high estimates are given in the references), only a third higher than the midestimate. Considering how close the low and midestimates are for the two sets of totals, there can be no objection to averaging them (line 299). In spite of the artificiality of the high for the consolidated, however, to be conservative this is also averaged with the calculated high. Now adding in transit deaths (from line 291), the overall result (line 300) is a total of 6,139,000 to 17,875,000 deaths in the camps or in transit to them, or a midestimate of 10,761,000.

Now, these figures include foreigners sent to the camps. To get a figure for the citizens who died we must determine the foreign dead. First, the foreign camp population involved POWs from many nations, estimates of which are consolidated in the table (line 308), and these are compared to a low estimate in the references of the total POWs in the camps (line 309). Both sets are in near agreement and are then consolidated (line 310). From the result, the number of POW camp-dead is calculated from the camp death rates (line 311).

There are also estimates of camp POW dead, which are consolidated and compared to the calculated dead (lines 321 to 322). The consolidated figures are generally higher, since they include overall POW deaths for specific nationals rather than a total for just one year. Accordingly, the consolidated figures are accepted as the final ones.

As to the foreign civilian camp-dead, there is one estimate in the references of the number of foreign civilians in the camps during 1945 (line 326). This can be compared to their overall camp population figures, which are half of the number of foreigners deported (line 327)—as determined elsewhere in the table and to be discussed below—but which should be higher, since they are for a longer period. In fact they arc higher and thus were used in calculating the transit- and camp-dead (lines 330 to 331).

The sum of the POW and foreign civilian camp-dead gives a range of 1,404,000 to 3,435,000 (line 337). These can now be subtracted from the overall camp-dead (line 300) to approximate the number of Soviet citizens who died in the camps, which gives a total (shown on line 399) of 4,735,000 to 14,440,000 dead, with a midestimate of

8,518,000. This alone is greater than the number of Soviet military killed in that other war against the Nazis (line 55).

Turning to the terror and repression, relevant estimates of those killed are listed in the table (lines 340 to 350). These include repatriated Russians and Soviet citizens executed, Ukrainians killed in the evacuation as Nazi armies advanced, execution of Nazi "collaborators," and some general estimates. These are consolidated (line 351) to give a range of 9,000,000 to 15,000,000 killed.

A problem with these numbers is that they probably include those killed in the deportations and camps (see lines 343 to 344) and therefore, prudently, should be reduced. Deportation and camp-dead figures are reproduced below the consolidated ones (lines 352 and 353). The most conservative approach is to subtract the high for the deportation and camp-dead from the consolidated low. This gives a minus result, which is then set to zero. Also, again conservatively, the deportation and camp high should be subtracted from the consolidated high, and the deportation and camp midestimates from the consolidated one. This gives (line 354) a range of zero to 3,929,000 dead from the party's terror in the Soviet Union during the war. The low of zero may trouble some readers, but keep in mind that these component estimates only play a role in arriving at an overall low for the period that should underestimate the actual democide, and certainly the zero underestimate of terror will contribute to this.

In putting together, now, deportations, camps, and terror-dead, the democide on the home front during the war amounts to a midestimate of 10,000,000 citizens, which may be on the high side by about half or too low by almost twice the number (line 405). When added to the Nazi war-dead (line 434), it means that 16,696,000 to 46,363,000 Soviets were killed during the war, with a midestimate of 29,625,000.

This huge number, largely unknown and unsuspected in the West, requires some testing. Fortunately, there are a number of separate estimates of the total war-dead in the references, and these are given in the table (lines 416 to 428). They are consolidated and shown for comparison to the overall war-period-dead (lines 434 to 435). Note that the consolidated midfigure—based on Dyadkin's and Tolstoy's independent demographic analysis[100]—is almost the same as that derived from the democide components. This is remarkable, since the latter are independently arrived at based on over a hundred distinct estimates of different events, and dozens of consolidations and calculations. Surely, this is partial validation of the procedures used here, not to mention of the midestimate itself. Note also that the democide low is lower than that for the consolidated overall estimates, and the high is higher.

As to the foreign democide, the deportation and terror components have yet to be shown. I give in the table (lines 153 to 219) estimates of foreigners deported into the Soviet Union from East Germany, Yugoslavia, Hungary, former Japanese territories, Poland, and Rumania. No estimates of Bulgarians or Koreans deported was available in the references, although such deportations presumably took place.

Reich and ethnic Germans found in Eastern Europe by Soviet forces were either deported to the Soviet Union or later, expelled to East or West Germany. The Soviets are responsible for all who died in deportations to the Soviet Union, but for the deaths of those expelled to the divided Germanies, the responsibility is not so clear. Although occupied by Soviet forces, the new Czech government itself played the major role in expelling their Sudenten Germans across the border, as did the Polish government in deporting Reich and ethnic Germans (especially from the former German Eastern Territories), and the Hungarian government in getting rid of their ethnic Germans. In all these expulsions from Eastern Europe up to 1950 (according to a West German Federal Government report), 2,200,000 ethnic and Reich Germans died or were missing. More than 1,300,000 were from East Prussia, East Pomerania, East Brandenburg, and Silesia; almost 300,000 were Sudenten Germans expelled by the Czechs; and the rest were deported to both German occupation zones from the Baltic area (including Memel), Danzig, Poland, Hungary, Rumania, and Yugoslavia.[101]

While it could be argued that as occupiers the Soviets bear the final responsibility for these expulsions and deaths (of the expulsion of 3,500,000 ethnic Germans from Czechoslovakia, Antonov-Ovseyenko says that this was "unmistakably a Stalin operation"),[102] to be prudent, only those ethnic and Reich Germans dying from deportations to the Soviet Union will be charged to Soviet democide. The loss of life in the expulsions to the divided Germanies by Eastern European nations will be counted elsewhere as genocide by the nations involved.[103]

This approach can be seen in those estimates of deported Reich and ethnic Germans given in the table, which are limited to those trucked into the Soviet Union, either for resettlement, labor camps, or "reconstruction work." The estimates are divided into Reich and ethnic

Germans, and each into the national or territorial source. Those estimates of the total Reich and ethnic Germans deported are shown
together (lines 180 to 184), and consolidated (line 185). This is then
compared to the separate consolidated totals for Reich and ethnic German deportations (lines 186 and 187), and the three sets are further
consolidated in one total (line 188). Taking into account that sums of
the separate mid- and high estimates of Reich and ethnic German
deportations are much smaller than that for both together (line 185),
conservatively, the two lows and midestimates are summed to get the
overall total, and the high is taken from the consolidated midestimate
(line 185). This gives a deportation to the Soviet Union, in the years
1944 to 1945, of 430,000 to 700,000 Germans (line 188).

The deportations of other foreign ethnics and nationalities into the
Soviet Union are estimated subsequently (lines 190 to 220). Including
the Germans, the consolidated estimates for all of these are summed
and shown in the table (line 225). There is one overall estimate of the
number of deported foreigners (line 223), but it excludes Poles. This
estimate is then adjusted (line 224) to add Poles (for after June, 1941),
and this gives us two sets of estimates, one based on that by
Swianiewicz[104] and the other based on the sum of the consolidated
totals for the different ethnics and nationalities (lines 224 to 225).
There are significant differences between the two sets. Accordingly,
they are consolidated into one set of estimates by taking the lowest
low, the highest high, and averaging the midestimates (line 226). To
halve the result, the deportation death rates are applied to calculate the
overall foreign deportation-dead (excluding in the camps). This gives
a toll of 142,000 to 775,000 deported foreign dead (line 227).

Estimates of the cost of Soviet terrorism in Eastern Europe are given
in the table (lines 358 to 386). There is only one estimate in the
references for that among the Germans, which is probably much too
low. There are no estimates for Soviet terror among the Bulgarians,
Czechs, Koreans, Japanese, or Yugoslavs, although the references
make clear that such was pervasive. While incomplete, these estimates
do provide some minimal indication of the extent of terrorism. They
sum (line 390) to a very conservative range of 397,000 to 790,000
foreigners killed, with a midestimate of 526,000.

Overall, in terrorism, deportations, and Soviet camps (lines 403 to
405), a midestimate of 3,053,000 foreigners were killed, with a low of
2,030,000 and a high of 5,000,000.

Added to the total citizens killed (line 412), Soviet democide during the World War II period cost 7,014,000 to 24,503,000 lives—probably 13,053,000. This is a very prudent figure, given the lack of estimates of Soviet terrorism and repression at home and in occupied territories, probably incomplete deportation estimates, and the use of an unknown number of prisoners and undesirables as cannon fodder in the war (e.g., clearing mine fields by forcing former prisoners to walk through them is surely democide). With this in mind, and considering that the low is a sum of all the available low estimates, it is most probably a gross underestimate. But in absolute terms, for this period alone, even a democide of 7,014,000 would be a crime against humanity of the first magnitude.

Epigraph quoted in Conquest (1970, p. 19). Pasternak was a Russian poet and novelist.

Notes

1. Mihajlov (1987).
2. Quoted in Kulischer (1948, p. 276).
3. Timasheff (1948, Table 1, p. 155).
4. Tolstoy (1981, p. 280).
5. Dyadkin (1983, p. 49).
6. Eason (1959, p. 601).
7. Elliot (1972, p. 226); Conquest, *et al.* (1984, p. 36); Timasheff (1948, Table 1, p. 155).
8. Elliot (1972, p. 55).
9. Medvedev (1979, p. 140). Medvedev's figures are from the Soviet demographer M. Maksudov; he gives about 7,500,000 civilians killed in the repression and fighting. I subtracted 500,000 civilians killed in the fighting itself.
10. Tolstoy (1981, p. 282). These are Jews "massacred at Babi Yar and elsewhere."
11. Kulischer (1948, p. 276).
12. Tolstoy (1981, p. 282).
13. Ibid.
14. Elliott (1982, pp. 7–9)
15. Conquest (1968, p. 491).
16. Heller and Nekrich (1986, p. 393); Conquest (1968, p. 491).
17. Hingley (1970, p. 191).
18. Heller and Nekrich (1986, p. 393).
19. Ibid., p. 453.

20. Dujardin (1978, p. 51).
21. *The World Almanac* (1986, p. 510).
22. Ibid., p. 333.
23. Ibid.
24. Misiunas and Taagepera (1983, p. 45); *Mass Deportations* (1981, pp. 20–21).
25. *Mass Deportations* (1981, pp. 20–21).
26. Misiunas and Taagepera (1983, p. 47).
27. Ibid.
28. Ibid., p. 67.
29. Quoted in Tolstoy (1981, p. 282). No doubt those killed in these penal battalions are counted as battle-dead but should actually be added to Stalin's side of the ledger. But there is no way of estimating what this number should be, and it is therefore ignored.
30. See appendix 7.1. Rosefielde (1981, Table 4, p. 65) gives the same estimate.
31. According to the encyclopedia *Rossiya-SSR* (Solzhenitsyn, 1975a, p. 205).
32. Kravchenko (1946, p. 404).
33. Ibid., p. 405–6.
34. Solzhenitsyn (1975a, p. 221).
35. Medvedev (1979, p. 117).
36. Panin (1976, p. 66).
37. Solzhenitsyn (1978, p. 8).
38. Ibid., p. 10.
39. Tolstoy (1981, p. 283).
40. Fleischhauer and Pinkus (1986, p. 80).
41. Conquest (1970a, pp. 64–65).
42. Ibid., pp. 65–66; Pearson (1983, p. 194); Fleischhauer and Pinkus (1986, p. 87).
43. Sheehy and Nahaylo (1980, p. 19).
44. Kuper (1981, p. 145).
45. Nekrich (1978, p. 116).
46. Conquest (1970a, p. 102).
47. Ibid., p. 162.
48. Tolstoy (1981, pp. 261–2).
49. Misiunas and Taagepera (1983, p. 68).
50. Schoenberg (1970, p. 32).
51. Misiunas and Taagepera (1983, p. 70).
52. Quoted in Tolstoy (1981, pp. 267–68).
53. Ibid., p. 268.
54. Quoted in de Zayas (1979, p. 63).
55. Ibid., pp. 63–64.
56. McWhirter and McWhirter (1977, p. 435).
57. Conquest (1978, p. 26).
58. de Zayas (1979, p. 75).

59. Schimitzek (1966, p. 249n.6). All population figures are for 1939.
60. Peers (1979).
61. Tolstoy (1981, p. 269).
62. Hingley (1974, p. 363).
63. Ibid., p. 364.
64. Tolstoy (1981, p. 269).
65. Gluckstein (1952, p. 148); Kusnierz (1949, pp. 220–29).
66. Hingley (1974, p. 361).
67. Lane (1948, p. 53).
68. Kusnierz (1949, p. 229).
69. Ibid., p. 190.
70. Ibid., p. 191.
71. Quoted in Markham (1949, p. 509).
72. Ibid., p. 517.
73. Ibid., p. 410–11.
74. Tolstoy (1981, p. 267); Herling (1951, p. 143).
75. Nagy (1948, p. 60).
76. Herling (1951, p. 143); Tolstoy (1981, p. 267).
77. Tolstoy (1981, p. 267).
78. Nagy (1948, p. 104).
79. See appendix 7.1.
80. Schoenberg (1970, p. 18).
81. Schimitzek (1966, p. 316, n203).
82. de Zayas (1979, p. 203n31). This excludes 300,000 ethnic Germans who fled the Soviet Union and were subsequently forcefully repatriated by the Soviets and sent to labor camps.
83. See appendix 1.2.
84. See appendix 7.1.
85. *The World Almanac* (1988, p. 333).
86. Tolstoy (1981, p. 343). See also Tolstoy (1977, 1986), Elliott (1982), and Bethell (1974).
87. Quoted in Johnson (1983, p. 430); italics added.
88. Quoted in Elliott (1982, p. 192).
89. Tolstoy (1981, pp. 283–84).
90. Tolstoy (1979, p. 515).
91. Elliott (1982, p. 202).
92. Ibid.
93. Ibid.
94. Tolstoy (1979, p. 515).
95. Swianiewicz (1965, p. 44).
96. See appendix 1.2.
97. Conquest, et al. (1984, p. 36).
98. Small and Singer (1982, p. 91).
99. See, for example, Conquest (1970a) and Nekrich (1978).
100. Dyadkin (1983, p. 49); Tolstoy (1981, p. 280).
101. Schoenberg (1970, pp. 32–33).

102. (1982, p. 275).
103. Similar to this book on Soviet democide, this will be done in a book-length detailing of 20th-century democide.
104. (1965, p. 42).

8

15,613,000 Victims: Postwar and Stalin's Twilight Period, 1945–1953

> *We were wretched, and we could not rise above our wretchedness. Should this have been our dream—to perish so that those who looked unmoved on our destruction might survive? We could not accept it. No, we longed for the storm! [World War III]. . . . Romain Rolland's generation in their youth were depressed by the constant expectation of war, but our generation of prisoners was depressed by its absence. . . . World war might bring us either a speedier death (they might open fire from the watchtowers, poison our bread, or infect us with germs, German fashion), or it just might bring us freedom. In either case, deliverance would be much nearer than the end of a twentiy-five-year sentence.*
>
> —Solzhenitsyn

On 2 May 1945, Soviet forces captured Berlin. On 7 May, the German Provisional Government under Admiral Doennitz unconditionally surrendered; the next day the war in Europe was over. The Soviets then looked to the East and waited. Finally, three days after the first atomic bomb was dropped on Hiroshima, with Japan already defeated, the Soviet Union declared war and launched an invasion of Manchuria against the Japanese army. Five days later, on 14 August 1945, Japan surrendered. By the end of the month, the Soviets had occupied all of Manchuria and Sakhalin Island.

World War II was over. This erected a political boundary historians and students of international conflict will always note: a division between war and peace, between death and life for millions. But in Soviet history this boundary only shuts down one death machine, the most visible one of clashing armies that historians and journalists write about. To the other death machine—terror against "enemies of the people," social prophylaxis, purges, deportations, labor camps, and utopian campaigns—this historical boundary was nonexistent.

In Soviet-occupied Eastern Europe and Asia, the end of World War II may have been noted by booming cannons and celebrating soldiers, but little else. Terror, executions, and the deadly deportations continued unabated. Among those the Soviets deported to Siberia or other inhospitable regions from the Soviet-occupied countries of Europe were 50,000 East Germans,[1] 120,000 Hungarians,[2] 500,000 to 600,000 Balts (from 1945 to 1952),[3] 107,000 German-Rumanians,[4] 400,000 Japanese from Sakhalin,[5] over 850,000 Rumanian-Bessarabians and North Bukovians (from 1944 to 1949),[6] over 1,000,000 Rumanians from Moldavia (from 1950 to 1952),[7] over 150,000 Bulgarian peasant families,[8] almost 2,000,000 Czechs and Slovaks,[9] and 4,500,000 Poles in 1945 and after.[10] As before and during the war, "enemies of the people" were swept from the conquered territories into the Soviet labor camps to replace the millions who had died. To the camps and forced settlements,

> each convoy triumphantly brought in a fresh haul: Koreans, Mongols, Japanese from Sakhalin, Russian refugees and Chinese from Northern China, Persians, Armenians and Turks from the border districts, natives of all the occupied European countries, people from Eastern and Western Germany, members of the Western Occupation Forces in Berlin or Vienna who have fallen into the hands of the Russians, and sailors and fishermen seized during conflicts in Russian coastal waters. Finally, there are prisoners, sentenced as war criminals, from all the armies defeated in the Second World War.[11]

By this period it was no longer extraordinary that some of these lethal deportations were by quota. This was true of the 1949 deportations of the Baltic people, for example. A quota was given to each administrative-territorial unit. To meet the quota Soviet officials in the unit then drew up a list. If those on the list were not at home, then *others not on the list* were picked up.[12] From 200,000 to 456,000 Balts were thus deported[13] and tens of thousands, perhaps more than a hundred thousand, died as a consequence.

At least regarding the March 1949 deportation of 50,000 to 60,000 Estonians,[14] Taagepera raises the question of genocide:

> The swath cut by deportation was so wide that the issue of genocide ought to be considered . . . . Most Estonian deportees never returned, having largely perished. In the case of "kulaks," all members of a population group, identified through *past* socio-economic status, were deported, regardless of their individual *present* behavior. There was no legal way to leave the condemned social group. In the case of children, the guilt was hereditary. If destroying a social group entirely, with no consideration of personal behavior, is genocide, then the March 1949 deportation would seem to qualify.[15]

Of all the foreigners deported in this postwar period, probably about 1,329,000 were killed during the deportation or in their destination camps or settlements (see appendix 8.1). About a million were repatriated to their occupied home countries by 1947. Of the POWs captured by the Soviets, many were never returned. Some 1,150,000 German POWs alone vanished into the USSR, of whom only 9,628 were classified as war criminals.[16] The former prime minister of Rumania, General Nicolai Radescu, pointed out that even by 1949 at least 180,000 Rumanian POWs remained to be repatriated, and he believed a "great number" were by then probably dead.[17]

In some occupied areas, Soviet deportations and terror were not accepted without a fight. In the Baltic states, a large-scale resistance war against the Soviets continued well into the 1950s. Beginning in 1944 with the reoccupation of the Baltic states, the Forest Brothers, as the anti-Soviet freedom fighters called themselves, were organized in Lithuania, Latvia, and Estonia. In Lithuania alone, they numbered 30,000 to 40,000 fighters at their peak. For all three states, the ratio of the population involved was about the same as that of the Vietcong fighting the Americans and South Vietnam government forces during the Vietnam War.[18] Guerrilla casualties in Lithuania alone were about 20,000 (Soviet estimate) to 50,000,[19] but they killed about 4,000 to 13,000 Soviet collaborators and caused Soviet forces of repression about 20,000 (Soviet figure) to 80,000 (guerrilla figure) losses.[20]

In Poland a similar resistance war was waged by anti-Soviet Poles and remnants of the Home Army. From 1945 to 1948, about 20,000 were killed during the resistance, including 4,000 Soviet soldiers.

Many captured freedom fighters were executed; 50,000 were deported to Siberia.[21] Even in the Soviet Union itself, there was rebellion, particularly in the Ukraine. From 1945 into the 1950s, the Ukrainian Insurrection Army (UPA) fought against Soviet troops. In 1945 they had at least 5,000 to 10,000 freedom fighters, and their commander claimed a force of 200,000.[22] Whatever their number, Khrushchev said himself that thousands were lost in the struggle with Ukrainian nationalists.[23]

These were only side shows, however, and lacking Western aid and attention, these guerrillas were bound to be defeated. In the postwar years, the NKVD especially sought Nazi "collaborators" and "sympathizers" throughout former occupied Soviet territory. This was a massive and deadly purge in its own right, quite apart from the routine pursuit of "enemies of the people." "Collaborators" were given special attention and shown no mercy, regardless of their numbers.

According to calculations of the Institute for the Study of the History and Culture of the USSR in Munich, about 3,000,000 were sentenced for collaboration with the Nazis, even including civilian or military prisoners in Germany during the war.[24] But this does not include outright executions, which must have been considerable. For example, in an interview, Stalin told Mikolajczyk, a Polish leader, "that he had ordered the execution of 20,000 Ukrainians who had been collaborating with the Germans and later captured by the Red Army."[25] Lest this number pass too quickly through the mind, it is equal to the total battle-dead of Mussolini's Italo-Ethiopian War of 1935-36, for whose aggression the League of Nations imposed sanctions on Italy.[26]

Now, liquidating Nazi collaborators was one special interest. Another was eliminating ideological infection. During the war, political impurities had been introduced into the country not only by the Nazis, but also by friends and allies. The party worried about those "contaminated" by contact with American Lend-Lease officials, diplomats, guards, military observers, and reporters. They feared that Westerners and their "propaganda" had created soft, rotten spots in the body politic. With the war now past, the satellization of Eastern Europe well in progress, and the country again self-quarantined, the party gave particular attention to excising these rotten parts. Wartime contact with foreigners by ordinary citizens was a ticket to a labor camp.

Then there was the problem of maintaining party purity and control. Postwar purges were certainly necessary, at least from the view of

Stalin at the top. And such were carried out. There was the Leningrad Purge in 1949, through which possibly 2,000 or more party members were murdered.[27] The number may even be many times this, given that Levytsky calls this purge the "darkest chapter in post-war soviet history."[28] Reminiscent of the Great Terror, the arrests included every main official in the Leningrad Province and City party secretariats, and even reached down into the town councils and trade union organizations.[29] In 1951, there was also a purge in Georgia of Beria's supporters. It was directed against Mingrelians, Beria's Georgian ethnic group.[30] Of those purged, thousands were murdered.[31] In all such purges throughout 1948-49, hundreds of thousands must have been sentenced to the camps, including the close relatives of those purged— wives sometimes receiving twenty-five years.[32]

All this seems hardly new, but there was a fresh twist to these purges and the general terror. Jews became specific targets. About 1947, for example, the party launched the Crimea Purge, which involved wide-scale pogroms and the murder of Jewish intellectuals, and which lasted until Stalin's death. Generally, Jews in especially powerful positions were targeted.[33]

Anti-Jewish propaganda and purges were on the upsurge in the years before Stalin's death and large-scale preparations were being made to deport all Jews to camps or remote resettlements (the party's "final solution"). Lists of Jews to be deported from central cities had been drawn up; those who remained would have yellow stars sewn on their sleeves. A pamphlet had been published, but not yet distributed, titled "Why Jews Must Be Resettled from the Industrial Regions of the Country."[34]

The alleged Jewish doctor's plot revealed in January 1953 was part of this. Among others, a number of Kremlin physicians responsible for treating Stalin and other high party men were arrested, including nine Jewish doctors,[35] for plotting to assassinate party leaders.[36] Stalin died before this "Zionist plot" was fully developed and the associated purge and executions worked out, but it did result in a countrywide panic against Jewish doctors, many of whom were driven out of hospitals.[37] After Stalin's death the plan to deport Jews was canceled.

Day by day, routine interrogations, executions, deportations of citizens, and sentences to forced labor—that is, common terror— continued until Stalin's death in March 1953. Deportations of Soviet nations and other citizens also took place after the war. About 1949, perhaps over 20,000 Armenians were deported,[38] about 40,000 Caucasian Greeks in 1947,[39] and perhaps another 100,000 ethnic Greeks in 1949.[40] Some 80,000 Georgian Muslims were deported in 1947[41] and possibly up to 2,000,000 Western Ukrainians from 1944 to the 1950s.[42] Many were trucked to labor camps.

The death rate in the camps throughout this period remained high. At general labor, such as timber-cutting and mining, new inmates still could not expect to survive three or four years, and their treatment in the camps was not much better than during the bad years of the war. Note that of the 3,000 people arrested in Kursk in 1943 and sent to camps, no more than 60 were alive in 1951—98 percent were killed.[43]

Besides the deadly camp conditions, inmates faced another dangerous risk that became evident in the early years of the war. When camp authorities were confronted by the loss of control over prisoners, either because of the approach of Nazi forces during the war or through natural disaster, prisoners were massacred en masse. For example, in 1949 there was an earthquake at Ashkhabad that demolished the local camp. The camp was then surrounded by the militia, who "fired on all survivors. Out of 2,800, thirty-four came out."[44]

With all the deportations, terror, purges, and raw killing during Soviet history, it is easy to slide over this bizarre example of inhumanity. But imagine this ruined camp after the earthquake. Dazed prisoners standing about, some milling in fear, the hurt crying for help, some lying on the ground or sitting on ruins in shock, groups of prisoners beginning to dig for survivors in the ruins, others helping the injured to open areas, and so on. We all have seen such pictures on television after major earthquakes have occurred in inhabited areas. Yet, were these survivors helped? No, they were surrounded by armed men, who systematically fired upon them until nearly all were dead.

New waves of prisoners flowed into the camps to replace these and other dead—perhaps a peasant who had taken an ear of corn from a collective's field (stealing from the people), a worker who had been absent from his job too often (sabotage), a grocer who had wrapped a fish in a newspaper showing Stalin's picture (anti-Soviet behavior) or a girl who had held hands with a foreigner (treason). Some real examples:

> A tailor laying aside his needle stuck it into a newspaper on the wall so it wouldn't get lost and happened to stick it in the eye of a portrait of

Kaganovich. A customer observed this. . . . 10 years (terrorism).

A saleswoman accepting merchandise from a forwarder noted it down on a sheet of newspaper. There was no other paper. The number of pieces of soap happened to fall on the forehead of Comrad Stalin. . . . 10 years.

A tractor driver. . . . lines his thin shoes for warmth with a pamphlet about the candidate for elections to the Supreme Soviet . . . .— Counter-Revolutionary Agitation—10 years. . . .

A sailor sold an Englishman a "Katyusha" cigarette lighter—a wick in a piece of pipe with a striking wheel—as a souvenir for one pound sterling. Subversion of the Motherland's dignity—10 years.

A shepherd in a fit of anger swore at a cow for not obeying: "You collective-farm wh——!" . . . a term [in camp]. . . .

A *deaf and dumb* carpenter . . . was laying the floors in a club. Everything had been removed from a big hall, and there was no nail or hook anywhere. While he was working, he hung his jacket and his service cap on a bust of Lenin. Someone came in and saw it. . . . 10 years [for counterrevolutionary agitation] . . .[45]

[T]he historian Ky——tsev received twenty-five years for committing ideological errors in his book.[46]

All are examples of people who had *done something. Being something* was also as much a basis for a camp sentence. When the historian Ky——tsev got twenty-five years for his ideological errors,

> shouldn't his wife get her sentence too? Ten years. But why leave out his old mother, aged seventy-five, and his sixteen-year old daughter? Both got sentences for failure to inform on him. And all four were sent off to different camps without the right to correspond with one another.[47]

During 1948 to 1950, just "belonging to a Baptist community could mean twenty to twenty-five years in a camp."[48] Having had bourgoisie parents, a grandfather in the White armies during the civil war, or a purged son was sufficient to be arrested and sent to the camps. But this was nothing new. And then there were those few who carried the stigma of having been camp inmates, who had managed to survive their sentence, who somehow avoided resentencing, and who got released. They were all rearrested around 1947 to 1948.[49]

But also *doing or being nothing* still did not keep one out of the camps, as when good citizens were rounded up to meet an arrest quota. Clearly, as in previous periods, Soviet life continued to be a roulette wheel.

The total population of the camps hardly changed much in numbers after the war. Dallin and Nicolaevsky claimed that in "Russia itself" estimates of forced laborers reached as high as 30,000,000.[50] Andics says the largest number of forced laborers in the camps was nearly 14,000,000 at the end of the war.[51] Krasnov mentions a camp population in 1949 of 20,000,000, and says that calculations at the time counted 10,000,000 political prisoners in seven severe regime-camp systems.[52] As shown in appendix 8.1, taking into account all these and lower estimates for this period, the labor camps probably reached a population of 12,000,000 in 1948 to 1950, dropping to 10,000,000 in the years just before Stalin's death.

Given this variation in camp population, the estimated number killed in either transit to or in the camps themselves for this eight-year period ranges from a low of 3,295,000 to a high of 29,032,000. A prudent estimate is that overall 11,388,000 were murdered, including 960,000 foreigners.

Some of the prisoners died from medical experiments done on them. Stalin, like Hitler, saw the advantage of exploiting expendable prisoners for medical experiments:

> In 1946 a laboratory was opened in the Lubianka known as "The Chamber." There scientists practiced ghastly experiments on prisoners, employing drugs and poisons whose effects they wished to establish. The authorities may have borrowed the idea from what they had learned of SS practices in liberated Germany. "The Chamber" itself was abolished in 1953, but today torture in psychiatric hospitals remains a favoured Soviet penal measure.[53]

Those sent to the camps before the war were largely peasants and workers, with fewer numbers of party officials, bureaucrats, and intellectuals. But with the war, a new type of prisoner entered the camps. This was the former military officer or partisan. Used to deadly combat, familiar with weapons and tactics, brave and willing to take deadly risks, he was a volatile catalyst in camps of angry men full of hate for the regime, with little but slow death to look forward to, and even hoping for a nuclear war to free them.[54] (According to A. Knyazhynsky, "The prisoners believed that the democratic countries, after the destruction of brutal German imperialism, would wage war on the enemy that was even more dangerous than national socialism. . . .")[55] They were eager followers who sought leaders among these former officers or partisans.

In the late 1940s and early 1950s, demonstrations and rebellions broke out in a number of camps. In the summer of 1953 there were strikes in "all the camps."[56] In some camps the prisoners wrested control from the guards, but soon the Red Army appeared with tanks and cannons and destroyed the camps, rebels, and any other prisoners in the vicinity. Waves of strikes aimed at improving conditions swept the camps in the years 1953-55. The resulting repression was sometimes very bloody, with many prisoners being massacred. In Kinguir, for example, as a result of a strike more than 500 prisoners — Ukrainian men and women — were slaughtered in one night.[57]

A remarkable rebellion broke out in the Pechora camps in 1948. Led by a former regimental commander at Stalingrad, a Hero of the Soviet Union who had been arrested and sent to camp, it eventually involved around 60,000 inmates, including some guards. Virtually all were massacred by air force planes as they marched across flat, treeless tundra, toward the forests of the Northern Urals.[58] Some thought at first the planes had come from the West to help them.

It is worth dwelling for a moment on the number of prisoners who may have been killed in this rebellion, whether 40,000, 50,000, or around 60,000 (only 40 of those wounded survived, all were condemned to death, a few were amnestied).[59] It exceeds those killed in battle during the Yom Kippur War between Israel and her neighbors (16,401 dead), the Sino-Vietnamese War of 1979 between China and Vietnam (21,000 dead), or the Second Kashmir War of 1965 between India and Pakistan (6,800 dead).[60] All these wars are well-known by historians and students of war. Ignorance of them by a Western political scientist would suggest poor study and scholarship. Yet, very few know about the death of these tens of thousands of brave men in their cry for freedom from the slavery of the camps. This huge rebellion is not even tallied in Small and Singer's *Resort to Arms*,[61] our most systematically gathered list of civil wars and rebellions, even though this rebellion is far larger than the greater number of civil wars and rebellions they list.

Although few survived this and other rebellions, they were not in vain. They showed that in their size and composition, the camps were an increasing danger to the party. They were, as the camp strikes and rebellions had shown, huge, unstable centers of virulent political opposition. Moreover, the economic value of the inmate's labor compared to the economic cost of the camps was increasingly suspect. After Stalin's death, for these if not for humanitarian reasons, the camp population began to be reduced and some camps eliminated, while overall camp conditions were improved. In a decade or so, the camp death rate may have approached that in nearby "free" settlements (still very high, by the standards of European Russia).

Besides the usual terror, camps, and the rest, the citizens faced another party-made famine during 1946–47—grain was exported abroad throughout the famine and no foreign aid was requested. Said Khrushchev: "Their [Stalin and Molotov's] method was like this: they sold grain abroad, while in some regions people were swollen with hunger and even dying for lack of bread."[62] The party had forced peasants to turn over "excessive amounts of grain, sometimes not even leaving enough for seed."[63] Grain reserves were emptied by expropriation, but even then the party still demanded millions of tons of grain, even in the midst of drought. Peasants implored local and central government officials for help. Khrushchev, then first party secretary in the Ukraine, finally wrote Stalin asking for authorization to "set up a temporary rationing system and retain some agricultural produce to feed the rural population. Stalin crudely rejected the request in a reply sent by telegram."[64] Peasants starved to death, while even resorting to cannibalism.[65] Perhaps as many as 1,000,000 died.[66]

The total murdered from purges, famine (while the party's fault and practical intention, I conservatively pin only half the toll on it), the usual terror, deportations and camps, is from 5,868,000 to 35,906,000 human beings—probably about 15,613,000, as shown in figure 8.1. Foreigners made up about 3,165,000 of this total.

The estimates themselves are given in table 8.1, and are from appendix 8.1. Figure 8.2 plots the components so that they may be compared to previous periods. As can be seen, most of the deaths in this period are due to the camps, a killing machine that ground up more human beings in this twilight period than ever before.

Figure 8.3 compares this period's total democide and annual democide rate to previous periods. Almost nine people per thousand were killed per year, an annual death rate thirty-three times that for motor vehicle accidents (including pedestrians) in the United States.[67]

In estimating the death toll under Stalin, analysts usually focus on the 1930s. Obviously, it was the most dramatic bloodbath of modern times, what with collectivization and the Great Terror. The postwar Stalin period is usually an afterthought. Even such an astute historian as Paul Johnson can misgauge these numbers when he says of Stalin's

FIGURE 8.1
Range in Postwar II Democide Estimates*

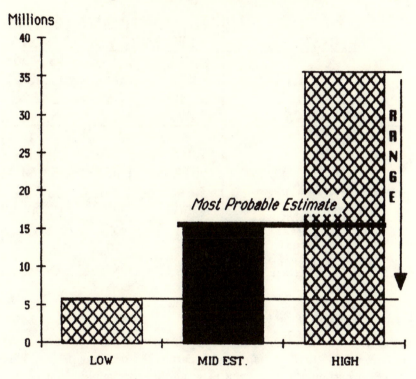

*From appendix 8.1

postwar period that "500,000 people were judicially murdered (or just murdered) by the state. . . ."[68] As we have seen, even the minimum number for this twilight period of Stalinism is 5,868,000.

Appendix 8.1

After the end of the war, foreign deportations, terror, and guerrilla warfare against soviet occupation continued into this period without a pause. Thus, as mentioned in the previous appendix, there is some artificiality in ending one period at 1945 and beginning the other with 1946. For example, this results in some events that took place over the

TABLE 8.1
Postwar and Stalin's Twilight Period Democide

ASPECTS*	DEAD ESTIMATES (000)		
	LOW	MID EST.	HIGH
DEMOCIDE	**5,868**	**15,613**	**35,906**
PERIOD RATE	2.27%	7.07%	17.45%
ANNUAL RATE	0.28%	0.88%	2.18%
FOREIGNERS	1,877	3,165	5,171
COMPONENTS			
TERROR	1,160	1,376	1,591
CAMP/TRANSIT	819	1,557	3,131
DEPORTATION	3,640	12,348	30,684
FAMINE	250	333	500
OTHER KILLED	311	423	667
WAR/REBELLION	61	90	167
FAMINE/DISEASE	250	333	500

*From appendix 8.1. Rates for citizens.

years 1944 to 1948 being included in this period and some events for the years 1945 to 1946 being made part of the previous period. This makes it particularly important to watch out for double-counting between the two periods.

Two other major problems exist in the estimates. First, after Germany's defeat, many millions of ethnic Germans were uprooted and expelled from Poland, Czechoslovakia, Rumania, and other East European nations, to the Eastern and particularly Western German occupation zones. Millions of Germans died as a result. Since the Eastern European nations involved were under Soviet domination, do the Soviets bear the major responsibility for these deaths? In the early postwar years, the Soviets did not exercise complete control over Eastern Europe, especially Poland and Czechoslovakia, the major expelling countries. And the German expulsions were clearly directed and managed by the East European governments involved. Unless there is evidence to the contrary, or the deportations were to the Soviet Union, the expelling countries are assigned the responsibility for the German dead.

FIGURE 8.2
Democide Components for Seven Periods*

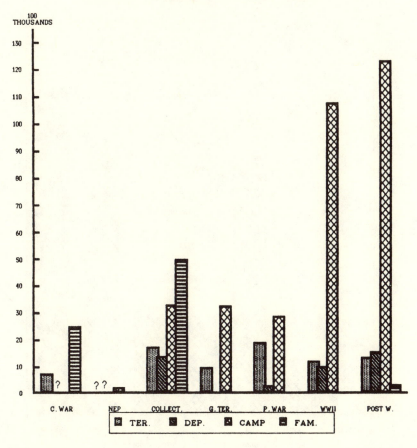

*From tables 2.1– 8.1

A second problem concerns the postwar purges and terror by Eastern European governments against their own populations. Since these governments were dominated by the Soviet Union, to what extent are these the resulting deaths to be counted as Soviet democide? When killing in Eastern Europe was done by Soviet forces or secret police, or the deaths were due to deportations to the Soviet Union, surely they should be counted as Soviet democide. All other deaths, such as those in labor camps ostensibly set up by Eastern European governments or in apparently indigenous purges and terror will be treated as the re-

FIGURE 8.3
Soviet Democide and Annual Rate by Period*

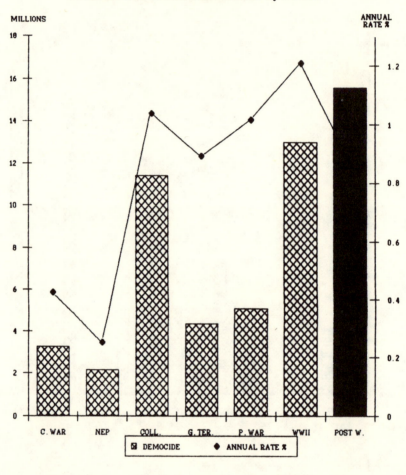

*From tables 2.1– 8.1

sponsibility of the governments allegedly involved. This may absolve the Soviets of much democide, but there is no way around it here without making assumptions that go beyond the references. In any case, this appears the most conservative approach.

With all this as qualification, table 8A presents estimates of Soviet democide during this period. Consider first the deportations of Soviet nations and ethnic groups (lines 9 to 23). There is an ambiguity in

TABLE 8A
15,613,000 Victims during the Postwar and Stalin's Twilight Period:
Soviet Murder: Sources, Calculations, and Estimates*

LINE	EVENT/PROCESS/STRUCTURE/EPISODE	BEGIN YEAR	M	END YEAR	M	DEAD ESTIMATES(000)			SOURCE	NOTES
						LOW	MID	HIGH		
	FAMINE									
1										
2	famine	1946		1947				2	Sorlin,68,201	"The Soviets now admit that thousands of people starved to death."
3	famine	1947					1,000		Heller & Nekrich,86,469	Stalin has major responsibility.
4	Ukraine/Byelorussia famine	1947						?	Conquest,86,335	mainly Ukraine/Byelorussia, while Stalin exported grain
5	*CONSOLIDATED FAMINE DEAD*	1946		1947		500	665	1,000		
6										
7	*DEPORTED POPULATIONS:DEAD*									
8	SOVIET NATIONS/ETHNIC GROUPS									
9	Armenians	1949c.				30			Nekrich,78,105	
10	Baltic/Ukraine/Byelorussian Finns	1945		1946c.			?		Forced Labor,52,32	
11	Greek-Soviets	1947c.					?		Nekrich,78,105	to Siberia
12	Greek-Soviets	1949		?			100		Bousceren,63,48	
13	Greeks (Caucasion)	1947					40		Hingley,70,210	
14	Greeks (Caucasion)	1947					40		Conquest,70s,111	mainly deported to Kazakhstan.
15	Georgian Muslims	1947					80		Nekrich,78,104	
16	Kurds/Khemshins	1940s					?		Nekrich,78,104	
17	Poles/Balts/Soviets	930s?		1955			8,000		Schoenberg,70,10	deported/resettled/interned
18	Ukrainians (Western)	1944		1950s				2,000	Conquest,86,334	arrested/exiled/deported, most of deported were innocent peasants
19	Ukrainians (Western)	1946		1950			300		Heller & Nekrich,86,456	
20	Ukrainians/Byelorussians	1944		1950			300		Heller & Nekrich,86,745	"political unreliable" and "alien class" elements from newly annexed western parts
21	Ukrainians/Byelorussians/Moldavians	1945		?			?		Heller & Nekrich,86,469	to Siberia
22	Ukrainians/Russians	1945		?			500		Bousceren,63,48	
23	CONSOLIDATED DEPORTED	1946		1953		1,250	1,750	2,500		(deportation of 500 Ukrainians assumed counted
24										in the million for previous period. Appendix 71, line 124]
25										
26	CALCULATED NATIONS/ETHNIC DEAD	1946		1953		113	228	538		[only for 50% assumed resettled; other 50% assumed picked up by camp/forced labor figures, below]
27										
28	FOREIGNERS DEPORTED									
29	ESTONIANS									
30	Estonians deported	1944		1946		55			Taagepera,80,381	From A Purre
31	Estonians deported	1944		1952			124		Mass Deportations,81,13	
32	Estonians deported	1949				50		60	Taagepera,80,393	
33	Estonians deported	1949					30		Swianiewicz,65,42	based on diverse estimates
34	Estonians deported	1949	12				60		Misiunas & Taagepera,83,96	
35	Estonians deported	1940		1980			140		Vizulis,85,105	
36	CONSOLIDATED DEPORTED	1944		1953		50	60	100		
37										
38	LATVIANS									
39	Latvians deported	1944		1952			136		Mass Deportations,81,13	
40	Latvians deported	1949	12			50			Misiunas & Taagepera,83,96	
41	Latvians deported	1940		1980			150		Vizulis,85,105	
42	Latvians deported	1945c.					34		Swianiewicz,65,42	
43	CONSOLIDATED DEPORTED	1944		1953		50	84	100		

TABLE 8A (continued)

#	Category	From	To	Number (000s)	Source	Remarks
44	**LITHUANIANS**					
45	Balts Lithuanians	1944	1952	245	Mass Deportations,81,18	based on census.
46	Balts Lithuanians	1945	1950	300	Remeikis,80,42	deported/killed
47	Balts Lithuanians	1947 12:	1949 7c	220	Misiunas & Taagepera,83,96	prisoners deported.
48	Balts Lithuanians	1945c.		38	Swianiewicz,65,42	general estimates.
49	Balts Lithuanians	1940		300	Vizulis,85,105	natives, deported to Siberia and similar uninhabitable or inhospitable places, about half Lithuanians.
50	Balts Lithuanians		1953			
51	CONSOLIDATED DEPORTED	1944		147 / 220 / 300		
52						
53	**BALTS OVERALL**					
54	Balts deported	1940	1951	2,000	Schmid,85,21	
55	Balts deported	1940	1953	600	Schmid,85,21	
56	Balts deported	1940	?	600	These Names,82,VI	
57	Balts deported	1941	1949	500	Schmid,85,21	
58	Balts deported	1941	1951	500	Vardys,67,58n4	
59	Balts deported	1944	1946	266	Misiunas & Taagepera,83,70	
60	Balts deported	1945	1951	600	Shtromas,86,193	
61						
62	Balts deported	1945	1952	500	Mass Deportations,81,17	to Siberia
63	Balts deported	1945	?	150	Bouscaren,63,48	
64	Balts deported	1946 7	1949 6	550	Forced Labor,52,32	
65	Balts deported	1949		200 … 456	Shtromas,86,212n33	from diverse estimates.
66	CONSOLIDATED DEPORTED	1944		335 / 500 / 600		
67	SUM BALTS DEPORTED	1944		247 / 364 / 500	[sum of lines 36, 43, and 51]	
68	AVERAGE BALTS DEPORTED	1944		291 / 432 / 550	[average of lines 66 and 67]	
69	CALCULATED DEAD	1944		26 / 56 / 118	[only for 50% assumed resettled; other 50% assumed picked up by camp/forced labor figures, below]	
70						
71	Balts deported dead	1944	?	100 / 78	Misiunas & Taagepera,83,100	deported that died of cold and hunger.
72	CONSOLIDATED BALTS DEAD	1944		63 / 78 / 118	[low and mid-estimates are the average of those of line 69 with the low of line 71]	
73						
74	**GERMANS**					
75	Germans deported	1945	1947	?	Netti,51,72	large numbers of prisoners deported from time to time.
76	Germans deported	1945	?	40	Possony,75,25	politicals.
77	Germans deported	1946	1962c	30 / 50	Stewart-Smith,64,368	from East Germany.
78	CONSOLIDATED DEPORTED	1946	1953	30 / 40 / 50	[some deportations in 1945 assumed counted in the previous period]	
79	CALCULATED DEAD	1946	1953	3 / 5 / 11	[only for 50% assumed resettled; other 50% assumed picked up by camp/forced labor figures, below]	
80						
81	German deported dead	1945	?	100 / 125	de Zayas,79,70,204	among deported Reich-Germans, 100,000-125,000 deed a conservative estimate
82						
83	AVERAGE GERMAN DEAD	1946	1953	51 / 65 / 68	[average of lines 79 and 83, high is the average of the high estimate of line 79 and the mid-estimate of line 81]	
84						
85	**HUNGARIANS**					
86	Hungarian peasants deported	1945	?	75	Bouscaren,63,48	peasants from southern frontier region; by context, to the USSR.
87	Hungarians deported	1945	?	120	Bouscaren,63,48	to Siberia
88	Hungarians deported	1945	?	180	Dushnyck,75,412	POWs and civilian deportees still held as of 1960.
89	Hungarians deported	1951 3		17	Stowe,51,177	from Uzhorod.
90						
91	CONSOLIDATED DEPORTED	1953		120 / 180 / 234	[1945 deportations assumed picked up in previous period]	
92	CALCULATED DEAD	1946	1953	11 / 23 / 50	[only for 50% assumed resettled; other 50% assumed picked up by camp/forced labor figures, below]	

TABLE 8A (continued)

Line	Category	From	To	1944	1948		Source	Notes
93	**RUMANIANS**							
94	Rumanians	1944		240			Herling,51,112	excludes Bessarabians/Bukovinians; includes Rumanian-Germans, from former Prime Minister Radescu
95								
96	Rumanians	1950	1952	1,000			Paceba,87,27	
97		1944	1949	850			Herling,51,113	from former Prime Minister Radescu
98	Roman-Bessarab'n Bukovinians	1946	1953	1,148	1,368	1,628		[1944-45 deportations assumed picked up in previous period]
99					180	350		[only for 50% assumed resettled; other 50% assumed picked up by camp/forced labor figures, below]
100	CALCULATED DEAD	1946	1953		103	350		
101	**BULGARIANS**							
102	Bulgarian peasants deportations	1944	1951	750	900		Stowe,51,123	[R.J Rummel calculation based on deportation of over 150 thousand peasant families (from Michael Padev) and assuming a low of 5 or high of 6 family members].
103								
104								by context to the USSR.
105	Bulgarian peasants deportations	1951		40			Stowe,51,123	
106	CONSOLIDATED DEPORTED	1944	1953	750	790	900		
107	CALCULATED DEAD	1944	1953	68	103	194		[only for 50% assumed resettled; other 50% assumed picked up by camp/forced labor figures, below]
108								
109	**CZECHS**							
110	Czechs deported	1952	?			50	Stewart-Smith,64,145	to labor camps in Czech and USSR.
111	Czechs/Slovacs deported	1945		1,340	2,000	2,050	Bouscaren,63,48	to Siberia
112	CONSOLIDATED DEPORTED	1945	1953	1,340	2,000	2,050		[only for 50% assumed resettled; other 50%
113	CALCULATED DEAD	1945	1953	121	260	441		assumed picked up by camp/forced labor figures, below]
114								
115	**POLES**							
116	Poles deported	1945	1948		50		Schmid,85,3	captured resistance fighters.
117	Poles deported	1945	?		4,500		Bouscaren,63,48	to Siberia
118		1946	1953	3,015	4,500	5,985		[50,000 assumed counted in previous period for 1945]
119	CONSOLIDATED DEPORTED	1946	1953	3,015	4,500	5,985		[only for 50% assumed resettled; other 50%
120	CALCULATED DEAD	1946	1953	271	585	1,287		assumed picked up by camp/forced labor figures, below]
121	**MHOLDAVIANS**							
122	Moldavians deported	?	1955	200		400	Dima,82,46	
123	CONSOLIDATED DEPORTED	1946	1955	200	266			
124	SUM CALCULATED DEAD	1946	1955	18	35	86		[only for 50% assumed resettled; other 50% assumed picked up by camp/forced labor figures, below]
125								
126	**FOREIGN DEPORTED DEAD**							
127	SUM DEPORTED	1946	1953	6,894	9,596	11,797		[sum of lines 68, 78, 90, 98, 105, 112, 118, and 123]
128	TOTAL CALCULATED DEAD	1946	1953	706	1,329	2,593		[sum of lines 72, 83, 91, 99, 107, 113, 119, and 124]
129								
130	*TERROR AND REPRESSION DEAD*							
131	*OCCUPIED STATES/TERRITORIES DEAD*							
132	Bulgarians	1944	9 1945 [3]		2		Gluckstein,52,135-6	Soviet conducted purge.
133	Bulgarians	1945	?		20		Johnson,83,437	"blootbath", from Maynard Barnes.
134	Germans	1945			350		de Zayas,79,70,204n36	Reich or ethnic Germans disappeared, from census.
135	Moldavian-Rumanians	1944	1959	100	200		Dima,82,74	
136	Poles	?	19477		936		Bouscaren,63,48	270,000 "perished"; another 666,000 unaccounted for border regions, [R. J Rummel contextual estimate]; 100,000
137	Yugoslavs	1951			10		Stowe,51,179	ethnics evicted, including also from major Hungarian, Rumanian, and Polish cities; many disappeared into USSR.
138								
139	Baits	1946	?	?	?			
140	Rumania	1946	?	?	?			
141								

TABLE 8A (continued)

#	Category	From	To	Est. 1	Est. 2	Est. 3	Source	Notes
142	Hungary	1946	?	?				
143	Japanese	1946	?	?				
144	N Koreans	1946	?	?				
145	Czechs	1946	?	?				
146	*CONSOLIDATED FOREIGN DEAD*	1946		826	876	926		[all Germans, 270,000 Poles, assumed counted in previous period]
147								
148	**DOMESTIC**							
149	Crimea Affair	1947c.	1953	?			Levytsky,72,193-7	wide-scale pogroms and killing of Jewish intellectuals
150	Georgia Affair	1951	?				Hingley,74,404	local purge of Beria supporters. [Rummel estimate from context]
151	Leningrad Affair	1949		2			Levytsky,72,190-3	"darkest chapter in post-war Soviet history."
152	Leningrad Affair	1949		2			Hingley,74,403	
153	purge	1948	?				Levytsky,72,188,190	Stalin Party purge; "bloody"
154	purge	1940	19517	1,000			Stewart-Smith,64,222	[half assumed for 1946-1953 period]
155	purges	1945	1953	500			Johnson,83,456	"murdered", judicially or otherwise
156	*CONSOLIDATED DEAD*	1946	1953	334	500	665		
157								
158	*REBELLION DEAD*							
159	*FOREIGN (SOVIET DEAD)*							
160	Polish resistance	1945	1948	4			Schmid,85,3	Soviet soldiers; 20,000 dead overall.
161	Baltic State's guerrilla war	1952		25	30		Mass Deportations,81,20-1	from context, these are assumed partisans
162	Lithuanian guerrilla war	1944	1952	20			Misiunas & Taagepera,83,278	"repression troops"; guerrilla estimate.
163	Lithuanian guerrilla war	1944	1952	80			Misiunas & Taagepera,83,278	"repression troops"; Soviet estimate
164	Lithuanian guerrilla war	1945	1955	50			Misiunas & Taagepera,83,278	losses on both sides, includes executions.
165	Lithuanian guerrilla war	1944	1948	20			Tolstoy,81,354	Soviet troops, from a Soviet historian.
166	Lithuanian guerrilla war	1945	1952	20			Shtromas,86,192	Soviet troops, from high communist official
167	Lithuanian guerrilla war	1944	?	20	30		Schmid,85,20-1	partisans killed; "comparable number"
168								of Soviets and Lithuanian collaborators killed.
169	Estonian guerrilla war	1945	1955	15			Misiunas & Taagepera,83,278	losses on both sides, includes executions
170	Latvian guerrilla war	1945	1955	25			Misiunas & Taagepera,83,278	losses on both sides, includes executions.
171	*CONSOLIDATED SOVIET DEAD*	1944	1955	29	40	100		
172								
173	**DOMESTIC**							
174	Vorkuta uprisers	1948		60			Roeder,58,22	killed as a result of the Vorkuta uprising among camp inmates.
175	Vorkuta uprisers	1948		30			Swianiewicz,65,47	most of about 60,000 massacred.
176	Ukrainian guerrilla war	1945	?				Tolstoy,81,354	Khrushchev says thousands lost.
177	Ukrainian guerrilla war	1944	?	2			Conquest,86,334	thousands shot.
178	Ukrainian guerrilla war	1944	1946	2			Stewart-Smith,64,127	5,000-10,000 guerrillas in 1945,
179	*CONSOLIDATED DEAD*	1944	1948	32	50	67		commander says 200,000 in 1944-46.
180								
181	*CAMP/FORCED LABOR POPULATION/DEAD*							
182	1946 POPULATION/DEAD							
183	forced laborers	1946c.		30,000			Dallin & Nicolaevsky,47,84	prisoners, the high of estimates "in Russia"
184	forced labor camps	1945	1946	14,000			Andics,69,105	largest number; at end of WWII.
185	convicts/exiles/post-war deportees	1945	?	40,000			Roeder,58,197	estimate generally accepted in the camps.
186	Germans	1946		3,000			Nickerson,47,223	prisoners being held (POWs?)
187	*CONSOLIDATED CAMP POPULATION*	1946		7,000	10,000	14,000		
188	*CALCULATED CAMP DEAD*	1946		700	2,000	3,920		
189								

TABLE 8A (continued)

	Category	Year	Year	Low	Mid	High	Source	Notes
190	**1947 POPULATION/DEAD**							
191	forced labor camps	1947		7,000		15,000	Stewart-Smith,64,135	
192	CONSOLIDATED CAMP POPULATION	1947		7,000	10,000	15,000		[mid-estimate assumed same as 1946]
193	CALCULATED CAMP DEAD	1947		700	2,000	4,200		
194								
195	**1948 POPULATION/DEAD**							
196	camps	1948			12,000		Conquest,68,531	from NKVD functionaries
197	forced labor	1948			10,000		Swianiewicz,65,44	from British government
198	forced labor camps	1948			20,000		Chyz,62,96	deportees; 20% women.
199	forced laborer	1948			17,000		Kosyk,62,17	from British Member of Parliament Stokes.
200	prisoners	1948		12,000	19,000		Kosyk,62,17,79	low from NKVD functionaries, mid-estimate for camps
201	CONSOLIDATED CAMP POPULATION	1948		10,000	12,000	20,000		
202	CALCULATED CAMP DEAD	1948		1,000	2,400	5,600		
203								
204	**1949 POPULATION/DEAD**							
205	camps	1948	1949		5,000		Elliot,72,43–4	added to camps.
206	camps	1949			13,000		Kosyk,62,17	from a member of the American government.
207	camps	1949			20,000		Krasnov,60,182–5	10 million political prisoners in severe regime camps.
208	CONSOLIDATED CAMP POPULATION	1949		10,000	12,000	20,000		(low assumed the same as for the previous year)
209	CALCULATED CAMP DEAD	1949		1,000	2,400	5,600		
210								
211	**1950 POPULATION/DEAD**							
212	camps	1950	1952	12,000		14,000	Conquest,78,223	probable maximum ever reached
213	camps	1950		8,000	12,000	20,000	Levytsky,72,184	concentration camps
214	forced labor	1950			10,000		Heller & Nekrich,86,493	British government estimate from S Swianiewicz.
215	Hungarian prisoners	1950			50		Stowe,51,176	to forced labor camps
216	prisoners	1950			15,000		Kosyk,62,17	from a source closely connected to the
217								Organization of Ukrainian Nationalists
218	Rumenian POWs	1950			230		Swianiewicz,65,43	doing forced labor in camps
219	CONSOLIDATED CAMP POPULATION	1950		8,000	12,000	20,000		
220	CALCULATED CAMP DEAD	1950		600	2,400	5,600		
221								
222	**1951 POPULATION/DEAD**							
223	prisoners	1950	1951		15,000		Kosyk,62,16	from Joseph Scholmer
224	prisoners	1951			10,000		Kosyk,62,17	from Israeli journalist and former camp inmate.
225	prisoners	1951		12,000	16,000	17,000	Kosyk,62,17,79	low from V. Andreyev, former camp inspector; mid-estimate
226								for camps, high from G. Yershov, former colonel of the Red Army
227								and post–WWII commandant of the repatriation camps
228	CONSOLIDATED CAMP POPULATION	1951		10,000	12,000	17,000		
229	CALCULATED CAMP DEAD	1951		1,000	2,400	4,760		
230								
231	**1952 POPULATION/DEAD**							
232	prisoners	1951	1952		20,000		Kosyk,62,17	
233	forced laborers	1952		4,000	10,000		Stewart-Smith,64,146	
234	CONSOLIDATED CAMP POPULATION	1952		4,000	10,000	20,000		
235	CALCULATED CAMP DEAD	1952		400	2,000	5,600		
236								
237	**1953 POPULATION/DEAD**							
238	camps	1953		15,000		20,000	Floyd,58,xiii	from O.C.Pfeiffer

TABLE 8A (continued)

Line	Item	Year	Year 2	Val 1	Val 2	Val 3	Source / Notes
239	camps	1953				12,000	Reddaway,73,1 — almost certainly "at least" this number.
240	camps	1953				10,000	Roeder,58,27 — katorzhniks. [R. J. Rummel estimate based on the context]
241	forced labor camps	1950	1954	3,000		6,000	Dyadkin,83,60 — from census, depending on death rate.
242	CONSOLIDATED CAMP POPULATION	1953		3,000	10,000	20,000	
243	CALCULATED CAMP DEAD	1953		300	2,000	5,600	
244							
245	OVERALL CAMP/FORCED LABOR DEAD						
	DEAD ESTIMATES						
246	camp dead	1945				8,500	Kosyk,62,79
247	camp dead	1946				6,000	Panin,76,93n
248	camp dead	1948				4,500	Kosyk,62,79
249	camp dead	1951				2,200	Kosyk,62,79
250	forced labor camp dead	1946				500	Legters,84,61
251	forced labor camp dead	1950				450	Dyadkin,83,60 — males; from census.
252	forced labor camp dead	1954			300		non-returned POWs by 1948 end; in 1948 Rumania
253	Rumanian camp dead	1949			230	600	Herling,51,103-5 — G. Yershov, former colonel of the Red Army / of 420 thousand POWs, 190 thousand returned
254							POWs, estimate from returned Rumanian POWs sent to camps
255	Rumanian camp dead	1944				230	Tolstoy,81,266
256	Rumanian camp dead	1945				200	Stowe,51,176-7 — of 150,000 alledged former Nazis sent to camps
257	German camp dead	1945	?			80	Dushnyck,75,405
258	CONSOLIDATED CAMP DEAD	1946	1953	1,000	6,000	17,000	[based on proportionating estimates (lines 247–257) for 1946–1953]
259	SUM CAMP DEAD	1946	1953	5,900	17,600	40,880	[sum of lines 188, 193, 202, 209, 220, 229, 235, and 243]]
260	AVERAGE CAMP DEAD	1946	1953	3,450	11,800	28,940	[average of lines 258 and 259]
261							
262	OVERALL DEAD						
263	MAXIMUM CAMP POPULATION	1946	1953	10,000	12,000	20,000	[among lines 187, 192, 201, 208, 219, 228, 234, and 242]
264	CALCULATED TRANSIT DEAD	1946	1953	190	548	1,744	
265	SUM CAMP/TRANSIT DEAD	1946	1953	3,640	12,348	30,684	[sum of lines 250 and 264]
266							
267	FOREIGN COMPONENT						
268	FOREIGN DEP CAMP POPULATION	1946	1953	3,447	4,798	5,899	[from line 137, assumed half of those deported]
269	CALCULATED FOREIGN CAMP DEAD	1946	1953	345	960	1,652	
270							
271	*OVERALL DEAD*						
272	COMPONENTS OF DEMOCIDE (CITIZENS)						
273	TERROR/SM	1946	1953	334	500	665	[from line 156]
274	DEPORTATIONS	1946	1953	113	228	538	[from line 26]
275	CAMP/TRANSIT	1946	1953	3,295	11,388	29,032	[line 265 minus line 269]
276	FAMINE	1946	1953	250	333	500	[50% of famine dead on line 5]
277	DEMOCIDE (CITIZENS)	1946	1953	3,991	12,448	30,735	[sum of lines 273 to 276]
278							
279	COMPONENTS OF DEMOCIDE (FOREIGNERS)						
280	TERROR/SM	1946	1953	826	876	926	[from line 146]
281	DEPORTATIONS	1946	1953	706	1,329	2,593	[from line 128]
282	CAMP/TRANSIT	1946	1953	345	960	1,652	[from line 269]
283	DEMOCIDE (FOREIGNERS)	1946	1953	1,877	3,165	5,171	[sum of lines 280 to 282)
284							
285	OVERALL COMPONENTS OF DEMOCIDE						
286	TERROR/SM	1946	1953	1,160	1,376	1,591	[sum of lines 273 and 280]
287	DEPORTATIONS	1946	1953	819	1,557	3,131	[sum of lines 274 and 281]

TABLE 8A (continued)

MURDER BY MARXISM

288	CAMP/TRANS/T	1946		3,640	12,348	30,684	[sum of lines 275 and 282]	
289	FAMINE	1946		250	333	500	[from line 276]	
290	OVERALL DEMOCIDE	1946		5,868	15,613	35,906	[sum of lines 286 to 288]	
291								
292	OTHER DEAD							
293	REBELLION	1944	1955	61	90	167	[foreign and domestic, sum of lines 171 and 179]]	
294	FAMINE	1946	1947	250	333	500	[50% of famine dead on line 5]	
295								
296	DEMOCIDE RATE							
297	population	1950		178,000			Dyadkin,83, 59	from census.
298	population	1950		178,500			Dyadkin,83, 49	from census.
299	population	1950		179,000			Eason,59,600	excluding territorial changes and immigration.
300	population	1950		180,000			Demographic Yearbook 1971,72,111	
301	population	1951		181,600			Dyadkin,83,24	
302	population	1952		184,780			Dyadkin,83,24	
303	population	1953		187,980			Dyadkin,83,24	
304	MID-PERIOD POPULATION	1949		176,150			[(sum of lines 297–300)/4)–((line 301)–((sum of lines 297–300)/4)]	
305	DEMOCIDE RATE (CITIZENS)	1946	1953	2.27%	7.07%	17.45%	[(line 278/line 304) X 100]	
306	ANNUAL DEMOCIDE RATE	1946	1953	0.28%	0.68%	2.18%	[line 305/8]	

*See notes to table 1A, appendix 1.1.

these estimates over which groups are from foreign territories occupied by the Soviet Union since 1939, such as West Ukrainians and West Byelorussians. An additional problem is the lumping together of some groups from these occupied territories with Soviet citizens (e.g., line 17). Accordingly, unless the estimates clearly and singularly concern foreigner deportations, they are treated as domestic. With this in mind, mostly during this period 1,250,000 to 2,500,000 people were deported in the Soviet Union (line 24—the range would be larger, but 500,000 Ukrainians are assumed to have been counted in the 1,000,000 deported during the last period). Of these deported (now applying the death rates determined in appendix 1.2), 113,000 to 538,000 probably died as a consequence (line 26), exclusive of those sent to camps.

Estimates of deported foreigners is next given in the table. Although the Soviets consider Lithuania, Estonia, and Latvia part of the Soviet Union, they were taken over by threat of force in 1939 and clearly annexed against their will. The Balts are therefore treated here as foreigners and their deportations are accordingly so classified in the table (lines 30 to 65). There are estimates of deportations from each Baltic nation and also estimates of the overall deportations of Balts. These are separately classified and then consolidated. The sum of the totals for the different Baltic nations is then compared to that for the overall estimates (lines 66 to 67). The two sets of results are fairly close, and lacking a reason to prefer one over the other, they are averaged (line 68). From this, the deportation dead is calculated (line 69).

There is one low estimate in the references of the number of Balts dying in the deportations (line 71). This is, however, an uncertain estimate based on the statement by Misiunas and Taagepera that of "several hundred thousand deportees . . . many, and possibly more than half, died of cold and hunger."[69] Moreover, this seems to apply to those resettled and to exclude those sent to camps. Now, clearly several hundred were deported, as shown by the consolidated and summed results (lines 66 and 67), but a reading of Misiunas and Taagepera strongly suggests that the calculated dead (line 69) seems far too low. Accordingly, the calculated low and midestimate are averaged with the low based on Misiunas and Taagepera's statement, while the calculated high is left unchanged. This gives a range of 63,000 to 118,000 Balts killed in the deportation (line 72), still much less than half of those deported (on line 68).

A similar procedure is used to determine a range of Germans deported. The average in this case is calculated from the very-low calculated dead (line 79) and a more explicit estimate that, conservatively, 100,000 to 125,000 Germans died from deportation (line 81). The result (line 83) gives a range of 51,000 to 68,000 dead.

Following this in the table, the deportation dead is calculated for the consolidated estimates of deported Hungarians, Rumanians, Bulgarians, Czechs, Poles, and Moldavians. These results, plus the averaged totals for the Balts and Germans, are summed (line 128) to get 706,000 to 2,593,000 foreign-dead from deportations (exclusive of those sent to camps), with a midestimate of 1,329,000. For comparison, this range is shown below the sum deported (line 127). Note that the midestimate of foreign dead is only 14 percent of the number deported, a prudent total.

Next is consolidated estimates (lines 132 to 139) of the costs of Soviet terror in occupied states and territories. These give a range of 826,000 to 926,000 dead (line 146—to avoid recounting those included in the previous period, the estimate of German dead is left out; moreover, 270,000 of the estimated Polish dead are assumed counted in the previous period). This range is probably very conservative, since in the references no specific estimates are available on North Korea, the Japanese territories, Hungary, the Baltic states, Rumania, and Czechoslovakia. While in some cases the number of dead may be small, overall it should be considerable and perhaps even double the toll estimated.

Next in the table are the estimates of the domestic dead from terror (lines 149 to 155). Only two are general estimates (line 154 to 155) and only one specifically covers the period (line 155). The latter is adopted as the consolidated midestimate (line 156). Lacking low and high estimates, these consolidated values are calculated by the one-third less, one-third greater rule.[70]

There are many estimates of the camp population and dead during this period. The population estimates have been divided into years (lines 182 to 241), consolidated, and, using the camp death rates from appendix 1.2, the annual camp-dead has been calculated.

Estimates of the camp-dead also have been collected together (lines 247 to 257). These are difficult to consolidate, however, because they are for different years and durations. However, since camp conditions remained generally bad during the period, we can assume the same death rates applied for all the years. Thus we can consolidate the estimates by first proportionating them over the whole period, 1946–53. For example, Kosyk gives an estimate of 4,500,000 camp-dead in the years 1948 to 1951 (line 249).[71] Conservatively assuming that all year-ranges for the estimates are inclusive of the last year, this estimate can be extrapolated by dividing it by four (the number of years), and multiplying the result by eight (the number of years in the period). This results in 9,000,000 camp-dead for the period. Doing this for each of the estimates, and consolidating all the results, gives a large range of 1,000,000 to 17,000,000 camp-dead (line 258).

This range now can be compared to the sum of the number of dead calculated for each year from the camp populations (line 259). The sum is several times higher, over five times higher at the low end. There appears no reason to favor one set of totals over the other, however, and the two are therefore averaged (line 260). To this average is added the calculated number of transit dead (line 264). The overall result (line 265) is a range of 3,640,000 to 30,684,000 camp-dead, with a midestimate of 12,348,000—more than a million-and-a-half dead per year.

This total, however, includes foreigners who died in the camps. Now, the foreign camp population is assumed half of the number of foreigners deported, and this latter number has already been calculated (line 127). Applying the camp death rates to half of this total (line 268) gives a range of 345,000 to 1,652,000 foreign dead. This can now be subtracted from the total camp-dead to get the range of citizens who died in the camps, the resulting midestimate of which is 11,388,000 (line 275).

The totals for the different components of domestic democide are shown together in the table (lines 273 to 176), and summed (line 277) to get a range of 3,991,000 to 30,735,000 citizens killed, with a midestimate of 12,448,000. This is a democide rate of 7.07 percent (line 305), or, for eight years, an annual democide rate (line 306) of 0.88 percent (almost nine killed of every thousand citizens per year)—the lowest rate since the NEP period.

The sum of the foreign democide components (lines 280 to 283) equals a range of 1,877,000 to 5,171,000 foreigners killed. Putting domestic and foreign democide together gives a middemocide estimate of 15,613,000 dead, overall, with a range of 5,868,000 to 35,906,000 for the period (line 290).

There is another source of violent deaths during the period. After occupation or reoccupation by the Red Army, revolts and large-scale guerrilla warfare broke out in the Ukraine, Baltic states, and Poland. Some of these were not completely suppressed until the early 1950s. Estimates of the resulting Soviet military deaths are given in the table (lines 160 to 170), which when consolidated give 29,000 to 100,000 Soviet dead (line 171).

Notes

1. Stewart-Smith (1964, p. 368).
2. Bouscaren (1963, p. 56).
3. Shtromas (1986, p. 193); *Mass Deportations* (1981, p. 17); *Forced Labor* (1952, p. 32).
4. Herling (1951, p. 106).
5. Bouscaren (1963, p. 56).
6. Herling (1951, p. 113).
7. Paceba (1987, p. 27).
8. Stowe (1951, p. 123).
9. Bouscaren (1963, p. 56).
10. Ibid.
11. Roeder (1958, p. 233).
12. Shtromas (1986, pp. 193, 212n.32).
13. Ibid., p. 212n.33.
14. Taagepera (1980, p. 393).
15. Ibid., p. 394.
16. Johnson (1983, p. 585). This estimate is included in appendix 8.1, line 315.
17. Quoted in Herling (1951, p. 103).
18. Misiunas and Taagepera (1983, pp. 81, 277). See also *Mass Deportations* (1981, pp. 20–21).
19. Ibid., p. 84.
20. Ibid., pp. 86, 88.
21. Schmid (1985, p. 3).
22. Stewart-Smith (1964, p. 127).
23. Tolstoy (1981, p. 354).
24. Swianiewicz (1965, p. 44).
25. Mikolajczyk (1948, pp. 99–100).
26. Small and Singer (1982, p. 90).
27. Hingley (1974, p. 403).
28. Levytsky (1972, p. 190).
29. Hingley (1974, p. 403).
30. Ibid., p. 404; Levytsky (1972, p. 197).
31. Hingley (1974, p. 404).
32. Levytsky (1972, p. 193).

33. Ibid., pp. 193–97.
34. Antonov-Ovseyenko (1981, p. 291).
35. Prpic (1967, p. 118).
36. Heller and Nekrich (1986, p. 503)
37. Ibid.
38. Nekrich (1978, p. 105).
39. Hingley (1970, p. 210).
40. Bouscaren (1963, p. 56).
41. Nekrich (1978, p. 104).
42. Conquest (1986, p. 334).
43. Conquest (1968, p. 533).
44. Ibid., p. 492n.
45. Solzhenitsyn (1975a, p. 293–94).
46. Ibid., p. 304.
47. Ibid.
48. Heller and Nekrich (1986, p. 495).
49. Conquest (1968, p. 365).
50. Dallin and Nicolaevsky (1947, p. 84).
51. Andics (1969, p. 105).
52. Krasnov (1960, p. 182).
53. Tolstoy (1981, p. 67). See also Deriabin (1972, p. 363). There are also reports of medical experiments on prisoners doing uranium mining to determine the effect on them of radiation ("Nuclear Gulag," 1987).
54. Solzhenitsyn (1978, pp. 47–48).
55. Quoted in Kosyk (1962, p. 81).
56. Roeder (1958, p. 23).
57. Swianiewicz (1965, p. 51).
58. Ibid., pp. 47–48; Roeder (1958, pp. 21–22).
59. Roeder (1958, p. 22).
60. Small and Singer (1982, table 4.2).
61. Ibid., p. 222.
62. Quoted in Dalrymple (1965, p. 474).
63. Heller and Nekrich (1986, p. 468).
64. Ibid.
65. Ibid.
66. Ibid., p. 469.
67. See table 1.3, chap. 1.
68. Johnson (1983, p. 456).
69. (1983, p. 100).
70. See the procedural section of the Methodological Appendix.
71. (1962, p. 79).

9

6,872,000 Victims: Post-Stalin Period, 1954–1987

> *Everything which goes on in the camp re-*
> *sembles one of those films which shows*
> *the tortures given by the Gestapo.*
>
> —Alexander Shatravka in 1984

With Stalin's death, the terror was gradually alleviated, though not really ended until the 1980s under Gorbachev. Beria, Stalin's chief enforcer and head of the KGB, was executed; many other lesser lights were purged.[1]

The "crimes" of the Stalin years, particularly the Great Terror (in which, be it remembered, top party members were executed) were secretly revealed by Khrushchev. As mentioned in the previous chapter, the camp population was gradually reduced and the camp regime improved in the post-Stalin 1950s. However, the death camps at Kolyma still continued into the early 1960s, when they were also subject to reform, and perhaps largely closed by the middle 1960s.[2]

The overall camp deathrate also was gradually reduced.[3] Commissions were sent to all camps to review sentences with the authority to release prisoners. Amnesties were declared. And the average citizen gradually became more secure in what he could say and do.

But all this was relative. Freedom of thought and expression, security from arbitrary arrest and imprisonment, the right to a fair trial, are not yet guaranteed to the Soviet citizen, even under Gorbachev. For example, in April 1989 the Soviet Presidium issued a decree making it illegal to insult or discredit the government.[4] Until recently, citizens who spoke out or demonstrated against the party could yet end up in labor camps, possibly to die from any of a number of causes with which the reader of Solzhenitsyn has become familiar,[5] not the least of which is being beaten or confined in a punishment cell. Even in reference to the late 1960s, Solzhenitsyn wrote that camps differed from Stalin's not in regime, but in composition—there were no longer many millions of those sentenced for political reasons, or for no reason at all.[6] In fact, numerous camp inmates had written Solzhenitsyn to point out that their conditions in the middle 1960s were just as bad as under Stalin.[7]

Moreover, while improved, the diet still barely sustained life, especially in strict regime camps. As late as 1977, a prisoner got 2,600 calories, 2,100 on a punishment diet, and 1,300 in the strict-punishment cells. Ignoring the diet's deficiency in vitamins and fats, in calories alone it was far below the international standard of 3,100 to 3,900 calories for a man working a very active, eight-hour day.[8]

In addition, something new was added for the especially important political prisoners. They often were interned in psychiatric hospitals for the insane, where they were kept under pain-inducing or mind-numbing drugs.[9]

As late as 1982, the American CIA claimed that there were at least 4,000,000 prisoners, including 10,000 prisoners involved in forced labor.[10] But these numbers may be on the low side. In the early 1980s, a former senior member of the Supreme Soviet who was in camp for bribery calculated that Soviet prisons and camps held about 5,000,000, with an additional 2,000,000 in investigative prisons waiting for trial or review of their sentences, and another 6,000,000 not in camps or prisons but doing mild forms of forced labor.[11]

The 1983–87 camp population was probably 4,000,000, even possibly as high as 5,000,000, inmates. The number of political prisoners can only be guessed but was likely in five figures.[12] Also, many alleged criminals were truly political prisoners (an anti-Soviet nuclear arms demonstrator may have been sentenced to five years for "hooliganism," a person caught trying to flee the Soviet Union over border barricades may have gotten ten years for treason).

For 1987 or early 1988, the CIA estimated that there still were 4,000,000 prisoners. Yuri Orlov, the former head of the Helsinki Monitoring Group, claimed that there were 5,000,000. Moreover, there were still claims that the courts had a quota to fill for forced labor.[13] And there is still a duty to work. Those not doing socially useful work, which is work legally contracted by the government or an enterprise sanctioned and registered by the government, are defined as parasites and subject to up to two years in prison.[14]

Life in the camps remains harsh and dangerous, although much improved over decades ago. Even then, note the opening quote by Shatravka.

In the generation after Stalin's death, general terror and repression have been reduced to its lowest level since the revolution. In the mid-1980s the secret police continued to be feared; people were still arrested and tortured and still disappeared. But then, they now had to have done something—demonstrate against the regime, sign a protest petition, refuse to work, criticize the party to foreign reporters, try to escape across the border, and so on. The average Soviet citizen no longer worried about being swept up in arbitrary arrests or purges, executed to meet a quota, deported because of his race, nationality, or ethnicity. Religious believers and especially Jews were still mistreated and discriminated against, but they no longer dreaded mass deportation to some inhospitable region to die from privation within a few years. The all-pervasive *fear*, that dominant characteristic of the Stalin years, was muted. Rather, there was sullen acquiescence. If the citizens ignored politics, quietly accepted the daily indignities and backwardness of Soviet life, shunned foreigners, worked without complaint, and did what they were told by the party, they were then relatively secure.

Also within a decade or so of Stalin's death, people were no longer executed en masse, and even outright executions of individuals for political "crimes" had apparently disappeared. By Western standards, however, an extraordinary number of executions still continued, ostensibly for economic and civil crimes (currency speculation, bribery, profiteering). In the middle 1960s, even "the illegal manufacture of such fripperies as hair ribbons and lipstick brought certain offenders before the firing squad. . . ."[15] By surnames about 30 percent of those executed for such crimes appear to have been Jewish, even though Jews made up only 1.5 percent of the population.[16] Even in the mid-1980s, perhaps about 900 a year still were formally executed, which does not count those secretly killed in prison or purposely by maltreatment in the camps or hospitals.[17] For example, in "the second half of 1984 alone, five prominent dissidents were killed or died from improper medical treatment. . . ."[18]

Mass deportations, a cause of death for millions in the Stalin years, were also eliminated in this period. Beforehand, however, hundreds of thousands of Moldavians had been deported to Kazakhstan and elsewhere.[19] Moreover, some deported POWs from the war were still being held in camps long after post-Stalin camp reforms and amnesties. Even by 1960, for example, the Soviets held about 60,000 Hungarian POWs and at least 120,000 civilian deportees.[20] After the Soviet repression of the 1956 Hungarian Revolution, thousands were executed and 63,000 deported to Siberia.[21] If anything shows the post-Stalin reform curve, this relatively small number of those deported surely does. If such a rebellion had occurred in Hungary in the late 1940s, the Soviets would probably have arrested, executed, and deported well over half-a-million.

In the last decades, however, no mass deportations are on record, although no doubt individuals and small groups were so liquidated.

In the thirty-four years after Stalin's death 1,695,000 to 12,467,000 people were murdered by the party. A prudent estimate is 6,872,000 killed, most in the early post-Stalin years. These estimates are illustrated in figure 9.1; the actual estimates and their components are given in table 9.1. Obviously, virtually all died in the camps, as is shown best in figure 9.2.

That 6,872,000 were murdered over the thirty-four years of this period actually is a sharp decline in Soviet democide. This can be seen from the annual democide comparisons shown in figure 1.4, chapter 1. Indeed, in terms of the annual democide rate, this period is by far the least bloody in Soviet history.

Apparently, the party has learned not to unleash forces that could consume itself. Moreover, the Stalin years (apparently, few yet talk about mass killing during the Lenin years) involved "mistakes," "over enthusiasm," "tactical blunders," in the dictatorship of the proletariat. As Khrushchev tried to do in the late 1950s, Gorbachev now is also setting about correcting these. The ideology still appears to remain, however. Marxism still seems true. Utopia is still to be achieved. The party need only refurbish (perestroika) the way.

Even after the unprecedented opening of the system to criticism, demonstrations and protests, public admission of the horror and deaths of the Stalin years (the Soviets now admit to 15,000,000 having died under Stalin),[22] and the first competitive elections since 1918 held in March 1989, the Soviet regime has yet to change fundamentally. This is the point of literary critic Andrei Sinyavsky's essay "Would I Move Back?" in which he expresses doubt about Gorbachev's reforms.[23]

FIGURE 9.1
Range in Post-Stalin Democide Estimates*

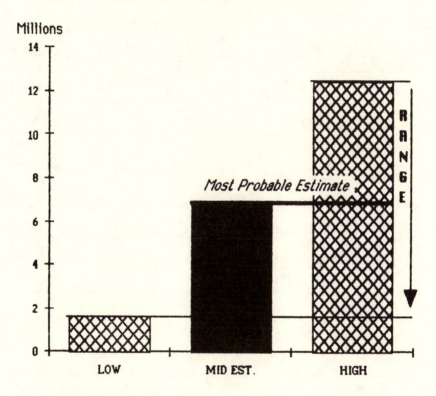

*From appendix 9.1

The party's totalitarian control of all aspects of Soviet life is still in place, although reserved and muted. Soviet law is still an instrument of political aims, the courts a handmaiden of the party. The secret police — the KGB — remains unshackled, all its tools of the trade available: universal surveillance, networks of informers, jails and prisons, interrogation rooms, and the camps. Now it is largely just watchful, waiting, probably still preparing dossiers on actual and potential enemies of the people.

It is true, as Vitali Korotich, the editor of the Soviet magazine *Ogonyok*, points out:

Fears do not come true as inevitably as they used to. The machine that

TABLE 9.1
Post-Stalin Period

ASPECTS*	DEAD ESTIMATES (000)		
	LOW	MID EST.	HIGH
DEMOCIDE	1,695	6,872	12,467
PERIOD RATE	0.66%	2.74%	4.94%
ANNUAL RATE	0.02%	0.08%	0.15%
FOREIGNERS	104	258	518
COMPONENTS			
TERROR	100	250	500
DEPORTATIONS	4	8	18
CAMP/TRANSIT	1,591	6,613	11,949
FAMINE		0	
OTHER KILLED	20	22	23
WAR/REBELLION	20	22	23
FAMINE/DISEASE			

*From appendix 9.1; rates for citizens

used to subjugate by crushing rather than persuading is worn out. But control through fear, discipline through fear, debate regulated by fear, they are all still alive in the souls and experience of millions. Fear can grab typewriters by the keys and plug up ears and mouths. Yet this fear is fading, and the nation is slowly coming back to life.[24]

But until this system of one-party rule is itself demolished and Marxism, the official religion, overthrown, the potential for a return to Leninism or Stalinism remains. Gorbachev, greater freedom of expression and criticism, and limited elections notwithstanding, this possibility casts a worrisome shadow over the present. Tremendous power remains in Gorbachev's hands and he and the Politburo remain supreme. Were Gorbachev to be replaced by hardliners convinced that the party and revolution could only be saved by a return to the tactics of previous periods, there is nothing to stop them. The machinery is there. With a little work, some cleaning, oiling, and cranking, it again

FIGURE 9.2
Democide Components for All Periods*

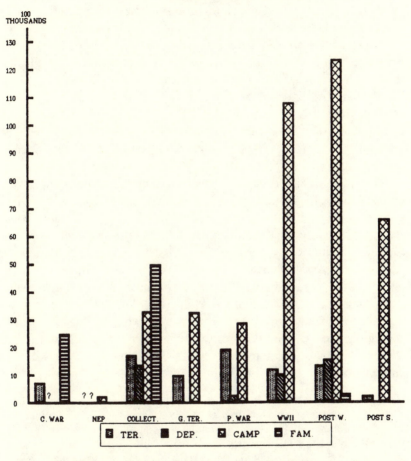

*From tables 2.1– 9.1

could grind up millions. Again, social "refuse" could stream into the gulag. Again, "traitors," "wreckers," and "enemies of the people" could be purged. And again, the people could live in daily fear.

And the party has not become any more humane. Genocide and mass killing remain policy options. The truth of this is well displayed by Soviet tactics in the Afghan War, even under Gorbachev, and right up to their withdrawal in February 1989. It is fitting, therefore, to end this book with a closer look at this war.

For the Soviet Union, Afghanistan offers a long, relatively undefendable border with Pakistan to the east; a second, flanking border with Iran to the west; and a good step towards the Gulf of Oman and the entrance to the world's most important waterway, the Persian Gulf. All that would separate Soviet land power from the gulf would be Pakistan's southwestern territory, largely inhabited by rebellious tribes open to communist subversion. Afghanistan was therefore strategically significant in Soviet aims to dominate southwest Asia and especially the Persian Gulf region. And by 1979, through pro-Soviet coups, assassinations, and subversion, the Soviets had reduced Afghanistan to a virtual satellite. But the communist Afghan government was widely unpopular and in late 1979 was near collapse from a widespread, anticommunist rebellion.

To at least ensure its control over Afghanistan, therefore, Soviet military forces began infiltrating the country in early December 1979, and on 24 December two airborne battalions took over Kabul airport, preparing the way for a massive airlift of infantry and tanks into the capitol. Simultaneously, Soviet forces crossed the Afghan border. Once Kabul was seized, top government officials were assassinated, puppets put in their places, and Soviet forces were launched against the rebels.

To control, cow, and defeat the Afghans the Soviets used indiscriminate terror, mass executions, massacres of whole villages, torture, starvation, the specific killing or maiming of children with mines that looked like toys,[25] poison gas,[26] and all the other techniques developed by the party in its long, bloody history.

> . . . Soviet forces in Afghanistan do not attempt to pacify areas where they encounter resistance; instead, they clear the areas of civilians. When they want to create collateral terror to produce a massive flight of refugees, the KDB (Punitive Desant Battalion) as well as regular regiments are sent to provide the population "with an example." Whole villages are destroyed beyond recovery and the population is slaughtered with extreme cruelty. Rape and the throwing of women from helicopters are frequent. Special chemicals are used to cause rapid decomposition of the corpses, a very effective means of deterrence for Muslims. The attacks on civilians are neither accidental nor a goal in themselves; they are simply a pragmatic and highly effective tactic. By such means, the Soviets have not only emptied whole areas, sending waves of refugees into Pakistan and Iran, but have also created forced migration within Afghanistan, resulting in artificially created famine. . . .[27]

Even before the invasion, Soviet advisors either approved or ordered the indiscriminate killing of civilians during military operations. In one case, they were involved in killing 1,200 villagers they suspected of helping the rebels.[28] After the invasion, as part of Soviet military sweeps, whole villages were massacred. For example, in December 1984, in the village of Haji Rahmatullah, Kunduz Province, 250 innocent people were murdered by Soviet forces. Two days later, in five nearby villages, 629 people also were massacred. In November 1985, 600 people were slaughtered in five villages on the Amu Darya in the Imam Saheb district of Kunduz Province.[29] In another case, 105 villagers who sought shelter in an underground tunnel were blown apart by explosives poured into the underground tunnel and ignited.[30]

All this killing was planned, a matter of policy. Such was pointed out by a Soviet army defector: "We were ordered by our officers that when we attack a village, not one person must be left alive to tell the tale. If we refuse to carry out these orders, we get it in the neck ourselves."[31] Said another Soviet defector interviewed in a Rand Corporation study:

> One day we had this punitive operation. The point is that our regiment was being fired upon every day. So one day we were given an order to fire at a certain village and then to comb that village thoroughly, and if we found any people that were still alive to kill all of them.[32]

Said yet another, "We were struck by our own cruelty in Afghanistan. We executed innocent peasants."[33]

One purpose of such massacres was to deter villagers from helping rebels and the rebels from making their attacks (be it recalled that such an atrocious technique of warfare—the lives of 400 peaceful villagers for that of one soldier killed by the resistance—was made infamous by the Nazis). Another purpose was to force Afghan civilians to abandon certain areas, to deprive them of their livelihood and to destroy food, agriculture, and pastoralism. Also to this end the Soviets used special incendiary weapons for burning wheat from the air or grain standing in the field.[34]

The Soviets took few prisoners; there were no known POW camps.[35] Those who surrendered or were taken prisoner were simply killed, often after torture to extract any information they had.[36] According to Amnesty International, even "clearly helpless civilians identified as belonging to certain groups—notably those traveling as refugees—are routinely seized and summarily executed or otherwise attacked and deliberately killed in violation of national and international law."[37]

The Soviets even tried to prevent relief or treatment from reaching the victims of their military action by bombing medical clinics.[38] A French doctor reported that hospitals operated by French medical organizations were systematically bombed.[39]

Overall, the Soviet-Afghan War possibly cost the lives of around 1,000,000 Afghans,[40] and as many as 15,000 Soviet soldiers and airmen were also killed.[41] The number of noncombatants or prisoners massacred by the Soviets must be in six figures. A UN Special Rapporteur noted that some give the toll of bombings and massacres as 500,000 Afghans, mainly civilians (32,755 civilians were reported killed in the first nine months of 1985 alone).[42] At least 35,000 Afghans were picked up by the secret police, never to be heard from again.[43] It is difficult to find any refugee without at least one family member killed. Out of prewar population of 15.5 million, at least 3,200,000 have fled to Pakistan, perhaps 2,200,000 to Iran.[44] Putting all this together, possibly the Soviets are guilty of murdering 100,000 to 500,000 Afghans. Perhaps a prudent estimate would be 250,000.

Surely, as Rosanne Klass points out, this was genocide.[45] And this latest in a long list of Soviet genocides shows that the Soviet Communist Party, if sufficiently provoked, again might do to its own subjects what it did to the Afghans. This is not only speculation. During April 1984, for example, in the region of Termez in southern Uzbekistan, there were widespread demonstrations by Uzbek students in support of the Afghan resistance. As a result, the Soviets reverted to their traditional response: "villages in Soviet Uzbekistan—inside the Soviet Union itself—were bombed by Soviet aircraft and attacked by Soviet troops."[46] Note this: Soviet citizens, as recently as 1984, were bombed from the air and attacked by troops because of student demonstrations.

Perhaps the last word on the incredible, bloody Soviet history recorded here, and the potential for humanistic reform from within the Communist party, should be left to those refugees from Uzbekistan who, along with those from other Muslim Soviet areas—Soviet citizens all—crossed over into Afghanistan and joined the freedom fighters.[47]

Appendix 9.1

Histories or specialized studies of the Soviet Union have almost entirely ignored deaths from terror and repression in the post-Stalin period. For while deaths there were hinted at or obliquely referred to

TABLE 9A
6,872,000 Victims during the Post-Stalin Period: Sources, Calculations, and Estimates*

LINE	EVENT/PROCESS/STRUCTURE/EPISODE	BEGIN YEAR	M	END YEAR	M	LOW	MID	HIGH	SOURCE	NOTES
1	*WARS/INTERVENTIONS*									
2	Hungary	1956						7.5	Small and Singer,82,93	Hungarian battle dead were 2,500.
3	Hungary	1956						7	Schmid,85,32	Hungarian dead were 20,000, 200,000 fled to the West.
4	Czechoslovakia	1968						nil	Schmid,85,27	No Soviet known killed; "at most a few hundred" Czechs killed
5	Afghanistan	1979	12	?				13.31	Elliot,88,3	Total admitted by the Soviets. Probably up to mid-1988
6	Afghanistan	1979	12	1938	5			13.31	Baltimore Sun,2/8/89,4	from a news conference of Soviet Gen. Alexei D. Lizichev
7	Afghanistan	1979	12	1985	12	10			"Afghanistan...",85	
8	Afghanistan	1979	12	1989?				15	Baltimore Sun,2/8/89,4	from Soviet Foreign Minister Shevardnadze.
9	CONSOLIDATED DEAD	1954		1988		20	21.50	23		
10								23		
11	*DEPORTATIONS*									
12	Hungarians	1956					2		Dashnyck,75,413	post-Hungarian Revolution
13	Hungarians	1956						63	Stewart-Smith,64,198	16,000 arrested and imprisoned; "many thousands" sent to
14										Soviet forced labor camps.
15	CONSOLIDATED DEPORTED	1956				42	63	84		
16	CALCULATED DEAD	1956				4	8	18		[50% of the deportation death rates applied to line 15]
17										
18	*CAMP/FORCED LABOR POPULATION/DEAD*									
19	*1954–1955 POPULATION/DEAD*									
20	prisoners	1953		1955			10,000		Kosyk,62,17	political prisoners; from B. Roeder, former German prisoner.
21	camps	1955		1955			12,000		Kosyk,62,79	[low assumed the same as for 1953]
22	CONSOLIDATED CAMP POPULATION	1953		1955		3,000	10,000	12,000	Kosyk,62,79	[excess camp death rate of Stalin years assumed decreased by 25%]
23	CALCULATED CAMP DEAD	1953		1955		150	1,000	1,680	Kosyk,62,79	
24	camp dead	1955		1956		300	600		Kosyk,62,79	
25	AVERAGE CAMP DEAD	1953		1955		300	950	1,290		[average of line 23 and of line 24 proportionated over 5 years; high is average of high of line 22 and proportionated mid-estimate of line 23]
26										
27	*1956–1960 POPULATION/DEAD*									
28	camps	1956					14,000		Kosyk,62,79	
29	forced labor	1956						6,000	Stewart-Smith,64,173	
30	prisoners	1957					23,000		Kosyk,62,16	
31	camps	1958					11,000		Kosyk,62,79	
32	CONSOLIDATED CAMP POPULATION	1956		1960		3,000	8,000	11,000		[excess camp death rate of Stalin years assumed decreased by 50%]
33	CALCULATED CAMP DEAD	1956		1960		750	4,000	7,700	Kosyk,62,79	
34	camp dead	1956		1958		433	1,300			
35	AVERAGE CAMP DEAD	1956		1960		736	3,083	4,933		[average of line 33 and of line 34 proportionated over 5 years; high is average of high of line 33 and proportionated mid-estimate of line 34]
36										
37	*1961–1970 POPULATION/DEAD*									
38	GULAG	1960		1976			2,500	5,000	Rosefielde,81,65	
39	camps	1962c.							Stewart-Smith,64,274	
40	camps	1965c.					2,000		Solzhenitsyn,78,493	
41	camps	1969c.						7,000	Hingley,70,261	concentration camps; from E. H. Cookridge; includes criminals.
42	CONSOLIDATED CAMP POPULATION	1961		1970		2,000	4,000	7,000		[excess camp death rate of Stalin years assumed decreased by 80%]
43	CALCULATED CAMP DEAD	1961		1970		400	1,600	3,920		

TABLE 9A (continued)

Line	Item	Year(s)	Low	Mid	High	Source / Notes
44	**1970–1982 POPULATION/DEAD**					
45	camps	1973 [2]		1,000		Reddaway,73,4 — a "confident", "conservative" estimate
46	camps/prisons/mental hosp.	1973 [2]		1,200		Reddaway,73,9
47	camps	1973c.	1,000		2,000	Possony,75,31
48						variation in current estimates; low from Brussels
49						Committee for the Defence of Human Rights in the USSR. officially sentenced during the year.
50	camps/prisons	1976		976		Heller & Nekrich,86,665
51	camps/prisons/forced labor	1977 [1]		2,108		Heller & Nekrich,86,666 — includes 495,711 serving terms "building the national economy."
52	forced labor	1977		2,100		Phillipps,83,163 — from Der Spiegel, 1/60.
53	GULAG	1977		4,000		Rosefielde,81,65
54	camps/prisons	1977c.		2,500		Heller & Nekrich,86,665 — from Valdimir Bukovsky memoir.
55	camps/prisons/forced labor	1977c.		5,000		Heller & Nekrich,86,665-6 — from Yuri Orlov, includes 2 million sentenced to work on "building the national economy."
56						
57	forced labor camps	1977c.	1,000		2,000	Glaser and Possony,79,482 — most Western estimates; little over 10,000 politicals.
58	GULAG	980c.	1,000		3,000	Garrard,82,76 — from The Committee for the Defence of Human rights (Brussels).
59	CONSOLIDATED CAMP POPULATION	1970 1982	2,000	3,000	4,000	[excess camp death rate of Stalin years assumed decreased by 90%]
60	CALCULATED CAMP DEAD	1970 1982	130	780	1,456	
61						
62	**1983–1987 POPULATION/DEAD**					
63	forced labor	1982		5,000		Satter,82 — at least 3 million in labor camps.
64	forced labor	1982		4,000		US News,11/22/82,31 — includes 10,000 politicals; from the CIA.
65	prisoners	1988	5,000		5,000	Bering–Jensen,88,28 — low from CIA; high from Helsinki Monitoring Group.
66	camps/prisons	1983c.	5,000	7,000	15,000	Sharansky,88,281 — mid-estimate from a former senior Supreme Soviet member; excludes about 6 million in short term forced labor ("chemists")
67						
68	CONSOLIDATED CAMP POPULATION	1983 1987	1,000	4,000	5,000	[low and mid-estimates assumed the same as during the previous years]
69	CALCULATED CAMP DEAD	1983 1987	25	200	350	[excess camp death rate of Stalin years assumed decreased by 95%]
70						
71	**TOTAL CAMP DEAD**	SUM DEAD 1954 1987	1,591	6,613	11,949	[sum of lines 25, 35, 43, 60, and 69]
72						
73	**TERROR/REPRESSION DEAD**					
74						
75	CITIZENS					
76	executed/dead	1954 1987		?		
77				?		
78	FOREIGNERS					
79	Hungarians	1957		?		
80	Czechs	1968 [12]		?		
81	Afghans	1979 [12] 1987	100	250	500	[based on Klass,87,19; Mackenzie,88,10; Braddock,88,50; Rubin,87,3,351]
82	SUM DEAD	1954 1987	100	250	500	
83						
84	**OVERALL DEAD**					
85	COMPONENTS OF DEMOCIDE (CITIZENS)	1954		?		
86	*TERROR/SYM*	1954		?		
87	*DEPORTATIONS*	1954	1,591	6,613	11,949	[from line 72]
88	*CAMP/TRANSIT*	1954		0		
89	*FAMINE*	1954		0		
90						
91	*DEMOCIDE (CITIZENS)*	1954 1987	1,591	6,613	11,949	[sum of lines 87 to 89]

TABLE 9A (continued)

92	**COMPONENTS OF DEMOCIDE (FOREIGNERS)**							
93	TERRORISM	1954	1987	100	250	500	[from line 82]	
94	DEPORTATIONS	1954	1987	4	8	18	[from line 16]	
95	CAMP/TRANSIT	1954	1987			7		
96	**DEMOCIDE (FOREIGNERS)**	1954	1987	104	258	518	[sum of lines 93 to 94]	
97								
98	**OVERALL COMPONENTS OF DEMOCIDE**							
99	TERRORISM	1954	1987	100	250	500	[from line 93]	
100	DEPORTATIONS	1954	1987	4	8	18	[from line 94]	
101	CAMP/TRANSIT	1954	1987	1,591	6,613	11,949	[from line 88]	
102	FAMINE	1954	1987			0	[from line 89]	
103	**OVERALL DEMOCIDE**	1954	1987	1,695	6,872	12,467	[sum of lines 99 to 102]	
104								
105	**OTHER DEAD** WAR	1954	1989	20	22	23		
106								
107								
108	**DEMOCIDE RATE**							
109	population	1959			208,800		Eason,59,599	census
110	population	1970			241,720		Dyadkin,83,16	census
111	population	1975			253,261		Dyadkin,83,16	census
112	MID-PERIOD POPULATION	1970			241,720			
113	**DEMOCIDE RATE (CITIZENS)**	1954	1987	0.66%	2.74%	4.94%	[(line 90/line 112) x 100]	
114	**ANNUAL DEMOCIDE RATE**	1954	1987	0.02%	0.08%	0.15%	[line 114/34]	

*See notes to table 1A, appendix 1.1.

in the literature, not enough detail is provided upon which to base an estimate of the toll. The terrorism component of democide is left a question mark in table 9A (lines 76 and 86). As best I can judge from the references, no significant deportations of citizens took place during this period.

The labor camps, however, still functioned, have been given some detailed attention in the references, and here and there are given estimates of the camp population. I have grouped these into years, made the usual range of estimates of the average population over these years, and then calculated the camp death toll for these years from an annual death rate. Now, the death rate in the camps began to be reduced after Stalin's death and within a decade or so was not much over that of the neighboring settlements. I have tried to reflect this change in the following way. The low, mid, and high estimates of the camp death rate (10, 20, and 28 percent per year) applied in previous periods is successively reduced as shown in the following table.

For example, in the appendix table, four estimates of the camp or forced labor population during 1956–60 have been classified together into one five-year period (lines 28 to 31) and consolidated (line 32). The resulting camp population range for the five years is 3,000,000 to 11,000,000 prisoners, with a midestimate of 8,000,000. Focusing on the latter, to now get a midestimate of the camp-dead for five years, the midpopulation is multiplied by 50 percent (from the above table for 1956–60) of the annual, mid-death rate of 20 percent, and the product

Years	% Rate Reduced	Resulting % Death Rate Low	Mid	High
1918–53	0	10	20	28
1954–55	25	7.5	15	21
1956–60	50	5	10	14
1961–70	80	2	4	5.6
1970–82	90	1	2	2.8
1983–87	95	0.5	1	1.4

in turn is multiplied by 5 to get the total dead for five years. That is, 8,000,000 x 0.5 x 0.2 x 5 = 4,000,000 camp dead, which is the product shown in the appendix table (line 33).

This product, however, is not the final estimate of camp dead during these five years, since there is also in the references a low and midestimate of the camp-dead for 1956 to 1958 (line 34). These are proportionated for five years (since the estimates are for three years, divide by three and multiply by five) and then averaged with the calculated camp-dead. The resulting range of camp dead for 1956 to 1960 is 736,000 to 4,933,000.

Even with the sharp reduction in the death rates after 1960, the total camp-dead over the whole post-Stalin period still varies from a low of 1,591,000 to 11,949,000, with a midestimate of 6,613,000 (line 72). This is due to the large number of camp inmates and deaths earlier in the period plus the many years—more than a generation—over which the death toll is accumulated.

I could find nothing to indicate that a significant number of prisoners died in transit. Moreover, there is reason to believe that the improvement in camp conditions also applied to transport to the camps. For these reasons, no transit deaths are included in the estimates.

Since the final estimates of those citizens killed during this period omit, for lack of data, those who may have died in transit to the camps, from terror and deportations, or in the deportation settlements, the overall democide total may be even more conservative than intended. This democide total entirely depends on camp deaths (line 90). In any case, the associated annual democide rate for this period is 0.08 percent (line 114), the lowest in Soviet history.

During this period the Soviet Union intervened by force in Hungary, Czechoslovakia, and Afghanistan. A midestimate of the number of Soviet military killed in these interventions is 21,500, most due to the war in Afghanistan (line 9).

Consequent on the Hungarian Revolution and its defeat by Soviet forces, 42,000 to 84,000 Hungarians were deported to the Soviet Union (line 15). The references give no estimates of those dying as a result of deportation, but we can calculate a range of the dead from the deportation death rates in appendix 1.2. However, since camp death rates declined during these years, there is also a question as to whether the same deportation death rates should apply during the late 1950s. To be conservative, therefore, the deportation death rates will be reduced by half, and no deportees will be assumed to have been sent off to the camps. This gives 4,000 to 18,000 Hungarian dead (line 16).

There are no estimates in the references of the cost of Soviet terror in Hungary or Czechoslovakia, but there are some estimates for such terror in Afghanistan. These together give a range of 100,000 to 500,000 Afghans killed (line 82). These dead almost entirely make up the foreign democide total shown in the table (line 96).

Finally, adding together the domestic and foreign democide components (line 99 to 102), the overall Soviet democide for the years 1954 to 1987 was 1,695,000 to 12,647,000 dead, with a midestimate of 6,872,000 (line 103).

Epigraph quoted from a 1984 letter written by Alexander Shatravka (1984). He was arrested and sent to a labor camp for activity associated with an unofficial Group to Establish Trust between the U.S.S.R. and U.S.A.

Notes

1. The KGB succeeded the MVD in 1954, which in turn succeeded the NKVD in 1946.
2. Conquest (1968, p. 516).
3. Conquest (1978, p. 65).
4. *The Honolulu Advertiser* (April 10, 1989), p. A-1.
5. Solzhenitsyn (1973, 1975, 1975a, 1978).
6. Solzhenitsyn (1978, pp. 493–94).
7. Ibid., p. 477.
8. Conquest (1978, p. 127).
9. Bloch (1977).
10. *U.S. News and World Report* (12 November 1982), p. 31.
11. Sharansky (1988, p. 281).
12. See appendix 9.1.
13. Bering-Jensen (1988, p. 28).
14. Ibid., p. 29.
15. Hingley (1970, p. 239).
16. Ibid.
17. Nuclear Gulag (1987).
18. Heller and Nekrich (1986, p. 727).
19. Dima (1982, pp. 46, 74).
20. Dushnyck (1975, p. 410).
21. Ibid., p. 413.

22. *The Sunday Star-Bulletin & Advertiser*, Honolulu (5 February 1989), p. A-20: in the Soviet weekly *Arguments and Facts*, more than 40,000,000 are reported to have been arrested, killed, or otherwise repressed and 15,000,000 to have died.
23. Sinyavsky (1989).
24. Korotich (1989).
25. Rubin (1987, p. 341).
26. An "ABC News" documentary on "Rain of Terror" (21 December 1981); Braddock (1988, p. 50); Bodansky (1987, p. 259).
27. Bodansky (1987, pp. 258–59).
28. Braddock (1988, p. 48).
29. Rubin (1987, pp. 342–43).
30. Braddock (1989, p. 49).
31. Quoted in ibid.
32. Quoted in ibid.
33. Quoted in ibid.
34. Rubin (1987, p. 343).
35. Ibid., p. 350.
36. Braddock (1988, p. 49).
37. Quoted in ibid., p. 51.
38. Rubin (1987, p. 344).
39. Braddock (1988, p. 51).
40. Klass (1987, p. 19).
41. *Baltimore Sun* (8 February 1989), p. 4.
42. Rubin (1987, p. 351).
43. Mackenzie (1988, p. 10).
44. Braddock (1988, p. 50); Rubin (1987, p. 351).
45. Klass (1987, p. 17).
46. Bennigsen (1987, p. 293).
47. Ibid., p. 293.

Appendix A

Methodology: Principles, Procedures, and Definitions

The statistical problem is clear, if not easily resolvable: how to determine within some range of error the most likely estimate of those murdered by the Communist Party of the Soviet Union (the de facto government), given all kinds of estimates in the literature of all kinds of genocides and mass murders over all kinds of events over all kinds of time periods, with no definitive, authoritative estimate available. There is no entirely satisfactory solution to this. Available estimates are neither comprehensive nor independent enough to apply formal probability models (sometimes there are only one or two estimates of a particular massacre), nor are the early Soviet census results and birth- and death rates reliable enough to be relied on for formal demographic analysis, as shown by the different estimates among demographers.

The approach has to be one of *reasonable approximation*, therefore, which involves (a) successively narrowing the range of estimates to what a reasonable analyst would arrive at in viewing all the available information, and (b) defining within this range a prudent figure that more or less reflects the central thrust of the statistics.

In doing this, it must be clear at the outset that we cannot expect to determine the actual number of deaths. Even were all Soviet archives opened and every record of those murdered by the police, secret police, or the military available, we then might have a figure closer to the truth, although still probably off by millions. This is because many people undoubtedly were killed or died without a record being made, especially in time of rebellion, civil war, the occupation of other countries, or mass movements like collectivization or the destruction of Ukrainian nationalism. Moreover, the numbers killed in some instances may have been exaggerated by the executioners, especially when they were given a quota of killed to fulfill. In regard to the difficulty of arriving at a definitive total, the Jewish holocaust is instructive. Although the Germans are noted for their rule-following and record-keeping, and the relevant German archives were available after the war and participants could be systematically interviewed, there is still considerable disagreement—a range of over a million—among experts over the number of Jews actually murdered.

Methodological Principles

The job here can only be to find a most likely and prudent total of Soviet murdered, where "most likely" means what a reasonable person would agree to on the basis of the evidence and analysis. Several statistical principles will be applied in doing this.

The Variation Principle

Dependence on only a few or one-sided estimates will obviously bias the results. While one cannot include every estimate appearing in every book or article by whomever, estimates should be selected that are at the extremes, as well as being reasonably authoritative and credible, such as from former camp prisoners (e.g., Solzhenitsyn), former Soviet officials, experts on the Soviet Union, and Western journalists formerly stationed there.

The Comprehensiveness Principle

As many estimates as possible should be included, even if redundant against other estimates, as long as they are independent in their sources. For example, if two estimates are based on the same source, only one should be included.

The Disaggregation Principle

Overall estimates should be subdivided into the smallest subestimates available (this a basic principle of estimation). For example, one should not simply rely on an estimate of the total killed by Stalin, but should subdivide this into the various campaigns, movements, deportations, camp deaths, massacres, and the like for which Stalin is reponsible. The sum of these subestimates then would tend to cancel out errors of exaggeration and underestimation and to achieve a more reliable overall estimate than would the total by itself. Such overall estimates should also be included, and where great disparities between the norm of these and the sum of the subestimates occur they should be reconciled (consolidated).

This disaggregation and reconciliation is done here by subdividing estimates into eight historical periods, and then within each period by further subdividing into groups killed, events, institutions, processes, and years. For example, estimates of labor-camp deaths are determined by separating by year estimates of camp populations and camp deaths. Then from the camp populations an estimated death toll from transit to the camps and in the camps themselves is calculated from a formula using estimated transit and camp death rate (see methodological procedure No. 4, below). This calculated total for each year is then compared to the estimates in the literature for camp deaths during the year, and the two kinds of estimates are then reconciled, using the consolidation principle given below.

The Error Range Principle

Overall low and high subestimates should be made for each case of genocide, massacre, etc., as well as a most probable (likely, prudent) estimate. The idea is that not all the low (high) estimates of all the different cases of genocide and mass murder can be correct, that some must be underestimating (overestimating) the true number, and that when all the lows (highs) are summed into a total for a period, the resulting low (high) is probably under (over) the true figure. Therefore, these total lows and highs will provide a probable range of error for the central estimate.

The Consolidation Principle

If two different sets of low, mid, and high estimates are to be reconciled into one set, then the lowest and highest of the two sets should be taken, and the average of the two midestimates should be calculated (unless there are qualitative or contextual reasons to select one or the other). For example, based on available estimates of the camp population, let the calculation of the number of dead in the labor camps for a given year be a low of 1,000,000, a midestimate of 2,000,000, and a high of 4,600,000. Let also the dead for this year be consolidated from a variety of sources as 850,000, 2,500,000, and 3,500,000. These two sets of figures for camp deaths follow, with their resolution (consolidation) below them.

1,000,000	2,000,000	4,600,000
850,000	2,500,000	3,500,000
850,000	2,250,000	4,600,000

As can be seen, the low is taken from that set with the lowest low, the high is taken from that with the highest, and the midfigure is the average.

If there are more than two sets, and unless there are qualitative or contextual factors to the contrary (such as an extremely-low low of camp deaths that was published during the 1940s by a historian and member of the British Communist Party), they should be resolved into one set of figures by also taking the lowest low and highest high.

The midfigure may or may not be based on the average, depending on what events or institutions are being dealt with and the nature of the different estimates. For example, there may be a large number of estimates near the high, which would cause the average also to be near the high, but this may seem undesirable if the historical context points to a figure closer to the low. Moreover, in cases of ambiguity or the lack of much historical material on an event, to be conservative a midestimate closer to the low is more desirable than one closer to the high.

This principle assures me that the final, prudential total for Soviet killing will be bracketed by the lowest reasonable lows and highs. And since these are the sum of lows or highs throughout, they in effect give the lower and upper bounds on the prudential estimate.

The What If . . . Principle

Major assumption should be altered to determine how the overall totals will change. In this way, these assumptions, the robustness and acceptability of the overall range of error, and the prudential estimate can be evaluated. It may be, for example, that an apparently high assumption about death rates in the camps has marginal impact on the totals when it is significantly lowered. This has been done in appendix 1.2

The Disclosure Principle

All estimates, their sources and relevant comments and qualifications, should be disclosed, as well as all calculations, formulas, and whatever else is done to reach the final totals. This is to enable an informed and detailed evaluation of the final figures by experts and to allow them to make additions and adjustments from their own perspective.

Methodological Procedures

A number of procedures were used to translate estimates into tables to which calculations and consolidation could be applied, and to carry out calculations on these estimates.

1. Translation of Qualitative Figures to Quantitative

Estimates of those killed are not always numerically precise. The following protocols have been used to translate from such qualititative assertions to usable numbers.

1.1 If a source says that the number killed is "close to," or "just over," or "about," or "nearly X," then X is made the estimate. If this is not also said to be a low or high, or conservative, or otherwise similarly qualified, it is treated as a midestimate.

1.2 If a source says that X is "conservative" or "prudent," or qualifies X by "at least" or "more than," or otherwise indicates X is a low figure, then X is treated as a low. To say "no more than," "Less than," "at most," or "approaches X," implies that X is a high. "As many as" is treated as suggesting a midestimate.

1.3 Qualitative approximations like "several thousand," or "thousands" are interpreted as a low of 2,000; a "couple of thousand" is interpreted as a midestimate of 2,000.

2. Filling in the Range

In some cases, when results are consolidated or there is only a single figure for a massacre or genocide available, the range of killed may have to be approximated. An analysis of available estimates suggests that the following procedure is very conservative.

2.1 If a low and midvalue is missing, but there is high, then the high can be halved to estimate the low. If there is a low, but no midvalue and high, then the low can be doubled to get the high.

2.2 If a midvalue is available but the low is missing, then the low can be estimated as two-thirds the midvalue; if a high is missing, it can be estimated as one-third higher then the midvalue.

3. Computing Camp and Deportation Deaths

When camp population or deportation figures are available for a period, but camp or deportation death estimates are not, then camp or deportation deaths can be calculated from the death rates determined in appendix 1.2. These are (low, midvalue, high):

3.1 Annual camp death rate (%) = 10, 20, 28. the annual camp population to which these rates are applied will be allowed to vary from year to year in line with the estimates in the references, even though such variation from one year to the next may appear unreasonable. This is because the aim here is not a definitive camp population or number of deaths for a year but rather a final democide figure for the period. Too high or too low estimates of the number of deaths are thus allowed to balance out over a number of years.

3.2 Deportation death rate (%) = 18, 26, 43. In all cases, the number of deportation deaths will be calculated for only half of the number deported; the other half will be assumed to have been sent to camps, and their deaths to be counted there.

4. Computing Transit Death Rates

The transit death rate (T) for a present period under consideration can be calculated from the previous and present period's camp populations and the past camp deaths. Now, the number of new prisoners into the camps between two periods is a function of the past camp population, the previous camp deaths, and the current population:

$$N = [P - (C - D)],$$

where N = number, new camp prisoners,
P = present camp population,
C = previous camp population,
D = previous number of camp deaths.

Moreover, the number of new prisoners added to the camps is a function of those originally sent to the camps and the transit death rate.

$$N = S(1 - R), B = N/(1 - R)$$

where B = number of prisoners that began transport to the camps,
R = transit death rate.

Then the number of transit deaths is:

$$T = B - N = [N/(1 - R)] - N = N[1/(1 - R) - 1],$$
$$= [P - (C - D)][(1/(1 - R)) - 1],$$

where T = transit deaths.

The transit death rate R is (low, midvalue, high) 0.03, 0.05, and 0.09, from appendix 1.2. All Soviet transit deaths have been calculated using the above formulae.

Definitions

Battle-Dead

Those combatants killed in a violent conflict, such as a war or revolution.

Democide

Any Actions by Government:
(1) designed to kill or cause the death of people (1.1) because of their religion, race, language, ethnicity, national origin, class, politics, speech, actions construed as opposing the government or wrecking social policy, or by virtue of their relationship to such people; (1.2) in order to fulfill a quota or requisition system; (1.3) in furtherance of a system of forced labor or enslavement; (1.4) by massacre; (1.5) through imposition of lethal living conditions of life;

(2) that cause death by virtue of an intentionally or knowingly reckless and depraved disregard for life, as in (2.1) deadly prison, or concentration, forced labor, or prisoner of war camp, conditions; (2.2) killing medical or scientific experiments on humans; (2.3) torture or beatings; (2.4) encouraged or condoned murder, rape, looting, and pillage; (2.5) a government-made famine or epidemic; (2.6) forced deportations and expulsions.

Qualifications and clarifications. (a) "government" includes de facto governance, as by the Communist Party of the Soviet Union; or by a rebel army over a region and population it has conquered from a government, as by the rule of the White armies over parts of Russia during the civil war;

(b) "actions by governments" comprise official or authoritative actions by government officials, including the police, military, or secret service; or such nongovernmental actions (e.g., by brigands, church leaders, or a secret society) receiving government approval, aid, or acceptance;

(c) clause 1.1 includes directly targeting noncombatants during a war or violent conflict for other than military reasons (e.g., out of hatred or revenge, or to depopulate an enemy region);

(d) "relationship to such people" (clause 1.1) includes their relatives, colleagues, coworkers, teachers, or students.

(e) "massacre" (clause 1.4) includes the mass killing of prisoners of war or rebellions;

(f) "quota" system (clause 1.3) includes randomly selecting people for executor in order to meet a quota;

(g) "requisition" system (clause 1.3) includes taking from peasants or farmers all their food and produce, leaving them to starve to death;

(h) excluded from the definition is or are: (h.1) execution for what are internationally considered capital crimes, such as murder, rape, spying, treason, and the like, so long as evidence does not exist that such allegations were invented by the government in order to execute the accused; (h.2) actions taken against participants in a violent conflict, riot, or demonstration (e.g., killing people with guns in their hands is not democide); (h.3) the death of noncombatants killed during attacks on military targets (e.g., during bombing enemy logistics) or when targeted for militarily justifiable strategic or tactical reasons (e.g., an embargo of all food and supplies to an enemy country or region)—see (c), above.

Genocide

Any actions by government designed to kill or cause the death of people because of their religion, race, language, ethnicity, national origin, or class. Genocide is defined as a type of democide, and is included within clause (1.1) of its definition.

Murder

A crime defined as the premeditated or deliberative killing of another person, or the causing of the death of another through reckless and willful disregard for human life.

Politicide

Any actions by government designed to kill or cause the death of people because of their politics, speech, or actions construed as opposing the government or wrecking social policy. Politicide is defined as a type of democide, and is included within clause (1.1) of its definition.

References

"Afghanistan: Six Years of Soviet Occupation." United States Department of State Special Report No. 135, Washington, D.C., December 1985.

The World Almanac and Book of Facts 1986. New York: Newspaper Enterprise Association, 1985.

Ambartsumov, Yevgeny. "Remembering the Millions that Stalin Destroyed." *Moscow News* (July 1988): 12.

Andics, Hellmut. *Rule of Terror*. Translated by Alexander Lieven. London: Constable & Co., 1969.

Antonov-Ovseyenko, Anton. *The Time of Stalin: Portrait of a Tyranny*. Translated by Stephen F. Cohen. New York: Harper & Row, 1981.

Ashton, D. L. W. "Communist Concentration Camps—Today." *East-West Digest* 9 (September 1973): 664–76.

Backer, George. *The Deadly Parallel: Stalin and Ivan the Terrible*. New York: Random House, 1950.

Bawden, C. R. *The Modern History of Mongolia*. London: Weidenfeld and Nicolson, 1968.

Beck, F. and W. Godin. *Russian Purge and the Extraction of Confession*. Translated by Eric Mosbacher and David Porter. New York: Hurst & Blackett Ltd., 1951.

Bennigsen, Alexandre. "Afghanistan & the Muslims of the USSR." In *Afghanistan: The Great Game Revisited*, edited by Rosanne Klass. New York: Freedom House, 1987, pp. 287–99.

Bering-Jensen, Henrik. "The System of Forced Labor: Cruel and Usual Punishment." *Insight* (22 February 1988): 28–30.

Bethell, Nicholas. *The Last Secret: The Delivery to Stalin of over Two Million Russians by Britain and the United States*. New York: Basic Books, 1974.

Bloch, Sidney and Peter Reddaway. *Psychiatric Terror: How Soviet Psychiatry Is Used to Suppress Dissent*. New York: Basic Books, 1977.

Bodansky, Yossef. "Soviet Military Operations in Afghanistan." In *Afghanistan: The Great Game Revisited*, edited by Rosanne Klass. New York: Freedom House, 1987, pp. 229–85.

Bouscaren, Anthony T. *International Migrations Since 1945*. New York: Praeger, 1963.

Bowers, William J. *Legal Homicide: Death as Punishment in America, 1864–1982*. Boston: Northeastern University Press, 1984.

Braddock, Lee. "Moral Unequivalence: Afghanistan is Not the Soviets' Vietnam." *Policy Review* (Summer 1988): 42–51.

Bunyan, James. *The Origin of Forced Labor in the Soviet State 1917–1921: Documents and Materials*. Baltimore: The Johns Hopkins Press, 1967.

Carlton, Richard K., ed. *Forced Labor in the "People's Democracies."* New York: Frederick A. Praeger, 1955.

Chalupa, V. *Rise and Development of a Totalitarian State*. Leiden: H. E. Stenfert Kroese N. V., 1959.

Chamberlin, William Henry. *The Russian Revolution, 1917–1921*, Vol. 2. New York: Macmillan, 1935.

Charny, Israel W., ed. *Toward the Understanding and Prevention of Genocide: Proceedings of the International Conference on the Holocaust and Genocide*. Boulder, Colo.: Westview Press, 1984.

Church, George J. "Haunted by History's Horrors." *Time* (10 April 1989): 71–72.

Churchill, Winston S. *The Second World War: Vol. 4: The Hinge of Fate*. Boston: Houghton Mifflin Co., 1950.

Chyz, Martha. *Woman and Child in the Modern System of Slavery—USSR*. Translated by Olha Prychodko. New York: DOBRUS, 1962.

Conquest, Robert. *The Great Terror: Stalin's Purge of the Thirties*. New York: Macmillan, 1968.

_____. "The Human Cost of Soviet Communism." Washington: Committee on the Judiciary, United States Senate, 91st Congrss, 2d Session, 1970.

_____. *The Nation Killers: The Soviet Deportation of Nationalities*. London: Macmillan, 1970a.

_____. *V. I. Lenin*. New York: The Viking Press, 1972.

_____. *Kolyma: The Arctic Death Camps*. New York: The Viking Press, 1978.

_____. *The Harvest of Sorrow: Soviet Collectivization and the Terror-Famine*. New York: Oxford University Press, 1986.

_____. , ed. *The Last Empire: Nationality and the Soviet Future*. Stanford, Calif.: Hoover Institution Press, Stanford University, 1986a.

Conquest, Robert, Dana Dalrymple, James Mace, and Michael Novak. *The Man-Made Famine in Ukraine*. Washington, D.C.: American Enterprise Institute for Public Policy Research, 1984.

Coutouvidis, John and Jaime Reynolds. *Poland 1939–1947*. n.p.: Leicester University Press, 1986.

Costa, Alexandra. "Gorbachev's Russia." Speech at Austin College, Sherman, Texas, 1988.

"The Current Death Toll of International Communism." Paper. London: Foreign Affairs Research Institute, 1979.

Dallin, David J. and Boris I. Nicolaevsky. *Forced Labor in Soviet Russia*. New Haven: Yale University Press, 1947.

Dalrymple, Dana G. "The Soviet Famine of 1932–1934." *Soviet Studies* 15, no. 3 (1964): 250–84.

_____. "The Soviet Famine of 1932–1934: Some Further References." *Soviet Studies* 16, no. 4 (1965): 471–74.

_____. "Forward." In *50 Years Ago: The Famine Holocaust in Ukraine:*

Terror and Human Misery as Instruments of Soviet Russian Imperialism, by Walter Dushnyck. New York: World Congress of Free Ukrainians, 1983, pp. 5–9.

The Dark Side of the Moon. London: Faber and Faber Limited, 1946.

de Zayas, Alfred M. *Nemesis at Potsdam: The Anglo-Americans and the Expulsion of the Germans: Background, Execution, Consequences.* 2nd ed. London: Routledge & Kegan Paul, 1979.

d'Encausse, Hélène Carrère. *A History of the Soviet Union 1917–1953: Volume Two: Stalin: Order through Terror.* Translated by Valence Ionescu. New York: Longman, 1981.

Denikine, General A. *The White Army.* Translated by Catherine Zvegintzov. Westport, Connecticut: Hyperion Press, 1973.

Deriabin, Peter. *Watchdogs of Terror: Russian Bodyguards from the Tsars to the Commissars.* New Rochelle, New York: Arlington House, 1972.

Devedjiev, Hristo H. *Stalinization of the Bulgarian Society 1949–1953.* Philadelphia: Dorrance & Co., 1975.

Dima, Nicholas. *Bessarabia and Bukovina: The Soviet—Romanian Territorial Dispute.* New York: Columbia University Press, 1982.

Dolot, Miron. *Executor by Hunger: The Hidden Holocaust.* New York: W. W. Norton & Co., 1985.

Dragnich, Alex N. *Tito's Promised Land: Yugoslavia.* New Brunswick, N.J.: Rutgers University Press, 1954.

Dujardin, Jean-Pierre. "N'oublions Jamais Oui. Mais N'oublions Rien." *Le Figaro Magazine* (18 November 1978): 48–51, 150.

Dushnyck, Walter. "Human Rights in Communist Ruled East-Central Europe." In *Case Studies on Human Rights and Fundamental Freedoms: A World Survey*, edited by Willem Andriaan Veenhoven and Winifred Crum Ewing. vol. 1. The Hague: Martinus Nijhoff, 1975, pp. 379–443.

_____. *50 Years Ago: The Famine Holocaust in Ukraine: Terror and Human Misery as Instruments of Soviet Russian Imperialism.* New York: World Congress of Free Ukrainians, 1983.

Dyadkin, Iosif G. *Unnatural Deaths in the USSR, 1928–1954.* Translated by Tania Deruguine. New Brunswick, N.J.: Transaction Books, 1983.

Dziak, John J. *Chekisty: A History of the KGB.* Lexington, Mass.: Lexington Books, 1988.

Eason, Warren W. "The Soviet Population Today." *Foreign Affairs* 37 (July 1959): 598–606.

Eberstadt, Nick. "Introduction." In *Unnatural Deaths in the USSR, 1928–1954*, by Iosif G. Dyadkin. Translated by Tania Deruguine. New Brunswick, N.J.: Transaction Books, 1983, pp. 1–14.

Eckhardt, William and Gernot Köhler. "Structural and Armed Violence in the 20th Century: Magnitude and Trends." *International Interactions* 6, no. 4: pp. 347–75.

Eliot, Theodore L., Jr., "Gorbachev's Afghan Gambit," National Security Papers No. 9, Institute for Foreign Policy Analysis, Cambridge, Mass., 1988.

Elliot, Gil. *Twentieth Century Book of the Dead*. London: Allen Lane The Penguin Press, 1972.

Elliott, Mark R. *Pawns of Yalta: Soviet Refugees and America's Role in Their Repatriation*. Urbana, Ill.: University of Illinois Press, 1982.

Fabian, Béla. "Krushchev's Broken Promise on Slave Labor in Russia." *U.S. News & World Report* (7 September 1959): pp. 84–85.

Falk, Richard A., Gabriel Kolko, and Robert Jay Lifton, eds. *Crimes of War: A Legal, Political-Documentary, and Psychological Inquiry into the Responsibility of Leaders, Citizens, and Soldiers for Criminal Acts in Wars*. New York: Random House, 1971.

Fejtö, François. *Behind the Rape of Hungary*. New York: David McKay Co., 1957.

FitzGibbon, Louis. *Katyn*. New York: Charles Scribner's Sons, 1971.

_____. *Unpitied and Unknown: Katyn . . . Bologoye . . . Dergachi*. London: Bachman & Turner, 1975.

Fleischhauer, Ingeborg and Benjamin Pinkus. *The Soviet Germans: Past and Present*. London: C. Hurst & Co., 1986.

Floyd, David. "Preface." In *Katorga: An Aspect of Modern Slavery*, by Bernard Roeder. Translated by Lionel Kochan. London: Heinemann, 1958, pp. vii–xxxix.

Forced Labor in the Soviet Union. Department of State Publication 4716: European and British Commonwealth Series 37, 1952.

Garrard, John. "Gulag Literature." *Problems of Communism* (November-December 1982): 75–80.

Gerson, Lennard, D. *The Secret Police in Lenin's Russia*. Philadelphia: Temple University Press, 1976.

Glaser, Kurt and Stefan T. Possony. *Victims of Politics: The State of Human Rights*. New York: Columbia University Press, 1979.

Gluckstein, Ygael, *Stalin's Satellites in Europe*. Boston: The Beacon Press, 1952.

Gollancz, Victor. *Our Threatened Values*. Hinsdale, Illinois: Henry Regnery, 1948.

Grey, Ian. *The First Fifty Years: Soviet Russia 1917–67*. New York: Coward-McCann, 1967.

Gross, Feliks. *Violence in Politics: Terror and Political Assassination in Eastern Europe and Russia*. The Hague, Paris: Mouton, 1972.

Gross, Jan Tomasz. "Introduction." In *War Through Children's Eyes: The Soviet Occupation of Poland and the Deportations, 1939–1941*, by Irena Grudzinska-Gross and Jan Tomasz Gross. Translated by Ronald Strom and Dan Rivers. Stanford, Calif.: Hoover Institution Press, 1981, pp. 3–27.

Gross, Jan T. *Revolution from Abroad: The Soviet Conquest of Poland's Western Ukraine and Western Belorussia*. Princeton: Princeton University Press, 1988.

Grossman, Vasily. *Forever Flowing*. Translated by Thomas P. Whitney. New York: Harper & Row, 1972.

Grudzinska-Gross, Irena and Jan Tomasz Gross. *War Through Children's Eyes: The Soviet Occupation of Poland and the Deportations, 1939–1941*. Translated by Ronald Strom and Dan Rivers. Stanford, Calif.: Hoover Institution Press, 1981.

Harff, Barbara and Ted Robert Gurr. "Toward Empirical Theory of Genocides and Politicides: Identification and Measurement of Cases since 1945." *International Studies Quarterly* 32 (1988): 359–71.

Heller, Mikhail. *Cogs in the Wheel: The Formation of Societ Man*. New York: Alfred A. Knopf, 1988.

Heller, Mikhail and Aleksandr Nekrich. *Utopia in Power: The History of the Soviet Union from 1917 to the Present*. Translated by Phyllis B. Carlos. New York: Summit Books, 1986.

Herling, Albert Konrad. *The Soviet Slave Empire*. New York: Wilfred Funk, 1951.

Hingley, Ronald. *The Russian Secret Police: Muscovite, Imperial Russian and Soviet Political Security Operations 1565–1970*. London: Hutchinson & Co., 1970.

_____. *Joseph Stalin: Man and Legend*. London: Hutchinson & Co., 1974.

Holmes, Ronald M. and James De Burger. *Serial Murder*. Beverly Hills: Sage, 1988.

Ignotus, Paul. *Political Prisoner*. New York: Macmillan, 1960.

Ionescu, Ghita. *Communism in Rumania 1944–1962*. London: Oxford University Press, 1964.

Irredentism and Provocation: A Contribution to the History of German Minority in Poland. Warsaw: Zachodnia Agencja Prasowa, 1960.

Jakobson, Max. *The Diplomacy of the Winter War: An Account of the Russo-Finnish War, 1939–1940*. Cambridge: Harvard University Press, 1961.

Jasny, Naum. "Labor and Output in Soviet Concentration Camps." *The Journal of Political Economy* 59 (October 1951): 405–19.

Johnson, Paul. *Modern Times: The World from the Twenties to the Eighties*. New York: Harper & Row, 1983.

Khrushchev, Nikita. *Khrushchev Remembers*. Translated and edited by Strobe Talbott. Boston: Little, Brown and Company, 1970.

Kim, Myong-sik. *Liquidation in North Korea*. n.p.: The Institute for North Korean Studies, 1980.

Klass, Rosanne. "The Great Game Revisited." In *Afghanistan: The Great Game Revisited*, edited by Rosanne Klass. New York: Freedom House, 1987, pp. 1–29.

Koestler, Arthur. *The Yogi and the Commissar and Other Essays*. The Danube Edition. New York: Macmillan, 1967.

Korotich, Vitali. "Typing Out The Fear." *Time* (10 April 1989): 124.

Kostiuk, Hryhory. *Stalinist Rule in the Ukraine: A Study of the Decade of Mass Terror (1929–39)*. New York: Praeger, 1960.

Kosyk, Volodymyr. *Concentration Camps in the USSR*. London: Ukrainian Publishers, 1962.

Krasnov, N. N., Jr. *The Hidden Russia: My Ten Years as a Slave Laborer*. New York: Holt, Rinehart and Winston, 1960.

Kravchenko, Victor. *I Chose Freedom: The Personal and Political Life of a Soviet Official*. New York: Charles Scribner's Sons, 1946.

Krawchenko, Bohdan. "The Man-Made Famine of 1932–1933 and Collectivization in Soviet Ukraine." In *Famine in Ukraine 1932–1933*, edited by Roman Serbyn and Bohdan Krawchenko. Edmonton: Canadian Institute of Ukrainian Studies, University of Alberta, 1986, pp. 15–26.

Kulischer, Eugene. *Europe on the Move: War and Population Changes, 1917–47*. New York: Columbia University Press, 1948.

Kuper, Leo. *The Pity Of It All: Polarization of Racial and Ethnic Relations*. Minneapolis, Minn.: University of Minnesota Press, 1977.

———. *Genocide: Its Political Use in the Twentieth Century*. New York: Yale University Press, 1981.

Kusnierz, Bronislaw. *Stalin and the Poles: An Indictment of the Soviet Leaders*. London: Hollis & Carter, 1949.

Lane, Arthur Bliss. *I Saw Poland Betrayed: An American Ambassador Reports to the American People*. New York: Bobbs-Merrill, 1948

Latvian Deportations 1940–Present. Rockville, Maryland: The World Federation of Free Latvians, n.d.

Leggett, George. *The Checka: Lenin's Political Police*. Oxford: Clarendon Press, 1981.

Legters, Lyman. "The Soviet Gulag: Is It Genocidal?" In *Toward the Understanding and Prevention of Genocide: Proceedings of the International Conference on the Holocaust and Genocide*, edited by Israel W. Charny. Boulder: Westview Press, 1984, pp. 60–66.

Levytsky, Boris. *The Uses of Terror: The Soviet Secret Police 1917–1970*. Translated by H. A. Piehler. New York: Coward, McCann & Geoghegan, 1972.

Lewin, M. *Russian Peasants and Soviet Power: A Study of Collectivization*. Translated by Irene Nove, with the assistance of John Biggart. Evanston: Northwestern University Press, 1968.

Liebman, Marcel. *Leninism under Lenin*. Translated by Brian Pearce. London: Jonathan Cape, 1975.

Lubachko, Ivan S. *Belorussia under Soviet Rule 1917–1957*. Lexington, Kentucky: The University Press of Kentucky, 1972.

Luza, Radomir. *The Transfer of the Sudenten Germans: A Study of Czech-German Relations, 1933–1962*. New York: New York University Press, 1964.

Lyons, Eugene. *Workers' Paradise Lost: Fifty Years of Soviet Communism: A Balance Sheet*. New York: Funk & Wagnalls, 1967.

Mace, James E. "Famine and Nationalism in Soviet Ukraine." *Problems of Communism* (May–June 1984): 37–50.

———. "The Man-Made Famine of 1933 in the Soviet Ukraine: What Happened and Why?" In *Toward the Understanding and Prevention of Genocide: Proceedings of the International Conference on the Holocaust and Genocide*, edited by Israel W. Charny. Boulder: Westview Press, 1984a, pp. 67–83.

———. "Correspondence." *Problems of Communism* (March–April 1985): 134–38.

———. "The Man-Made Famine of 1933 in Soviet Ukraine." In *Famine in Ukraine 1932–1933*, edited by Roman Serbyn and Bohdan Krawchenko. Edmonton: Canadian Institute of Ukrainian Studies, University of Alberta, 1986, pp. 1–14.

Mackenzie, Richard. "A Brutal Force Batters a Country." *Insight* (5 December 1988): 8–17.

Maksudov, M. "Ukraine's Demographic Losses 1927–1938." In *Famine in Ukraine 1932–1933*, edited by Roman Serbyn and Bohdan Krawchenko. Edmonton: Canadian Institute of Ukrainian Studies, University of Alberta, 1986, pp. 27–43.

Manning, Clarence A. *Ukraine Under the Soviets*. New York: Bookman, 1953.

Markham, Reuben H. *Rumania under the Soviet Yoke*. Boston: Meador Publishing Co., 1949.

Mass Deportations of Population from the Soviet Occupied Baltic States. Stockholm, Sweden: Latvian National Foundation, 1981.

Maximoff, G. P. *The Guillotine at Work: Twenty Years of Terror in Russia (Data and Documents)*. Chicago: The Chicago Section of the Alexander Berkman Fund, 1940.

McCauley, Martin, ed. *The Russian Revolution and the Soviet State 1917–1921: Documents*. New York: Harper & Row, 1975.

McWhirter, Norris and Ross McWhirter. *Guinness Book of World Records*. New York: Bantam Books, 1977.

Medvedev, Roy A. *Let History Judge: The Origins and Consequences of Stalinism*. Translated by Colleen Taylor. New York: Alfred A. Knopf, 1972.

———. *On Stalin and Stalinism*. Translated by Ellen de Kadt. Oxford: Oxford University Press, 1979.

Melgounov, Sergey Petrovich. *The Red Terror in Russia*. London: J. M. Dent & Sons, 1925.

Mihajlov, Mihajlo. "Did Krushchev Lie About Soviet War Casualties?" *Human Events* (5 September 1987): 13, 16.

Mikolajczyk, Stanislaw. *The Rape of Poland: Pattern of Soviet Aggression*. New York: McGraw-Hill, 1948.

Misiunas, Romuald J. and Rein Taagepera. *The Baltic States: Years of Dependence 1940–1980*. Berkeley, Calif.: University of California Press, 1983.

Nagy, Ferenc. *The Struggle Behind the Iron Curtain*. Translated by Stephen K. Swift. New York: Macmillan, 1948.

Nam, Koon Woo. *The North Korean Communist Leadership, 1945–1965: A Study of Factionalism and Political Consolidation*. University, Ala.: The University of Alabama Press, 1974.

Nekrich, Aleksandr M. *The Punished Peoples: The Deportation and Fate of Soviet Minorities at the End of the Second World War*. Translated by George Saunders. New York: W. W. Norton & Co., 1978.

Nettl, J. P. *The Eastern Zone and Soviet Policy in Germany 1945–50*. New York: Oxford University Press, 1951.

Neufeld, Dietrich. *A Russian Dance of Death: Revolution and Civil War in the Ukraine*. Translated and edited by Al Reimer. Scottdale, Pennsylvania: Herald Press, 1980.

"A New Report: Soviet's Record on Slave Labor." *U.S. News and World Report* (22 November 1982): 31.

Nickerson, Hoffman. *The New Slavery*. Garden City, New York: Doubleday, 1947.

1939–1950 Population Movements Between the Oder and Bug Rivers. Warsaw: Zachodnia Agencja Prasowa, 1961.

1939–1945 War Losses in Poland. Warsaw: Zachodnia Agencja Prasowa, 1960.

North Korean Political System in Present Perspective. Seoul, Korea: Research Center for Peace and Unification, 1976.

Nove, Alec. *Stalinism and After*. New York: Crane Russak & Co., 1975.

"Nuclear Gulag." Produced by Channel 4 Television, Great Britain, 1987c.

Oren, Nissan. *Revolution Administered: Agrarianism and Communism in Bulgaria*. Baltimore: The Johns Hopkins University Press, 1973.

Pacepa, Ion Mihai. *Red Horizons: Chronicles of a Communist Spy Chief*. Washington D.C.: Regnery Gateway, 1987.

Panin, Dimitri. *The Notebooks of Sologdin*. Translated by John Moore. New York: Harcourt Brace Jovanovich, 1976.

Parvilahti, Unto. *Beria's Gardens: A Slave Laborer's Experiences in the Soviet Utopia*. Translated by Alan Blair. New York: E. P. Dutton, 1960.

Paul, David W. *Czechoslovakia: Profile of a Socialist Republic at the Cross-roads of Europe*. Boulder, Colorado: Westview Press, 1981.

Pearson, Raymond. *National Minorities in Eastern Europe 1848–1945*. New York: St. Martin's Press, 1983.

Peers, Lt. Gen. W. R. *The My Lai Inquiry*. New York: W. W. Norton, 1979.

Petersen, William. "Soviet Society Under Stalin: The Prototype of Totalitarianism." In *The Realities of World Communism*, edited by William Petersen. Englewood Cliffs, N.J.: Prentice-Hall, 1963, pp. 41–61.

Petrov, Vladimir. *Soviet Gold: My Life as a Slave Laborer in the Siberian Mines*. Translated by Mirra Ginsburg. New York: Farrar, Straus and Co., 1949.

_____. *Escape from the Future: The Incredible Adventures of a Young Russian*. Bloomington, Ind.: Indiana University Press, 1973.

Petrov, Vladimir and Evodkia. *Empire of Fear*. New York: Praeger, 1956.

Philipps, John. *The Tragedy of the Soviet Germans (A Story of Survival)*. Published by John Philipps, 1983.

Pilon, Juliana Geran. "Review of John J. Dziak's Checkisty: A History of the KGB." *Human Events* (26 March 1988): 286.

"Pipeline: Largest East-West Transaction." *Washington Times* (19 May 1982); included in the Congressional Record, 97th Congress, Second Session: Vol. 128-Part 9, 26 May 1982, pp. 11,950–51.

Possony, Stefan T. "From Gulag to Guitk: Political Prisons in the USSR Today." In *Case Studies on Human rights and Fundamental Freedoms: A World Survey*, edited by Willem A. Veenhoven and Winifred Crum Ewing. vol. 1. The Hague: Martinus Nijhoff, 1975, pp. 3–38.

Procyk, Oksana, Leonid Heretz, and James E. Mace. *Famine in the Soviet Ukraine 1932–1933: A Memorial Exhibition, Widener Library, Harvard University*. Cambridge: Harvard University Press, 1986.

Prpic, George J. *Fifty Years of World Communism: 1917–1967: A Selective Chronology*. Cleveland, Ohio: Institute for Soviet and East European Studies, John Carroll University, 1967.

Ramaer, J. C. *Soviet Communism: The Essentials*. 2d ed. Translated by G. E. Luton. Stichting Vrijheid, Vrede, Verdediging (Belgium), 1986.

Reddaway, Peter. "The Forced Labour Camps in the U.S.S.R. Today: An Unrecognized Example of Modern Inhumanity." Brussels: International Committee for the Defense of Human Rights in the U.S.S.R. (Report presented to the Press in Brussels on February 26, 1973).

Reitlinger, Gerald. *The Final Solution: The Attempt to Exterminate the Jews of Europe 1939–1945*. New York: A. S. Barnes, 1961.

Remeikis, Thomas. *Opposition to Soviet Rule in Lithuania 1945–1980*. Chicago: Institute of Lithuanian Studies Press, 1980.

Riasanovsky, Nicholas V. *A History of Russia*. 3d ed. New York: Oxford University Press, 1977.

Roeder, Bernhard. *Katorga: An Aspect of Modern Slavery*. Translated by Lionel Kochan. London: Heinemann, 1958.

Rosefielde, Steven. "An Assessment of the Sources and Uses of Gulag Forced Labour 1929–56." *Soviet Studies* 33 (January 1981): 51–87.

Rothstein, Andrew. *A History of the U.S.S.R.* Harmondsworth, Great Britain: Penguin Books, 1950.

Roucek, Joseph S. and Kenneth V. Lottich. *Behind the Iron Curtain: The Soviet Satellite States-East European Nationalisms and Education*. Calwell, Idaho: The Caxton Printers, Ltd., 1964.

Rubin, Barnett R. "Human Rights in Afghanistan." In *Afghanistan: The Great Game Revisted*, edited by Rosanne Klass. New York: Freedom House, 1987, pp. 335–58.

Rummel, R. J. *Understanding Conflict and War*. Vols. 1–5. Beverly Hills, California: Sage Publications, 1975–1981.

―――. "Libertarianism and International Violence." *The Journal of Conflict Resolution* 27 (March 1983): 27–71.

_____. "Libertarianism, Violence within States, and the Polarity Principle." *Comparative Politics* 16 (July 1984): 443–62.

_____. "A Test of Libertarian Propositions on Violence." *The Journal of Conflict Resolution* 29 (September 1985): 419–55.

_____. "War Isn't This Century's Biggest Killer." *The Wall Street Journal* (7 July 1986).

_____. "Deadlier than War." *IPA Review* (Institute of Public Affairs Limited, Australia) 41 (August-October 1987): 24–30.

_____. "As Though a Nuclear War: The Death of Absolutism." *International Journal on World Peace* 5 (July-September 1988): 27–43.

Rupen, Robert. *How Mongolia Is Really Ruled: A Political History of the Mongolian People's Republic, 1900–1978.* Stanford: Hoover Institution Press, 1979.

Russian Genocidal Policies: Mass Deportation of Roumanians from Besarabia. Detroit: Roumanian American National Committee, 1965.

Satter, David. "The System of Forced Labor in Russia." *The Wall Street Journal* (24 June 1982).

Scalapino, Robert A. and Chong-Sik Lee. *Communism in Korea.* parts 1–2, Berkeley: University of California Press, 1972.

Schechtman, Joseph B. *European Population Transfers 1939–1945.* New York: Oxford University Press, 1946.

Schimitzek, Stanislaw. *Truth of Conjecture? German Civilian War Losses in the East.* Warsaw: Western Press Agency, 1966.

Schmid, Alex P. *Soviet Military Interventions since 1945.* New Brunswick, N.J.: Transaction Books, 1985.

Schoenberg, Hans W. *Germans from the East: A Study of their Migration, Resettlement, and Subsequent Group History Since 1945.* The Hague: Martinus Nijhoff, 1970.

Serbyn, Roman. "The Famine of 1921–1923: A Model for 1932–1933?" In *Famine in Ukraine 1932–1933,* edited by Roman Serbyn and Bohdan Krawchenko. Edmonton: Canadian Institute of Ukrainian Studies, University of Alberta, 1986, pp. 147–78.

Serbyn, Roman and Bohdan Krawchenko, eds. *Famine in Ukraine 1932–1933.* Edmonton: Canadian Institute of Ukrainian Studies, University of Alberta, 1986.

Seton-Watson, Hugh. *The East European Revolution.* New York: Praeger, 1961.

Sharansky, Natan. *Fear No Evil.* Translated by Stefani Hoffman. New York: Random House, 1988.

Shatravka, Alexander. "Man of Peace finds None in Soviet Camp." *The Wall Street Journal* (21 December 1984): p. 18.

Sheehy, Ann and Bohdan Nahaylo. *The Crimean Tatars, Volga Germans and Meskhetians: Soviet Treatment of Some National Minorities.* Report No. 6, 3d ed. New York: Minority Rights Group, 1980.

Shtromas, Alexander. "The Baltic States." In *The Last Empire: Nationality and the Soviet Future*, edited by Robert Conquest. Stanford, Calif.: Hoover Institution Press, Stanford University, 1986, pp. 183–217.

Sinyavsky, Andrei. "Would I Move Back?" *Time* (10 April 1989): 129.

Sivard, Ruth Leger. *World Military and Social Expenditures 1985*. Leesburg, Va.: WMSE Publications, 1985.

Small, Melvin and J. David Singer. *Resort to Arms: International and Civil Wars, 1816–1980*. Beverly Hills, Calif.: Sage Publications, 1982.

Solovyov, Vladimir and Elena Klepikova. "Afghanistan and Russian History." *Worldview* 24 (January 1981): 4–6.

Solzhenitsyn, Aleksandr I. *The Gulag Archipelago 1918—1956: An Experiment in Literary Investigation I–II*. Translated by Thomas P. Whitney. New York: Harper & Row, 1973.

_____. "Repentance and Self-Limitation in the Life of Nations." In *From Under the Rubble*, by Aleksandr I. Solzhenitsyn. Translated by A. M. Brock. London: Collins & Harvill Press, 1975, pp. 105–43.

_____. *The Gulag Archipelago 1918–1956: An Experiment in Literary Investigation III–IV*. Translated by Thomas P. Whitney. New York: Harper & Row, 1975a.

_____. "America: You Must Think About the World." (Address delivered in Washington, D.C., on June 30, 1975). *Society* 13 (November/December 1975b): 14–25.

_____. *The Gulag Archipelago 1918–1956: An Experiment in Literary Investigation V–VII*. Translated by Harry Willetts. New York: Harper & Row, 1978.

Sorlin, Pierre. *The Soviet People and Their Society: From 1917 to the Present*. Translated by Daniel Weissbort. New York: Praeger, 1968.

Sorokin, Pitirim A. *Social and Cultural Dynamics: Volume 2: Fluctuation of Systems of Truth, Ethics, and Law*. New York: American Book Co., 1937.

Souvarine, Boris. *Stalin: A Critical Survey of Bolshevism*. New York: Longmans, Green & Co., 1939.

"Soviet Union: 102,000 in a Single Stalin Grave." *News Weekly* [Australia] (19 October 1988).

Stewart, George. *The White Armies of Russia: A Chronicle of Counter-Revolution and Allied Intervention*. New York: Macmillan, 1933.

Stewart-Smith, D. G. *The Defeat of Communism*. London: Ludgate Press Limited, 1964.

Stowe, Leland. *Conquest by Terror: The Story of Satellite Europe*. New York: Random House, 1951.

Sturdza, Michel. *The Suicide of Europe: Memoirs of Prince Michel Sturdza, Former Foreign Minister of Rumania*. Boston: Western Islands Publishers, 1968.

Svalastoga, Kaare. *On Deadly Violence*. Oslo, Norway: Universitetsforlaget, 1982.

Swettenham, John Alexander. *The Tragedy of the Baltic States: A Report Compiled from Official Documents and Eyewitnesses' Stories*. London: Hollis and Carter, 1952.

Swianiewicz, S. *Forced Labour and Economic Development: An Enquiry into the Experience of Soviet Industrialization*. New York: Oxford University Press, 1965.

Taagepera, Rein. "Soviet Collectivization of Estonian Agriculture: The Deportation Phase." *Soviet Studies* 32 (July 1980): 379–97.

Tawdul, Adam J. "Ex-Soviet Official Charges: 'Russia Warred on Own People.' " *New York American* (19 August 1935): 2.

Tchernavin, Vladimir V. *I Speak for the Silent Prisoners of the Soviets*. Translated by Nicholas M. Oushakoff. New York: Hale, Cushman & Flint, 1935.

These Names Accuse: Nominal List of Latvians Deported to Soviet Russia in 1940–41. 2d ed. Stockholm: The Latvian National Foundation, 1982.

Timasheff, Nicholas S. *The Great Retreat: The Growth and Decline of Communism in Russia*. New York: E. P. Dutton & Co., 1946.

Timasheff, N. S. "The Postwar Population of the Soviet Union." *The American Journal of Sociology* LIV (September 1948): 148–55.

Tolstoy, Nikolai. *Victims of Yalta*. London: Corgi Books, 1977

———. *Stalin's Secret War*. New York: Holt, Rinehart and Winston, 1981

———. *The Minister and the Massacres*. London: Century Hutchinson Ltd., 1986.

Toth, Zoltan. *Prisoner of the Soviet Union*. Translated by George Unwin. Old Woking: Gresham Books, 1978.

Tottle, Douglas. *Fraud, Famine and Fascism: The Ukrainian Genocide Myth from Hitler to Harvard*. Toronto: Progress Books, 1987.

Ulam, Adam. "Introduction." In *Execution by Hunger: The Hidden Holocaust*, by Miron Dolot. New York: W. W. Norton & Co., 1985, pp. vii–xii.

Ulam, Adam B. *A History of Soviet Russia*. New York: Praeger, 1976.

Vairogs, Dainis. *Latvian Deportations 1940–Present*. Translated by Martin T. Hildebrants. Rockville, Maryland: The World Federation of Free Latvians, n.d.

Váli, Ferenc A. *Rift and Revolt in Hungary: Nationalism versus Communism*. Cambridge: Harvard University Press, 1961.

Vardys, V. Stanley, ed. *Lithuania Under The Soviets: Portrait of a Nation, 1940–65*. New York: Praeger, 1965.

Vardys, V. Stanley. "The Baltic Peoples." *Problems of Communism* (September-October): 55–61.

Veenhoven, Willem Adriaan and Winifred Crum Ewing, eds. *Case Studies on Human Rights and Fundamental Freedoms: A World Survey*. vol. 1. The Hague: Martinus Nijhoff, 1975.

Vizulis, I. Joseph. *Nations Under Duress: The Baltic States*. Port Washington, N.Y.: Associated Faculty Press, 1985.

Weissberg, Alex. *Conspiracy of Silence*. London: Hamish Hamilton, 1952.

Weissman, Benjamin M. *Herbert Hoover and Famine Relief to Soviet Russia: 1921–1923*. Stanford, Calif.: Hoover Institution Press, 1974.

Werth, Alexander. *Russia at War: 1941–1945*. New York: E. P. Dutton, 1964.

Westwood, F. N. *Russia Since 1917*. New York: St. Martin's Press, 1980.

Wheatcroft, S. G. "On Assessing the Size of Forced Concentration Camp Labour in the Soviet Union, 1929–56." *Soviet Studies* 33 (April 1981): 265–95.

———. "Correspondence." *Problems of Communism* (March-April 1985): 132–34.

Wiles, Peter. "The Number of Soviet Prisoners: Part I: The NKVD in the 1941 Plan." (Paper available at the Library of Congress), n.p. (c. 1953).

Wilson, Richard and E. A. Crouch. "Risk Assessment and Comparisons: An Introduction." *Science* 236 (17 April 1987): 267–70.

Wright, Quincy. *A Study of War*. 2d ed. Chicago: The University of Chicago Press, 1965.

Wytwycky, Bohdan. *The Other Holocaust: Many Circles of Hell*. Washington, D.C.: The Novak Report on the New Ethnicity, 1980.

Zawodny, J. K. *Death in the Forest: The Story of the Katyn Forest Massacre*. Notre Dame, Ind.: University of Notre Dame Press, 1962.

Zinsmeister, Karl. "All the Hungry People." *Reason* 20 (June 1988): 22–30.

Zorin, Libushe. *Soviet Prisons and Concentration Camps: An Annotated Bibliography 1917–1980*. Newtonville, Mass.: Oriental Research Partners, 1980.

Name Index

Subject Index